William Shakespeare

HENRY V

Edited with a Commentary by A. R. Humphreys
Revised and introduced by Ann Kaegi

PENGUIN BOOKS

PENGUIN BOOKS

Published by the Penguin Group

Penguin Books Ltd, 80 Strand, London WC2R ORL, England

Penguin Group (USA) Inc., 375 Hudson Street, New York, New York 10014, USA

Penguin Group (Canada), 90 Eglinton Avenue East, Suite 700, Toronto, Ontario, Canada M4P 2Y3
(a division of Pearson Penguin Canada Inc.)

Penguin Ireland, 25 St Stephen's Green, Dublin 2, Ireland (a division of Penguin Books Ltd)

Penguin Group (Australia), 250 Camberwell Road, Camberwell, Victoria 3124, Australia
(a division of Pearson Australia Group Pty Ltd)

Penguin Books India Pvt Ltd, 11 Community Centre, Panchsheel Park, New Delhi – 110 017, India

Penguin Group (NZ), 67 Apollo Drive, Rosedale, North Shore 0632, New Zealand
(a division of Pearson New Zealand Ltd)

Penguin Books (South Africa) (Pty) Ltd, 24 Sturdee Avenue, Rosebank, Johannesburg 2196, South Africa

Penguin Books Ltd, Registered Offices: 80 Strand, London WC2R ORL, England

www.penguin.com

This edition first published in Penguin Books 1968
Reissued in the Penguin Shakespeare series 2010

2

Set in 11.5/12.5 PostScript Monotype Fournier
Designed by Boag Associates
Typeset by Palimpsest Book Production Limited, Grangemouth, Stirlingshire
Printed in England by Clays Ltd, St Ives plc

ISBN: 978-0-141-01379-4

www.greenpenguin.co.uk

Contents

General Introduction

Every play by Shakespeare is unique. This is part of his greatness. A restless and indefatigable experimenter, he moved with a rare amalgamation of artistic integrity and dedicated professionalism from one kind of drama to another. Never shackled by convention, he offered his actors the alternation between serious and comic modes from play to play, and often also within the plays themselves, that the repertory system within which he worked demanded, and which provided an invaluable stimulus to his imagination. Introductions to individual works in this series attempt to define their individuality. But there are common factors that underpin Shakespeare's career.

Nothing in his heredity offers clues to the origins of his genius. His upbringing in Stratford-upon-Avon, where he was born in 1564, was unexceptional. His mother, born Mary Arden, came from a prosperous farming family. Her father chose her as his executor over her eight sisters and his four stepchildren when she was only in her late teens, which suggests that she was of more than average practical ability. Her husband John, a glover, apparently unable to write, was nevertheless a capable businessman and loyal townsfellow, who seems to have fallen on relatively hard times in later life. He would have been brought up as a Catholic, and may have retained

Catholic sympathies, but his son subscribed publicly to Anglicanism throughout his life.

The most important formative influence on Shakespeare was his school. As the son of an alderman who became bailiff (or mayor) in 1568, he had the right to attend the town's grammar school. Here he would have received an education grounded in classical rhetoric and oratory, studying authors such as Ovid, Cicero and Quintilian, and would have been required to read, speak, write and even think in Latin from his early years. This classical education permeates Shakespeare's work from the beginning to the end of his career. It is apparent in the self-conscious classicism of plays of the early 1590s such as the tragedy of *Titus Andronicus*, *The Comedy of Errors*, and the narrative poems *Venus and Adonis* (1592–3) and *The Rape of Lucrece* (1593–4), and is still evident in his latest plays, informing the dream visions of *Pericles* and *Cymbeline* and the masque in *The Tempest*, written between 1607 and 1611. It inflects his literary style throughout his career. In his earliest writings the verse, based on the ten-syllabled, five-beat iambic pentameter, is highly patterned. Rhetorical devices deriving from classical literature, such as alliteration and antithesis, extended similes and elaborate wordplay, abound. Often, as in *Love's Labour's Lost* and *A Midsummer Night's Dream*, he uses rhyming patterns associated with lyric poetry, each line self-contained in sense, the prose as well as the verse employing elaborate figures of speech. Writing at a time of linguistic ferment, Shakespeare frequently imports Latinisms into English, coining words such as abstemious, addiction, incarnadine and adjunct. He was also heavily influenced by the eloquent translations of the Bible in both the Bishops' and the Geneva versions. As his experience grows, his verse and prose become more supple,

the patterning less apparent, more ready to accommodate the rhythms of ordinary speech, more colloquial in
diction, as in the speeches of the Nurse in *Romeo and
Juliet*, the characterful prose of Falstaff, and Hamlet's
soliloquies. The effect is of increasing psychological
realism, reaching its greatest heights in *Hamlet*, *Othello*,
King Lear, *Macbeth* and *Antony and Cleopatra*. Gradually
he discovered ways of adapting the regular beat of the
pentameter to make it an infinitely flexible instrument for
matching thought with feeling. Towards the end of his
career, in plays such as *The Winter's Tale*, *Cymbeline* and
The Tempest, he adopts a more highly mannered style, in
keeping with the more overtly symbolical and emblem-
atical mode in which he is writing.

So far as we know, Shakespeare lived in Stratford till
after his marriage to Anne Hathaway, eight years his
senior, in 1582. They had three children: a daughter,
Susanna, born in 1583 within six months of their marriage,
and twins, Hamnet and Judith, born in 1585. The next
seven years of Shakespeare's life are virtually a blank.
Theories that he may have been, for instance, a school-
master, or a lawyer, or a soldier, or a sailor, lack evidence
to support them. The first reference to him in print, in
Robert Greene's pamphlet *Greene's Groatsworth of Wit*
of 1592, parodies a line from *Henry VI, Part III*, implying
that Shakespeare was already an established playwright.
It seems likely that at some unknown point after the birth
of his twins he joined a theatre company and gained
experience as both actor and writer in the provinces and
London. The London theatres closed because of plague
in 1593 and 1594; and during these years, perhaps recog-
nizing the need for an alternative career, he wrote and
published the narrative poems *Venus and Adonis* and *The
Rape of Lucrece*. These are the only works we can be

certain that Shakespeare himself was responsible for putting into print. Each bears the author's dedication to Henry Wriothesley, Earl of Southampton (1573–1624), the second in warmer terms than the first. Southampton, younger than Shakespeare by ten years, is the only person to whom he personally dedicated works. The Earl may have been a close friend, perhaps even the beautiful and adored young man whom Shakespeare celebrates in his *Sonnets*.

The resumption of playing after the plague years saw the founding of the Lord Chamberlain's Men, a company to which Shakespeare was to belong for the rest of his career, as actor, shareholder and playwright. No other dramatist of the period had so stable a relationship with a single company. Shakespeare knew the actors for whom he was writing and the conditions in which they performed. The permanent company was made up of around twelve to fourteen players, but one actor often played more than one role in a play and additional actors were hired as needed. Led by the tragedian Richard Burbage (1568–1619) and, initially, the comic actor Will Kemp (d. 1603), they rapidly achieved a high reputation, and when King James I succeeded Queen Elizabeth I in 1603 they were renamed as the King's Men. All the women's parts were played by boys; there is no evidence that any female role was ever played by a male actor over the age of about eighteen. Shakespeare had enough confidence in his boys to write for them long and demanding roles such as Rosalind (who, like other heroines of the romantic comedies, is disguised as a boy for much of the action) in *As You Like It*, Lady Macbeth and Cleopatra. But there are far more fathers than mothers, sons than daughters, in his plays, few if any of which require more than the company's normal complement of three or four boys.

The company played primarily in London's public playhouses – there were almost none that we know of in the rest of the country – initially in the Theatre, built in Shoreditch in 1576, and from 1599 in the Globe, on Bankside. These were wooden, more or less circular structures, open to the air, with a thrust stage surmounted by a canopy and jutting into the area where spectators who paid one penny stood, and surrounded by galleries where it was possible to be seated on payment of an additional penny. Though properties such as cauldrons, stocks, artificial trees or beds could indicate locality, there was no representational scenery. Sound effects such as flourishes of trumpets, music both martial and amorous, and accompaniments to songs were provided by the company's musicians. Actors entered through doors in the back wall of the stage. Above it was a balconied area that could represent the walls of a town (as in *King John*), or a castle (as in *Richard II*), and indeed a balcony (as in *Romeo and Juliet*). In 1609 the company also acquired the use of the Blackfriars, a smaller, indoor theatre to which admission was more expensive, and which permitted the use of more spectacular stage effects such as the descent of Jupiter on an eagle in *Cymbeline* and of goddesses in *The Tempest*. And they would frequently perform before the court in royal residences and, on their regular tours into the provinces, in non-theatrical spaces such as inns, guildhalls and the great halls of country houses.

Early in his career Shakespeare may have worked in collaboration, perhaps with Thomas Nashe (1567–*c*. 1601) in *Henry VI, Part I* and with George Peele (1556–96) in *Titus Andronicus*. And towards the end he collaborated with George Wilkins (*fl*. 1604–8) in *Pericles*, and with his younger colleagues Thomas Middleton (1580–1627), in *Timon of Athens*, and John Fletcher (1579–1625), in *Henry*

VIII, *The Two Noble Kinsmen* and the lost play *Cardenio*. Shakespeare's output dwindled in his last years, and he died in 1616 in Stratford, where he owned a fine house, New Place, and much land. His only son had died at the age of eleven, in 1596, and his last descendant died in 1670. New Place was destroyed in the eighteenth century but the other Stratford houses associated with his life are maintained and displayed to the public by the Shakespeare Birthplace Trust.

One of the most remarkable features of Shakespeare's plays is their intellectual and emotional scope. They span a great range from the lightest of comedies, such as *The Two Gentlemen of Verona* and *The Comedy of Errors*, to the profoundest of tragedies, such as *King Lear* and *Macbeth*. He maintained an output of around two plays a year, ringing the changes between comic and serious. All his comedies have serious elements: Shylock, in *The Merchant of Venice*, almost reaches tragic dimensions, and *Measure for Measure* is profoundly serious in its examination of moral problems. Equally, none of his tragedies is without humour: Hamlet is as witty as any of his comic heroes, *Macbeth* has its Porter, and *King Lear* its Fool. His greatest comic character, Falstaff, inhabits the history plays and *Henry V* ends with a marriage, while *Henry VI, Part III*, *Richard II* and *Richard III* culminate in the tragic deaths of their protagonists.

Although in performance Shakespeare's characters can give the impression of a superabundant reality, he is not a naturalistic dramatist. None of his plays is explicitly set in his own time. The action of few of them (except for the English histories) is set even partly in England (exceptions are *The Merry Wives of Windsor* and the Induction to *The Taming of the Shrew*). Italy is his favoured location. Most of his principal story-lines derive from printed writings; but the structuring and translation of these narratives into dramatic terms is Shakespeare's own, and he invents much additional material. Most of the plays contain elements of myth and legend, and many derive from ancient or more recent history or from romantic tales of ancient times and faraway places. All reflect his reading, often in close detail. Holinshed's *Chronicles* (1577, revised 1587), a great compendium of English, Scottish and Irish history, provided material for his English history plays. The *Lives of the Noble Grecians and Romans* by the Greek writer Plutarch, finely translated into English from the French by Sir Thomas North in 1579, provided much of the narrative material, and also a mass of verbal detail, for his plays about Roman history. Some plays are closely based on shorter individual works: *As You Like It*, for instance, on the novel *Rosalynde* (1590) by his near-contemporary Thomas Lodge (1558–1625), *The Winter's Tale* on *Pandosto* (1588) by his old rival Robert Greene (1558–92) and *Othello* on a story by the Italian Giraldi Cinthio (1504–73). And the language of his plays is permeated by the Bible, the Book of Common Prayer and the proverbial sayings of his day.

Shakespeare was popular with his contemporaries, but his commitment to the theatre and to the plays in performance is demonstrated by the fact that only about half of his plays appeared in print in his lifetime, in slim paperback volumes known as quartos, so called because they were made from printers' sheets folded twice to form four leaves (eight pages). None of them shows any sign that he was involved in their publication. For him, performance was the primary means of publication. The most frequently reprinted of his works were the non-dramatic poems – the erotic *Venus and Adonis* and the more moralistic *The Rape of Lucrece*. The *Sonnets*, which appeared in 1609, under his name but possibly without his consent, were less successful, perhaps because the vogue for sonnet sequences, which peaked in the 1590s, had passed by then. They were not reprinted until 1640, and then only in garbled form along with poems by other writers. Happily, in 1623, seven years after he died, his colleagues John Heminges (1556–1630) and Henry Condell (d. 1627) published his collected plays, including eighteen that had not previously appeared in print, in the first Folio, whose name derives from the fact that the printers' sheets were folded only once to produce two leaves (four pages). Some of the quarto editions are badly printed, and the fact that some plays exist in two, or even three, early versions creates problems for editors. These are discussed in the Account of the Text in each volume of this series.

Shakespeare's plays continued in the repertoire until the Puritans closed the theatres in 1642. When performances resumed after the Restoration of the monarchy in 1660, many of the plays were not to the taste of the times, especially because their mingling of genres and failure to meet the requirements of poetic justice offended against the dictates of neoclassicism. Some, such as *The Tempest* (changed by John Dryden and William Davenant in 1667 to suit contemporary taste), *King Lear* (to which Nahum Tate gave a happy ending in 1681) and *Richard III* (heavily adapted by Colley Cibber in 1700 as a vehicle for his own talents), were extensively rewritten; others fell into neglect. Slowly they regained their place in the repertoire, and they continued to be reprinted, but it was not until the great actor David Garrick (1717–79) organized a spectacular jubilee in Stratford in 1769 that Shakespeare began to be regarded as a transcendental genius. Garrick's idolatry prefigured the enthusiasm of critics such as Samuel Taylor Coleridge (1772–1834) and William Hazlitt (1778–1830). Gradually Shakespeare's reputation spread abroad, to Germany, America, France and to other European countries.

During the nineteenth century, though the plays were generally still performed in heavily adapted or abbreviated versions, a large body of scholarship and criticism began to amass. Partly as a result of a general swing in education away from the teaching of Greek and Roman texts and towards literature written in English, Shakespeare became the object of intensive study in schools and universities. In the theatre, important turning points were the work in England of two theatre directors, William Poel (1852–1934) and his disciple Harley Granville-Barker (1877–1946), who showed that the application of knowledge, some of it newly acquired, of early staging conditions to performance of the plays could render the original texts viable in terms of the modern theatre. During the twentieth century appreciation of Shakespeare's work, encouraged by the availability of audio, film and video versions of the plays, spread around the world such an extent that he can now be claimed as a global author.

The influence of Shakespeare's works permeates the English language. Phrases from his plays and poems – 'a tower of strength', 'green-eyed jealousy', 'a foregone conclusion' – are on the lips of people who may never have read him. They have inspired composers of songs, orchestral music and operas; painters and sculptors; poets, novelists and film-makers. Allusions to him appear in pop songs, in advertisements and in television shows. Some of his characters – Romeo and Juliet, Falstaff, Shylock and Hamlet – have acquired mythic status. He is valued for his humanity, his psychological insight, his wit and humour, his lyricism, his mastery of language, his ability to excite, surprise, move and, in the widest sense of the word, entertain audiences. He is the greatest of poets, but he is essentially a dramatic poet. Though his plays have much to offer to readers, they exist fully only in performance. In these volumes we offer individual introductions, notes on language and on specific points of the text, suggestions for further reading and information about how each work has been edited. In addition we include accounts of the ways in which successive generations of interpreters and audiences have responded to challenges and rewards offered by the plays. The Penguin Shakespeare series aspires to remove obstacles to understanding and to make pleasurable the reading of the work of the man who has done more than most to make us understand what it is to be human.

Stanley Wells

The Chronology of Shakespeare's Works

A few of Shakespeare's writings can be fairly precisely dated. An allusion to the Earl of Essex in the chorus to Act V of *Henry V*, for instance, could only have been written in 1599. But for many of the plays we have only vague information, such as the date of publication, which may have occurred long after composition, the date of a performance, which may not have been the first, or a list in Francis Meres's book *Palladis Tamia*, published in 1598, which tells us only that the plays listed there must have been written by that year. The chronology of the early plays is particularly difficult to establish. Not everyone would agree that the first part of *Henry VI* was written after the third, for instance, or *Romeo and Juliet* before *A Midsummer Night's Dream*. The following table is based on the 'Canon and Chronology' section in *William Shakespeare: A Textual Companion*, by Stanley Wells and Gary Taylor, with John Jowett and William Montgomery (1987), where more detailed information and discussion may be found.

The Two Gentlemen of Verona	1590–91
The Taming of the Shrew	1590–91
Henry VI, Part II	1591
Henry VI, Part III	1591

Introduction

Shakespeare's *Henry V* can seem at once impossibly remote and eerily familiar. This dual impression is not unique to *Henry V* nor is it limited to Shakespeare's historical dramas, but it is one to which they are particularly susceptible due to their distinctive mix of historic personages and events, on the one hand, and enduring struggles for power on the other. The serial topicality of *Henry V* is among its most striking features. In Shakespeare's day persistent threats of invasion by Spain and intensifying conflict in Ireland gave added resonance to plays about England's illustrious warrior king and his stunning victory at Agincourt. The performance history of *Henry V* has been closely tied to the fortunes of war, yet what sets Shakespeare's play apart from other contemporary plays featuring celebrated battles is not so much its depiction of war as the arresting manner in which it both exploits and exposes the power of speech to persuade. The fashioning of speech into a sophisticated political, military and theatrical instrument, an instrument of power, is a hallmark of the play and marks the emergence in *Henry V* of a challenging form of political drama in which audiences are subjected to competing and incompatible claims by successive speakers that put our judgement to the test.

The suggestion that what distinguishes *Henry V* is not

so much its anatomy of war as its anatomy of the power
of persuasion may seem odd, as it is often described as
Shakespeare's war play and has frequently been performed
and twice filmed at times of war or in the aftermath of
military conflict. Yet there are as many battle scenes in
Henry IV, Part I, and considerably more in the *Henry VI*
plays. Unless additional business has been devised, the
closest audiences come to witnessing a major battle scene
in *Henry V* is the second assault on Harfleur, an attack that
the town's defenders successfully repulse. As for the famed
battle of Agincourt, apart from the sound of several military signals (IV.4.0, IV.5.5, IV.6.0, 34, IV.7.52) and one
stage direction calling for '*Excursions*' (military skirmishes
or sorties across the stage; IV.4.0), the only sustained military engagement we witness is an anticlimactic encounter
between two misapprehending cowards: the terrified
Monsieur Le Fer and the bombastic Pistol – just the sort
of 'brawl ridiculous' (IV.Chorus.51) from which the
Chorus seeks to distract us with stirring words. In marked
contrast to *Henry IV, Part I*, where he shows courage by
fulfilling his pledge to kill the intrepid Hotspur 'in single
fight' (V.1.96–100), in *Henry V* we never see Henry engage
in single combat with an esteemed martial adversary. Yet
unlike the King of France, who delegates command on
the battlefield to the Constable, Henry risks his life by
leading his army into battle at Harfleur and again at
Agincourt, where, faced with overwhelming odds, he spurns
repeated offers of ransom. In so doing Henry V outdoes
his famous ancestor King Edward III, who surveyed the
clash of armies at Crécy from a nearby hill while his son
Edward, the Black Prince, 'played a tragedy, | Making
defeat on the full power of France' (I.2.106–7). At
Agincourt, however, the only military command we hear
Henry utter, aside from his instructions to the English

Herald, is his chilling order to kill defenceless French prisoners (IV.6.37, IV.7.61). If we believe we have witnessed the re-enactment of an epic conflict, that is either because the Chorus has conjured up a vivid impression of the clash of armies in our minds or because elaborate battle scenes have been devised for performance. That *Henry V* should be known as Shakespeare's war play when it contains relatively few scenes of combat, and those few are at odds with the stuff of legend and the Chorus's rousing account of an epic struggle, is one of many paradoxes that mark the play's reception.

However, it is neither for its evocation of battle nor for its cogent exploration of the motives for, prosecution of and political capital to be made from war that the play advances its most pressing claim for continued attention. *Henry V* remains an important and compelling drama above all because of its enduring and unrivalled capacity to test our desire to remember, our inclination to forget and our openness to persuasion. In *Hamlet* we listen to the prince ponder the ethics of revenge. In *Henry V* it is we the audience who are directly urged to 'Work, work ... [our] thoughts' (III.Chorus.25) while simultaneously being encouraged to abandon judgement, yield unthinkingly to the enticing oratory of the King and his Chorus on a matter of war and 'Follow, follow!' (17). Unless we remain vigilant we risk being 'marvellously mistook' (III.6.79), as our capacity to remember and willingness to forget are probed at every turn. With the possible exception of *Julius Caesar*, no other Shakespearian play brings home so forcefully, and not even *Julius Caesar* brings home as insistently, the political value of controlling how the past is remembered and the relative ease with which historical remembrance can be manipulated for political ends.

The refashioning of the past into a patriotic epic and so into political myth is the principal function of the choruses, beginning with the Prologue's comparison of 'warlike Harry' (5) to the Roman god of war and concluding with the Epilogue's memorial sonnet to 'This star of England' (6). But the version of history promoted in the choruses proves unreliable. Even as we are encouraged by the Chorus to respond unthinkingly to its rousing account of Henry V's wars in France, the dramatic sequence prompts us to note the difference between what we hear and what we see and to recall the actual as distinct from the (mis)reported sequence of events. Meanwhile, the play's inclusion of dissonant voices – the Eastcheapers, the conspirators, the quarrelsome captains, the common soldiers, Burgundy and Katherine – opens up alternative versions of history to the official version sponsored by the Chorus. While the famous victories of Henry V are central to Shakespeare's historical drama, the need to exercise discernment in responding to a play of persuasion that draws audiences one way and then another on a matter of war lies at the heart of Shakespeare's testing theatre of judgement. For much of its performance history the latter has been sacrificed in favour of a version of the former modelled on the choruses, resulting in a potentially stirring but comparatively slight drama. *Henry V*, its audiences and our times deserve better.

THE TWO VERSIONS OF *HENRY V*
AND THE CLIMATE OF WAR

Henry V depicts a military expedition against a country that is an irritant but does not pose an imminent threat to the invading power. The ensuing conflict causes the invaded land, formerly 'this best garden of the world' (V.2.36), to 'grow to wildness' (55) and its people to 'grow like savages' (59). Perhaps it is unsurprising that it has proved the most critically divisive of Shakespeare's plays in modern times. Changing attitudes to war, and especially to military invasions of dubious warrant, have contributed to this modern critical phenomenon, but the emergence of opposing responses to *Henry V* is also bound up with the way it arouses expectations one moment and upsets them the next. The existence of two very different surviving early versions of *Henry V*, one exceptionally short and the other unusually long, raises the intriguing possibility that Shakespeare's play may also have divided its earliest interpreters. Most modern editions of *Henry V*, including the present one, are based on *The Life of Henry the Fifth*, the version included in the first collected edition of Shakespeare's plays, now commonly known as the first Folio, which was compiled by two of Shakespeare's former fellow actors, John Heminges and Henry Condell, and printed posthumously in 1623. A very different version of *Henry V* was issued as a quarto in August 1600, bearing the descriptive title *The Chronicle History of Henry the Fifth, with His Battle Fought at Agincourt in France. Together with Ancient Pistol*. Although *The Chronicle History* (known as the first Quarto) was the only version printed in Shakespeare's lifetime, his name is notably absent from its title page, the only one of five Shakespeare plays printed that year not to record Shakespeare's authorship. Its title page purports to offer the play 'As it hath been sundry times played' by the Lord Chamberlain's Men (the playing company of which Shakespeare became a principal shareholder in 1599); however, this claim and Shakespeare's direct involvement in devising the acting script from which *The*

Chronicle History supposedly derives remain in doubt (see 'Textual Issues' in Further Reading).

The two versions are distinguished not only by their sharply differing lengths (*The Chronicle History* is half the length of *The Life*) but also by their divergent representations of Henry V and his French campaign. *The Chronicle History* omits all of the choruses (including the Prologue and Epilogue), removes or truncates the longest speeches, leaves out entire scenes and transposes others, reduces the number of roles and makes consistent changes to names (the most notable being the elimination of the Dauphin from Agincourt through the reassignment of his speeches to Bourbon). The representation of Henry V, the motives for and conduct of his war are transformed by the omission of Act I, scene 1 and lines 115–35 of Act I, scene 2, removing any hint of a financial motive for Canterbury's interpretation of the Salic law and the bishops' eagerness to sanction – and fund – Henry's war; any suggestion in Act II, scene 1 that Henry is responsible for Falstaff's death; Cambridge's hint that deeper motives than bribery prompted him to join the conspiracy (II.2.155–60); Jamy, Macmorris and the quarrel over Macmorris's 'nation' in Act III, scene 2; most of the Harfleur episode, including Henry's famous rallying speech (III.1) together with his most savage threats to the townspeople (III.3.11–41); much of Henry's disquieting exchange with his soldiers on the night before Agincourt in Act IV, scene 1; the lengthy section of Henry's soliloquy on ceremony and the burdens of kingship (IV.1.223–77); any mention of the hanging of Nym (IV.4.68–71); the whole of Burgundy's evocative description of the havoc caused by Henry's invasion (V.2.34–67); much of the dialogue between Henry and Princess Katherine; and the edgy sexual banter between Burgundy and Henry (V.2.277–322) – material crucial to Henry's characterization. The 'short' version thus dispenses with much of the material that detracts from a straightfor-wardly heroic and patriotic account of Henry V and his French wars, resulting in a pacier, more jingoistic and considerably more orthodox play. The 'long' and 'short' versions of *Henry V* are thus not merely distinct but potentially opposing. Many argue that *The Chronicle History* supplies the idealized heroic and patriotic war play that some have taken *The Life* to be.

Shakespeare's unsettling account of a celebrated English king and his French wars in the 'long' Folio version of *Henry V* appears all the more daring if we reflect on the historical circumstances in which the play-wright devised his heterodox drama. The play was (most probably) written and first performed in 1599, the last year of a tumultuous century and at the end of the most militarist decade in Elizabethan history, during which time people in England lived in fear of imminent invasion by Spain. The failure of the 'Glorious Armada' of 1588 did not end fears of a Spanish naval assault. Rapid Spanish rearmament meant that the threat of invasion persisted, with further invasion scares over the next decade and annually from 1596 (the year the port of Calais fell to Spain) until 1599 prompting sudden mobilizations of men and shipping to strengthen England's defences followed by their abrupt disband-ment when the rumours of an armada proved false or severe storms scattered the Spanish fleet. Forced musters of men became a regular occurrence, and trained bands of citizen militia were frequently to be seen performing military drills on London fields and in provincial churchyards.

War and the threat of invasion shaped late-Elizabethan

culture and influenced Shakespeare's theatre of war in
Henry V in myriad ways. 'Art of war' writing prolifer-
ated, particularly manuals on the orderly conduct of war
and the attributes of an ideal general, generating an enter-
tainingly quarrelsome battle as rival captains vehemently
denounced one another's theories in print (Jorgensen,
Shakespeare's Military World, pp. 72–3). Shakespeare
gently mocks the appetite for such literature and the argu-
mentative character of the Elizabethan manual debate in
the person of Captain Fluellen. A fiercely loyal Welshman
with a temperament as 'hot as gunpowder' (IV.7.175),
Fluellen nonetheless allows his fondness for 'disputations
. . . touching or concerning the disciplines of the war'
(III.2.92–4) to get in the way of the fighting during the
heat of the battle for Harfleur, much to the annoyance
of Captain Macmorris, who notes that 'it is no time to
discourse, . . . there is throats to be cut, and works to be
done' (104–9). Fluellen's comically pedantic obsession
with 'the disciplines of the pristine wars of the Romans'
(79) parodies the advice to study the 'ancient Roman disciplines for the wars . . . and accommodate them to the
service of our time' (Preface, pp. Aiii^v–Aiv^r) offered by
Leonard and Thomas Digges in their influential guide to
military tactics *An Arithmeticall Militare Treatise, Named
Stratioticos* (1579), a book that Shakespeare may have
come upon when it was reissued in 1590 by his fellow
Stratfordian Richard Field (who printed Shakespeare's
Venus and Adonis in 1593).

While London's bookstalls filled up with war manuals,
war plays were in vogue in its playhouses. Christopher
Marlowe set the pattern with his ground-breaking
conqueror play *Tamburlaine the Great* (*c.* 1587–8), which
proved so popular that he promptly wrote a sequel (*c.*
1588). In devising his own conqueror play just over a

decade later, Shakespeare repeatedly summons up remembrance of Marlowe's seminal two-part drama: Pistol's bombastic speeches parody the 'high astounding terms' of Marlowe's Scythian shepherd (*Part One*, Prologue, l. 5); Henry's threatening speech at Harfleur recalls the threat of total war levelled by Tamburlaine at the siege of Damascus, only to distinguish Henry's instruction to 'Use mercy' (III.3.54) after Harfleur surrenders from Tamburlaine's order to put the citizens of Damascus 'to the sword' (*Part One*, V.1.134); and Henry's betrothal to Princess Katherine, his 'capital demand' (V.2.96) in the peace negotiations with France, has disturbing parallels with Tamburlaine's rape of and subsequent marriage to Zenocrate, daughter of the Sultan of Egypt. Several of the playhouses in which 1590s war plays were regularly performed were sited near the city's wartime training grounds (de Somogyi, *Shakespeare's Theatre of War*, pp. 124–6), including two, the Theatre and the Curtain, that have strong Shakespearian connections, the former as the home of Shakespeare's playing company until they built the Globe Theatre on Bankside in 1599 and the latter as the company's temporary home during the Globe's construction and quite possibly the 'wooden O' (Prologue.13) in which *Henry V* was first performed. Playgoers travelling to the first production of *Henry V* may well have passed within sight of actual soldiers rehearsing for battle in nearby fields. There is also evidence to suggest that captains and soldiers made up a significant portion of theatre audiences during this period (see R. B. McKerrow (ed.), *The Works of Thomas Nashe* (1904–10), vol. 1, p. 212). All of these factors would have lent a sense of immediacy to performances of war plays such as *Henry V* irrespective of their historically remote settings.

Several features of *Henry V* would have made its
temporal setting seem considerably less remote in 1599.
Contemporary wartime anxieties account for the presence in *Henry V* of material that is often omitted in
modern performances yet would have blurred the
boundary between past and present for the play's first
audiences. Continuing fears of a Spanish armada may
have prompted Shakespeare's choice of a maritime
metaphor when Henry recounts how, when Edward III
was waging war in France, 'the Scot on his unfurnished
kingdom | Came pouring, like the tide into a breach'
(I.2.148–9). Henry's preoccupation with the 'ill neighbourhood' of Scotland (136–221) also would have struck
a chord after Elizabeth I's agents uncovered successive
plots by Catholic earls in Scotland to join in league with
Spain in the post-Armada years, and after the discovery
in the 1590s that a number of Scottish nobles were fuelling
revolt in Ireland. The lengthy debate by Henry and his
war council over the threat of incursion posed by the
Scots is now frequently omitted; however, inveterate
distrust of England's 'giddy neighbour' (145) to the north
and prevailing concerns about the need for England to
protect itself from invasion by Spain while simultaneously fighting defensive wars abroad would have made
this discussion of homeland security highly topical in
1599. In August 1599, just months after Elizabeth had sent
over into Ireland the largest army to have been dispatched
abroad since the reign of Henry VIII, England was
plunged into its largest invasion scare since 1588. False
reports that the Spanish had landed on the Isle of Wight
caused panicked scenes in London as heavy chains were
drawn across the Thames and the city's thoroughfares to
hinder the rumoured invaders. As outlined below,
Shakespeare probably wrote *Henry V* sometime between

February and September 1599, with the spring or early summer the most likely date of completion. If so, the debate about homeland defence in *Henry V* could not have been more timely.

While Elizabeth's testy relations with Scotland can be detected behind the protracted ruminations on 'the main intendment of the Scot' (I.2.144) by Henry's war council, the impact of Elizabeth's widening wars in Ireland on Shakespeare's account of Henry V's wars in France is more far-reaching and more diffuse. *Henry V* was written at the height of the Nine Years War in Ireland (1594–1603). The shift to open and sustained warfare in Ireland came less than a year before Shakespeare wrote *Henry V*, after an English force several thousand strong was slaughtered by Irish rebels in August 1598 and the Munster Plantation (a colony of 'New English' settlers) was overrun two months later. Ireland was Elizabeth's second kingdom; Spain viewed it as England's Achilles' heel and began supplying money, munitions and eventually also soldiers to support the revolt so as to threaten England with encirclement. To counter that menace and suppress the uprising, record numbers of Englishmen were hastily conscripted into military service at the end of 1598 and the first six months of 1599. This crisis in Irish affairs lies behind the repeated intrusion of Ireland into *Henry V*, a play set during Henry V's campaigns (1414–22) in the Hundred Years War (1337–1453) between England and France, fought more than a century before Henry VIII became the first English king to assume the title King of Ireland in the 1540s. The period of Lancastrian rule under Henry V and Henry VI acquired new meaning with the outbreak of open war in Ireland. Where the prospect of possessing forfeited 'rebel' lands in Munster and establishing themselves as landed gentry had offered New

English adventurers an opportunity unseen on such a scale since the time of Henry V and his conquests in France (MacCaffrey, *Elizabeth I*, p. 344), so the loss of the Munster colony called to mind the loss of England's possessions in France in the last phase of the Hundred Years War. The descriptions of Henry's '*poor soldiers*' (III.6.84) closely chime with Elizabethan reports of the famished nakedness of the poorly provisioned, disease-ridden (III.5.57, III.6.153, III.7.148, IV.2.14) and ill-shod (IV.8.68–71) royal army in Ireland. The unusually explicit topical reference in the fifth chorus to 'the General of our gracious Empress . . . from Ireland coming' (30–31); the inclusion of Macmorris; and other curious references to Ireland in the play, such as the cluster of mocking references to 'a kern of Ireland' (III.7.51), 'strait strossers' (52) and 'foul bogs' (55); Pistol's mispronunciation of an Irish ballad refrain, '*Calen o custure me!*' (IV.4.4); the anachronistic greeting, 'brother Ireland', Isabel addresses to Henry (see note to V.2.12); and Henry's equally anachronistic pledge to Katherine, 'England is thine, *Ireland is thine*, France is thine' (V.2.236–7; added emphasis) would have encouraged the play's first audiences to draw analogies between Henry V's wars in France and the ongoing wars in Ireland and, more narrowly, between the victor at Agincourt and the general whose triumphal return 'from Ireland' is anticipated in the fifth chorus (though whether these comparisons were favourable is open to question). The general alluded to is almost certainly Robert Devereux, the second Earl of Essex, whom Elizabeth had dispatched to Ireland in March 1599.

The thinly veiled reference to Essex makes it possible to date *Henry V* with unusual confidence to the period between February and September 1599 with internal evidence pointing to the spring or early summer as the most likely date of completion. After months of stalling Essex had finally accepted the Irish commission in February 1599. An ardent militarist, acclaimed 'Great England's glory and the world's wide wonder' by Edmund Spenser (*Prothalamion* (1596), l. 146), Essex had captured the public's imagination with his exploits at Rouen, Lisbon, Cadiz and the Azores. He left for Ireland on 27 March, cheered on by crowds of Londoners (John Stow, *Annales* (1615), pp. 787–8) confident that their popular hero would return 'Bringing rebellion broachèd on his sword' (V.Chorus.32). Contrary to popular expectations, Essex returned unauthorized to England on 28 September, having concluded a humiliating truce without Elizabeth's permission. Forty-eight hours later Essex was under house arrest. However, it had already become apparent by July that Essex's campaign might end in failure. If the play was written in the spring or early summer, the Chorus's unfavourable comparison of the popular support for Essex (characterized as 'lower', V. Chorus.29) to that merited by Henry V – 'Much more, and *much more cause*, | Did they this Harry' (34–5; added emphasis) – was prescient. Its use of the ambiguous phrase 'Bringing rebellion broachèd on his sword' (see note) allows for the possibility that Essex's return to the capital might threaten 'the peaceful city' (33) (Patterson, *Shakespeare and the Popular Voice*, pp. 84–7). And so it proved when on 8 February 1601 Essex attempted to launch a popular uprising in London in a bid to depose his rivals at court. Ill-conceived and clumsily executed, the attempted coup proved an abject failure: in rapid order Essex was captured, tried and beheaded.

CHRONICLING ENGLAND

It was in this wartime climate that the English history
play emerged to become one of the dominant genres of
the Elizabethan stage, and Shakespeare was at the forefront of its invention. Historical writing had long been
among the favourite reading matter of England's book-
buying population. When William Caxton established
the first printing press in England in 1476 one of the first
books he printed was *The Chronicles of England* (1480).
Designed for a lay readership, *Caxton's Chronicles* (as it
came to be known) would go through thirteen printings
in fifty years. The break with Rome under Henry VIII
gave impetus to the task of writing England, its history,
institutions, land and language; however, it was during
the reign of Elizabeth I that the project of writing the
English 'nation' into being reached fruition. Elizabeth's
war years sharply heightened patriotic interest in the
history of England and of London, its burgeoning capital,
and a glut of histories issued from the presses. English
history plays complemented, supplemented and, for those
unable to read, substituted for these multiplying volumes
of printed history. Many playgoers in Shakespeare's day
and after derived their knowledge of England's past from
stage plays. In his *Apology for Actors* (1612) Thomas
Heywood maintained that history plays had so widely
'instructed such as cannot read in the discovery of all our
English chronicles' that scarcely anyone 'cannot discourse
of any notable thing recorded' (F3^r). The growing body
of writing on the history of England helped to fashion
a distinctive sense of 'Englishness'; in so doing it helped
to generate (in Benedict Anderson's phrase) the 'imagined political community' of an emerging English (and

nascent British) nation. The contribution made by the
theatre to this generational project of writing the *nation*
of England into being was unique, for the playhouse
provided a vibrant forum and the English history
play provided a popular means for Elizabethan audiences
to participate in that imagined community and in the twin
processes of *remembering* and *forgetting* on which a shared
sense of national history crucially depends and that
Shakespeare foregrounds so trenchantly in *Henry V*.

Shakespeare's dramatic writing on English history
drew on and helped to create the avid public appetite for
all forms of writing on England's past. His English chronicle plays comprise nearly a third of his known dramatic
output, particularly if we include his possible collaboration on *Sir Thomas More* (c. 1592–5, revised c. 1603–4)
and *Edward III* (c. 1592–3). In the first Folio's table of
contents Shakespeare's plays are listed under one of three
headings, 'Comedies', 'Histories' and 'Tragedies'. Of the
ten plays grouped as Histories, all were written in the
1590s with the exception of *Henry VIII* (*All is True*),
which dates to 1613. In choosing plays for inclusion as
Histories the Folio's compilers were clearly guided by
the 'Englishness' of the history treated in the plays they
selected. The Histories are listed in the table of contents
in chronological order by reign, commencing with *King
John*, which begins soon after the king was crowned in
1199, and concluding with *Henry VIII*, which ends with
the birth of Princess Elizabeth and anticipates the reign
of James VI and I. The eight intervening plays span a
tumultuous period in medieval English history from 1397
to 1485. The Folio's chronological listing has sponsored
a modern performance tradition in which these eight plays
are performed as a historical cycle that begins with the
deposition and murder of Richard II and concludes with

the death of Richard III and the accession of the first
Tudor monarch, Henry VII, who brought the civil wars
to an end by uniting the Yorkists and the Lancastrians
through marriage. In their preoccupation with political
violence Shakespeare's English histories show 'the very
age and body of the time his form and pressure' (*Hamlet*,
III.2.23–4). Civil war, factionalism and political assassi-
nation had made the Low Countries and France vulner-
able to Spanish domination; all three, and the bane of
civil war in particular, feature prominently in
Shakespeare's Histories – except for *Henry V*.

In place of civil war, *Henry V* presents a war of invasion led by a king of England in which a numerically
greatly superior opponent suffers a humiliating defeat at
the hands of a 'beggared host' (IV.2.41). In what would
prove the last English history he wrote during Elizabeth's
reign (1558–1603) Shakespeare reminded contemporary
audiences of a time when their ancestors emerged victorious from a battle undertaken against seeming impossible odds and forced their enemies to sue for peace. The
posture of readiness, long endured by the English in their
defensive wars with Spain, is displaced on to the French,
who are reminded by the Dauphin 'that defences, musters,
preparations, | Should be maintained, assembled, and
collected, | As were a war in expectation' (II.4.18–20).
Where the preceding histories portray England divided
against itself, in *Henry V* Shakespeare creates the illusion
of a kingdom uniquely united in war against a foreign
adversary by omitting the anti-Lancastrian and dissenting
Lollard revolts Henry V had had to quell in the first
eighteen months of his reign, isolating the Cambridge
conspiracy as the only internal challenge to Henry's
regime and suppressing its political motive to depose
Henry in favour of Edmund Mortimer, Richard II's lineal

heir. He also makes the King of France a more regal
opponent by omitting his name and any mention of the
'old disease of frensie' from which Charles VI report-
edly suffered (Holinshed, *Chronicles*, vol. 3, p. 547). Far
from being a distracted ruler troubled by bouts of mental
illness, in *Henry V* the King of France is the first to apprehend the gravity of the threat posed by Henry (II.4.48–
9). The first two acts are given over to the preparations
for war while the remaining three depict a radically fore-
shortened version of Henry V's French wars, portraying
events from his first invasion of France in 1414 to the
battle of Agincourt in 1415 before proceeding directly to
Henry's betrothal to Princess Katherine, which sealed the
peace treaty signed at Troyes cathedral in 1420. The
intervening four-year period of sustained fighting is
omitted, as is Henry's second French campaign, which
was triggered by the Dauphin's rejection of the Treaty
of Troyes and ended with Henry's death in 1422, probably from dysentery. This structure gives the play a double
climax in the form of Henry's decisive victory at
Agincourt and his betrothal to Katherine, war and peace,
followed by the abrupt anticlimax of the Epilogue.
Shakespeare would return to his abiding preoccupation
with civil war in his next play, *Julius Caesar*, seen by a
Swiss visitor at the Globe Theatre on 21 September 1599,
one week before Essex's unauthorized return from
Ireland. (The reference in the fifth chorus of *Henry V* to
the senators and plebeians of 'th'antique Rome' fetching
in 'their conquering Caesar' (26–8) and the playwright's
first ever mention of Mark Antony (III.6.14) together
suggest that Shakespeare was already casting his mind
forward to *Julius Caesar* as he was completing *Henry V*.)
In the years to follow Shakespeare would draw on Roman
history for *Antony and Cleopatra* and *Coriolanus*, on ancient

British legend for *King Lear* and *Cymbeline* and on Scottish history for *Macbeth*; however, it would be another fourteen years before he returned to the recent English past to write one of his last plays, *Henry VIII (All is True)*, probably in collaboration with John Fletcher. *Henry V* thus marks an important transition in the playwright's use of history on the stage.

The last of Shakespeare's Elizabethan chronicle histories, *Henry V* is also the last of a series of four plays known as the second tetralogy, so called because the plays that comprise the series (*Richard II*, *Henry IV, Parts I* and *II* and *Henry V*) were written after an earlier quartet of plays on the reigns of Henry VI and Richard III known as the first tetralogy. Although composed *after* the first tetralogy, the second tetralogy surveys the tumultuous twenty-three-year period in medieval English history (1397–1420) that immediately *preceded* the protracted wars over the royal succession portrayed in the earlier tetralogy. The events leading up to and following immediately upon the deposition and murder of Richard II are the subject of the first play in the second tetralogy. The next two plays, *Henry IV, Parts I* and *II*, treat the 'scambling and unquiet' (I.1.4) reign of Richard's successor, the usurper Henry Bolingbroke, who was the father of Prince Hal, the future King Henry V. *Henry V* brings the second tetralogy to a close, but its Epilogue recollects what came after: the premature death of Henry V and the coronation of his infant son Henry VI, 'Whose state so many had the managing | That they lost France, and made his England bleed' (11–12) – a history, it reminds audiences, 'Which oft our stage hath shown' (13). The chronological listing of Shakespeare's Histories in the first Folio thus suppresses one of the defining features of his double cycle of English history plays; namely, that it circles back on itself. The Epilogue to *Henry V* anticipates the death of Henry V, whose solemn funeral procession begins *Henry VI, Part I*. To the extent that the order of composition discloses the order of the writer's imagination, the reign of Henry V emerges as central and his untimely death as structurally and conceptually pivotal to a nostalgic project of recovery in which chronological order is subordinate to the order of remembrance, the linear narrative of time transformed by Shakespeare into a dramatic narrative that encircles irrecoverable loss. *Henry V* is the capstone of that narrative, the play that revives a fleeting vision of England's heroic past and 'Awake[ns] remembrance of [its] valiant dead' (I.2.115).

THE SPECTRE OF HENRY V

Henry V holds a unique place in Shakespeare's historical imagination, but Shakespeare was by no means the only Elizabethan playwright to detect in Henry V's short reign material likely to excite the interest of wartime audiences. By the time a version of Shakespeare's *Henry V* was performed in London playgoers had already had the opportunity to see as many as three other plays about England's conqueror-king since the mid 1580s. The most popular, and the one that had the greatest influence on Shakespeare's *Henry V* and *Henry IV* plays, was *The Famous Victories of Henry the fifth: Containing the Honourable Battell of Agin-court*, an anonymously written work printed by Thomas Creede in 1598. *Famous Victories* may have been performed by the Queen's Men as early as 1588, when anticipation of the threatened Spanish Armada was at its height. The text betrays nothing of the panic that reports of an approaching armada generated in the capital just over a decade later. A bellicose play for a bellicose time, *Famous Victories* reflects a national mood of defiance, confidently alternating scenes of clowning with scenes of conquest that pander unabashedly to jingoist and chauvinist sentiments: if the King of France does not consent to give his daughter in marriage to Henry, Henry will 'so rouse the towers over his ears | That I would make him be glad to bring her me | Upon his hands and knees' (sc. xviii, ll. 71–3). The French soldiers (though not the French king) are boastful or stupid; the innovative tactics used by the English to secure victory are twice noted; King Henry exhibits no sign of a conscience (troubled or otherwise) before battle; a bluff warrior, he proves a brisk wooer – 'Ay but I love her, and must crave her – | Nay, I love her, and will have her!' (sc. xviii, ll. 35–6); for her part, having gained her father's consent, the French princess is eager to be wed – 'I had best whilst he is willing, | Lest when I would he will not' (sc. xx, ll. 48–9).

The appeal these earlier Henry V plays held for Elizabethan audiences living amid the rumours and reports of war can be gleaned from a passage in Nashe's *Pierce Penniless* (1592) in which he observes 'what a glorious thing it is to have Henry the fifth represented on the stage, leading the French king prisoner, and forcing both him and the Dauphin to swear fealty' (*Works*, vol. 1, p. 213). *Famous Victories* ends with a similar spectacle of French humiliation in which Burgundy and the Dolphin (probably a deliberate misspelling) are made to swear fealty and kiss Henry's sword (sc. xx, ll. 34, 35), a crowd-pleasing piece of stage business that Shakespeare notably omits by having *Henry V* conclude just after Henry demands oaths of submission from the French peers but before they are performed (V.2.362–6). For audiences living under renewed threat of invasion and subject to alarmist reports of Spanish landings in Devon, Cornwall, Wales, Ireland and on the Isle of Wight, the appeal of Henry V and his against-the-odds victory at Agincourt is obvious.

In Shakespeare's English history plays the reign of Henry V similarly occasions a mixture of eager anticipation and nostalgic longing. His *Henry VI* plays are haunted by the spectre of Henry V, whose reign becomes the focus of intense yearning for a former, idealized age of heroic conquests abroad and unity at home. Speakers in these plays repeatedly summon up remembrance of Henry V and his triumphs over the French. Even the ardent French patriot Joan la Pucelle (Joan of Arc), self-proclaimed scourge of the English, acknowledges the glory he achieved through his victories in France. Yet 'Glory', she observes, 'is like a circle in the water, | Which never ceaseth to enlarge itself | Till by broad spreading it disperse to naught' (*Henry VI, Part I*, I.2.133–5). So it is with Henry V, the foremost exemplar of English martial glory: 'With Henry's death the English circle ends; | Dispersèd are the glories it included' (136–7).

Tellingly, it is not Henry's life but his death that links the two tetralogies, where it serves as a poignant reminder of former glory. *Henry VI, Part I* begins with the funeral procession of Henry V, whose eulogy is laden with foreboding:

> Posterity, await for wretched years,
> When at their mothers' moistened eyes babes shall suck,
> Our isle be made a nourish of salt tears,
> And none but women left to wail the dead. (I.1.48–51)

The premature death of its conquering hero has left England feminized and infantilized. His passing signals the demise of a masculine heroic ideal – 'arms avail not, now that Henry's dead' (47). The military victories Henry V achieved in France are the benchmark against which succeeding kings are measured and found wanting, such is the conviction that 'England ne'er lost a king of so much worth' (7). The reign of Henry VI sees the loss of his father's conquests and the advent of civil war, accentuating the desire for a return to an idealized past epitomized by the reign of the deceased king. Paradoxically, rather than securing the throne for his son, the glory achieved by Henry V ends up fuelling the sedition that deprives his son of both crown and life, because Henry VI's opponents are able to cite his squandering of his father's legacy as evidence of his unworthiness to rule.

In the plays of the second tetralogy the focus on Prince Hal, the future King Henry V, grows steadily more intense. The one play in which Henry V does not appear as either prince or king is *Richard II*, where his absence provokes his father to enquire 'Can no man tell me of my unthrifty son?' (V.3.1). Although *Henry IV, Parts I* and *II* are titled after the reigning king, Prince Hal appears in more scenes and speaks considerably more lines than does his ailing father. Yet Shakespeare's depiction of Hal as a politically knowing, role-playing heir to a tainted royal title significantly complicates the received legend of the prodigal prince. Although Hal's pledge at the outset of *Henry IV, Part I* that he will 'so offend, to make offence a skill, | Redeeming time when men think least I will' (I.2.214–15) heightens the sense of anticipation that surrounds his long delayed accession to the throne at the end of *Henry IV, Part II*, it also frames his future 'sudden' reformation as a premeditated political stratagem devised by an astute tactician. The Prologue to *Henry V* draws on the climate of expectation built up over the preceding

seven plays; however, the ensuing depiction of Henry V
and his French campaign is considerably more complex
and disquieting than may have been anticipated of a ruler
so long the object of nostalgic idealization. For the 'long'
version of *Henry V* awakens remembrance of an English
legend in such a way as to expose how such national
legends are 'perfected', by reminding us of what we must
forget to remember if they are to be sustained.

SHAKESPEARE'S THEATRE OF
JUDGEMENT

The two figures in *Henry V* who are most determined to
control how the past is remembered for political ends are
Henry and his admiring Chorus. Yet even as the Chorus
strives to fashion our thoughts, the dramatic sequence
casts doubt on the choric version of events. In this artfully
constructed drama the baffling inconsistencies between
the choric commentary and the dramatic action play an
essential part in promoting a theatre of judgement in the
face of the strenuous efforts of the King and his Chorus
to exploit eloquence to influence remembrance. Although
the relentlessly flattering portrait of Henry V sketched
in the choruses could hardly be more disambiguated, the
Chorus frames the play with a pair of strikingly discor-
dant speeches as Prologue and Epilogue and proves an
unreliable narrator throughout. As regards the Prologue,
it is hard to imagine a dramatic apostrophe more at odds
with its theatrical occasion. Dramatic prologues and
epilogues routinely seek the audience's pardon for
supposed 'faults' in a play or performance, but few express
as little confidence in the theatre as a mode of representation as does the Prologue to *Henry V*. For the prologue

to a play about a famous royal martialist to apologize for
the inadequacy of the 'crookèd figure' (15) of the actor
and the 'wooden O' (13) of the theatre 'to bring forth |
So great an object' (10–11) as the battle of Agincourt
does not inspire confidence in playgoers recently parted
from their money. Given the popular success of the *Henry
VI* plays with their numerous battle scenes and bouts of
sword fighting, the Prologue's poor opinion of the
theatre's capacity to create credible martial spectacle
appears perverse.

   Although the Prologue disparages the shortcomings
of theatrical spectacle, it expresses no such reservations
about the capacity of speech to work on the listener's
imagination or about the power of the imagination to
'Piece out . . . imperfections' (23) in the theatrical representation of Henry V and his French wars. On the
contrary, the Chorus will exploit a heady combination of
flattery, exhortation, hyperbole and 'invention' (2; the
generation of material with which to move and convince)
to persuade listeners 'Gently to *hear*, kindly to judge, our
play' (34; added emphasis). While playbook prefaces were
customarily addressed to 'Gentlemen Readers' (Erne,
Shakespeare as Literary Dramatist, pp. 47–50), in the
theatre the Prologue's 'gentles all' (8) flatters the many
playgoers ranked beneath the gentry. Though subsequent
choruses are more strident, this early posture of extreme
obsequiousness and apologetic deference is never entirely
abandoned. Exhorting us one moment, cajoling and
imploring us the next, the strain required to convince us
that we are witnessing a heroic epic becomes palpable.
In the absence of 'A kingdom for a stage, princes to act, |
And monarchs to behold the swelling scene' (3–4), the
Prologue resorts to verbal amplification to overcome the
physical limitations of the stage. With its rhetoric of 'a

thousand parts' (24), it is the first in a series of choric speeches redolent of the abundant style. If the Prologue is to be believed, hyperbole must substitute for theatrical illusion because it alone has the power to foster the impression of plenitude and amplitude needed to induce us to 'make imaginary puissance' (25) and *see* 'warlike Harry ... Assume the port of Mars' (5–6) in our minds. The impression of heroic greatness is dependent on rhetorical invention and amplification, effective spectacle on affective speech.

'Think, when we talk ... you see' (Prologue.26) is the formula that informs the choruses. At key moments the Chorus invites us to imagine scenes of splendour the play makes no attempt to stage: 'The well-appointed King at Hampton pier ... and his brave fleet' (III.Chorus.4–5); 'The Mayor and all his brethren ... With the plebeians swarming at their heels', pouring out of London to 'fetch their conquering Caesar in' (V.Chorus.25–8). These lengthy passages of description draw needless attention to the limits of Elizabethan staging. The declared aim of the Chorus is to encourage us to tolerate 'th'excuse | Of time, of numbers, and due course of things' (V.Chorus. 3–4) in the performance, yet as Shakespeare nowhere else deemed the practice of abridgement he routinely adopted in composing history plays merited comment, much less an apology (44), the stated motives of the Chorus are suspect. The true purpose of these evocative speeches is not to inform us but to arouse our emotions and shape our thoughts. For it is by conjuring up a stirring vision of epic grandeur in our minds, a vision expressly *not* depicted on stage, that the Chorus entices us to accept its version of history as true in defiance of the evidence of our own eyes. As the stage direction calling for the entrance of '*the King and his poor soldiers*' (III.6.84), the

Constable's dismissive appraisal of Henry's army as a 'poor and starvèd band' (IV.2.14) and Henry's frank admission 'We are but warriors for the working-day' (IV.3.109) make plain, what we should witness is an altogether grimmer, more prosaic struggle, if one no less moving for its potent mix of humour and horror.

'Still be kind,' entreats the solicitous Chorus, 'And eke out our performance with your mind' (III.Chorus.34–5). In *The Winter's Tale* Paulina instructs Leontes that if he wishes to see the statue of his wronged wife move and speak to him 'It is required | You do awake your faith' (V.3.94–5). Moments later Hermione '*slowly descends*' from her plinth (V.3.103). Keeping faith with the Chorus in *Henry V* brings no such tangible reward for audiences, as what we see (directors permitting) doesn't merely fall short of the Chorus's vivid verbal scene-painting; on a number of occasions the ensuing action is blatantly at odds with the choric account, not least because the Chorus fails to acknowledge the existence of the Eastcheapers. The second chorus, for example, courteously announces that 'the scene | Is now transported, gentles, to Southampton' (34–5). Despite reiterating the shift in locale (41–2), what follows is not the anticipated sight of English youth, 'on fire' (1) with expectation, hurriedly preparing to embark from Southampton but a pub fight in Eastcheap between two of Falstaff's drinking companions over a brothel keeper and an unpaid debt. The Chorus's claim that 'honour's thought | Reigns solely in the breast of every man' (3–4) is similarly contradicted not only by the treachery of the three conspirators, whose existence the Chorus does acknowledge (21–30), but also by Pistol's cynical decision to join Henry's army as a supplier of provisions in anticipation that 'profits will accrue' (II.1.107). Later, rather than seeing an army of 'culled and choice-drawn cavaliers', supported by 'the nimble gunner', sweeping its way to victory at Harfleur as promised by the Act III Chorus (24, 32), we witness an army debilitated by sickness (III.3.55–6) undertake a second unsuccessful assault on the town's walls, during which a reluctant crew of Eastcheapers have to be beaten forward by Fluellen (III.2.20–1). Contrary to what the Act IV Chorus affirms, we do not see the English king on the eve of Agincourt 'Walking from watch to watch, from tent to tent . . . With cheerful semblance, and sweet majesty', dispensing to all 'A little touch of Harry in the night' (28–47). It may be that here, as elsewhere, the Chorus is relating an episode that has already occurred, yet when he has the opportunity to offer a group of sleepless soldiers words of encouragement we witness Henry do the very opposite by reporting that a trusted commander believes they are 'Even as men wrecked upon a sand, that look to be washed off the next tide' (IV.1.95–6), then heatedly quarrelling with them. These marked discrepancies between the choric report and the dramatic sequence draw attention to the gulf between the idealized account and the unembellished event.

Of the many discontinuities between the choric narrative and the ensuing action, none is more jarring or more salutary than that created by the abrupt transition from the Prologue to the opening scene. Working on our 'imaginary forces', the Prologue invites us to 'Suppose' that we see the combined forces of France and England crammed within the confines of the theatre (18–20). Moments later there step on to the stage not 'two mighty monarchies' (20), as we had been led to anticipate, but two scheming clerics calculating how best to block or moderate a bill, presently being re-urged in Parliament, that would divest the Church of 'the better half' (I.1.8)

of its landed wealth and use some of the funds to relieve
the poor, the sick and the elderly (15–17). This highly
equivocal scene provides an important template for the
play. Because the bill must receive royal assent before it
can become law, determining whether or not Henry can
be induced to oppose the measure is crucial to the two
bishops. It is in this context that Canterbury recounts
'The noble change' (*Henry IV, Part II*, IV.5.155) from
'wildness' to sobriety that Henry appeared to undergo
the moment his father died. Canterbury appears to offer
an adulatory account of Henry's spiritual reformation:

> Never was such a sudden scholar made;
> Never came reformation in a flood
> With such a heady currance scouring faults;
> Nor never Hydra-headed wilfulness
> So soon did lose his seat, and all at once,
> As in this King. (I.1.32–7)

Yet, by underscoring the singularity of the sudden and
improbable change from 'Hydra-headed wilfulness' to 'a
paradise | T'envelop and contain celestial spirits' (I.1.30–
31), his thrice repeated 'never' can also sound incredu-
lous. The archbishop has difficulty explaining how a
seemingly dissolute prince, who never appeared to devote
any time to private study, came to possess the skills of
an accomplished statesman. Henry's 'discourse of war'
(43) may be accounted for by his having experienced
combat during his father's troubled reign, but as he point-
edly distanced himself from his father's court, preferring
the companionship of the Boar's Head tavern to affairs
of state, his ability to address matters of policy and reli-
gion with seeming ease and fluency on becoming king is
no less wondrous than his sudden reformation. As

Canterbury observes, it 'is a wonder how his grace should glean it, | Since his addiction was to courses vain, | His companies unlettered, rude, and shallow' (I.1.53–5).

The key to the riddle of Henry's duplex reformation is supplied by Canterbury in his second panegyric. If we listen closely as each of Henry's virtues is listed, his defining skill as a ruler becomes apparent:

> *Hear* him but reason in divinity,
> And all-admiring, with *an inward wish*,
> You would desire the King were made a prelate.
> *Hear* him *debate* of commonwealth affairs,
> You would say it hath been all in all his study.
> *List* his *discourse* of war, and you shall *hear*
> A fearful battle rendered you *in music*.
> Turn him to any cause of policy,
> The Gordian knot of it he will unloose,
> Familiar as his garter; that, when he *speaks*,
> The air, a chartered libertine, is still,
> And the *mute wonder lurketh in men's ears*
> To steal his *sweet and honeyed sentences*.
>   (I.1.38–50; added emphasis)

Every instance Canterbury cites of Henry's proficiency as a ruler is rooted in Henry's virtuosity as a public speaker. Such is the seductive power of the king's copious, captivating, almost cloying speech that he doesn't just sound the part, according to the archbishop Henry's eloquence so enchants his listeners that 'with an inward wish' they desire him to be the person his speech enables him successively to resemble. Significantly, the response Henry's oratory solicits is not dialogue or debate but 'mute wonder'. A pattern of Henry using exceedingly protracted speeches to silence dissent is readily detectable

in the play: the Southampton conspirators say little in
their own defence after Henry's prolonged tirade; the
Governor of Harfleur surrenders the town immediately after Henry's sustained threatening speech; and
Katherine, having hardly spoken as Henry displays at
length his mastery of the plain style favoured by Hotspur
in *Henry IV, Part I*, falls silent after Henry's forced kiss.
Revealingly, when Henry's disguise obliges him to debate
with his soldiers on equal terms (IV.1.90–222) he ends
up engaged in a bitter quarrel over ethics that climaxes
in an intemperate exchange of gages. Willing obedience
is the aim of the orator king, as it is of his tireless accom-
plice in persuasion the Chorus, and Williams's blunt
reminder that subjects are constrained to obey angers this
self-styled 'king of good fellows' (V.2.240).

Canterbury's damaging disclosure that he has already
discussed matters 'touching France' with the king and
pledged 'to give a greater sum' to fund Henry's wars than
the clergy had given to any of his predecessors (I.1.75–
81) means that when Henry publicly charges this scheming
cleric to 'justly and religiously unfold' (I.2.10) whether
or not the Salic law bars him from claiming the French
crown, he knows full well (as do we) that the archbishop
will support his claim and has a financial motive for doing
so. This revelation compounds those niggling doubts and
insinuations that unsettle Canterbury's apparently lauda-
tory portrait of the king and detracts from Henry's heroic
image even as it is being constructed and seemingly vener-
ated. This corrosive quality is not unique to Canterbury;
paradoxically, the unreliable choruses ensure it is integral
to the play's design. Incorporating such verbal slippages
and dramatic discontinuities at the outset attunes our ears
to dissonance and our eyes to dissimulation. By the end
of their exchange Canterbury, who initially appeared to

subscribe, however knowingly, to the legend of Hal's miraculous reformation, concurs with Ely that the transformation of the profligate prince into the reformed king was premeditated:

> It must be so, for miracles are ceased;
> And therefore we must needs admit the means
> How things are perfected. (I.1.67–9)

The statement 'we must needs admit the means | How things are perfected' is an apt gloss on *Henry V*. While the apparently fulsome praise Henry receives from the two clergymen invites us to embrace the legend of his reformation unthinkingly, the stark disparity between the appearance of piety and the crass shoring-up of riches in the opening scene, like that between the Prologue's invocation of 'a Muse of fire' (1) and the cynical voices that succeed it, encourages us to reflect critically on the historical legend and to exercise judgement in responding to the play. Above all the opening exchange between these two wily bishops cautions us to be wary of the Chorus's stirring invocations of an imperial pageant by directing attention to how such sanitized accounts of royal power are constructed and the political ends they serve. 'Yet sit and see,' the Chorus urges, 'Minding true things by what their mockeries be' (IV.Chorus.52–3). So numerous, manifest and consistent are the discrepancies between the Chorus's pronouncements and the ensuing action that the idealized choric account is gradually exposed as a distortion of 'true things' – so long, that is, as audiences and directors resist the Chorus's urgent solicitations, remember the sequence of events and respond judiciously to beguiling oratory, 'Not working with the eye without the ear, | And but in purgèd judgement trusting neither' (II.2.135–6).

Fluellen provides an object lesson in the hazards of failing to measure words against deeds when he mistakes Pistol to be courageous. The Boy has already confided that 'Pistol . . . hath a killing tongue, and a quiet sword' (III.2.34), yet Fluellen claims that he witnessed an unnamed ensign, subsequently revealed to be Pistol, 'do . . . gallant service' defending the bridge (III.6.12–15). Only later do we discover that Fluellen's high regard for Pistol did not in fact arise from the *sight* of Pistol's 'gallant service' but from the *sound* of his 'prave words' at such bridge. Fluellen's comical confusion of sound with sight in his muddled simile, ''a uttered as prave words at the pridge as you shall see in a summer's day' (III.6.62–3), exemplifies his tendency to mistake words for deeds. In advising his fellow captain, 'you must learn to know such slanders of the age' (III.6.78–9), Gower recalls the words of Ely in the opening scene and reaffirms the play's preoccupation with the power of speech to shape perceptions of the truth.

Our ability to distinguish between seeming and substance (and to remember the sequence of events) is similarly tested, and not just by the choruses. The greatest tests of our judgement follow the battle of Agincourt. After hearing the disproportionate losses suffered by the French Henry attributes his victory entirely to God: 'O God, Thy arm was here! | And not to us, but to Thy arm alone, | Ascribe we all!' (IV.8.105–7). By omitting any mention of the tactics employed to defeat the French, Shakespeare allows Henry's claim that divine intervention alone could account for such a resounding upset to appear more credible. The one notable exception is the playwright's retention of Henry's command to kill the French prisoners (IV.6.37). Yet many may be lured by Gower's misconstruing of events (IV.7.5–10) into

believing that the order is given after the king learns that
the boys have been killed when in fact Shakespeare departs
from the chronicles of Hall and Holinshed in making
Henry's order precede the raid on the English camp,
radically altering its motivation.

An earlier scene provides weightier grounds for ques-
tioning whether Henry's account of the battle is any
more accurate than Gower's by exposing another, far-
reaching cause for the stunning collapse of the French
army at Agincourt. Whether we do so depends yet again
on our willingness to exercise our faculties of memory
and judgement. After their initial boisterous assault on
the English has been repulsed Orleans observes to
Bourbon and the Constable that the scattered French
forces would still be of sufficient number to overwhelm
their opponents 'If any order might be thought upon'
(IV.5.21). When Henry hears a fresh alarm sounded in
the field he promptly commands his soldiers to execute
their prisoners in the mistaken belief that just such a
regrouping is underway (IV.6.35–8). Fatally, the French
nobles refuse to observe any such collective discipline.
The responses of Bourbon and the Constable – 'The
devil take order', 'Disorder that hath spoiled us, friend
us now! | Let us on heaps go offer up our lives' (IV.5.22,
17–18) – clarify both why their first impetuous and over-
confident attack failed and why the French nobility are
slaughtered in such numbers. Formerly the subject of
lewdly convivial banter, in battle their adherence to a
medieval chivalric code founded on individual feats of
valour against opponents of noble blood impels even the
most level-headed among them to bury shame in death
once they believe that their honour has been sullied irre-
deemably by their initial, shameful repulse at the hands
of Henry's 'beggared host' (IV.2.41). Sent to the field

'with spirit of honour edged, | More sharper than [their] swords' (III.5.38–9), their devotion to an aristocratic code of chivalric honour costs them the battle and many of them and their untitled foot soldiers their lives. As the staggeringly disproportionate casualty lists graphically testify, such a single-minded pursuit of personal repute is perilously outdated in a war in which the chivalric ideal of fellowship in arms is evoked by Exeter's report of the deaths of Suffolk and York (IV.6.7–27) only to be brutally displaced by Henry's merciless order to execute defenceless prisoners. In *Henry IV, Part I* the death of Hotspur is felt as a present loss; in *Henry V* the sentimental deaths of Suffolk and York occur as if in another, older world. Agincourt bears out Exeter's blunt warning to the King of France that Henry is prepared to abandon his posture as 'the native and true challenger' in a chivalric trial-by-combat and enforce his will through 'Bloody constraint' (III.2.71; cf. 79, 93–4). Unlike the French, the military discipline Henry imposes is strategic, collective and ruthless, as Bardolph, Nym and the French prisoners discover to their cost. The bookish concern with 'the Roman disciplines' (III.2.71; cf. 79, 93–4) that preoccupies Fluellen finds no echo in his king, who prudently consults the chronicles before declaring war on France merely to ascertain what other hazards may arise from such a decision and how best to counter them (I.2.146–54). Where the French commanders are preoccupied with their status and repute – a preoccupation Henry avowedly shares (I.2.226–34; IV.3.28–9) – as a military leader he imposes strict discipline on his army and ensures that it is ordered by military rank, each rank having its particular martial function. Such is Henry's confidence that his officers know their offices that his terse order before battle is framed as a statement of fact: 'You know your places' (IV.3.78).

In his Crispin Crispian oration (IV.3.18–67) Henry seeks
to rally the daunted spirits of his followers by appealing
to their shared desire to be remembered 'with advantages'
(50). The King is as acutely aware as the Chorus that how
history is remembered depends on whose history is told
and who does the telling. Of the many kings that appear
in Shakespeare's English histories, none is more anxious
than Henry V to control *which* story of his reign the 'good
man' shall 'teach his son' (56). His title as King of England
tainted by his father's deposition of Richard II and
Richard's subsequent murder, Henry V has every reason
to be concerned how his history is reported. The perceived
legitimacy and consequent stability of his reign and of the
Lancastrian dynasty are critically dependent on whether
he can achieve sufficient popular renown as a conquering
hero to expunge his father's crime from the collective
memory of his subjects and allay the threat of civil war
over the disputed succession by securing their devoted
loyalty. As we have seen, Shakespeare's early history plays
are haunted by the spectre of Henry V; on the night before
Agincourt we discover that Henry V is haunted by his
father's act of treason: 'Not today, O Lord, | O not today,
think not upon the fault | My father made in compassing
the crown!' (IV.1.285–7). Fearful that God may avenge his
father's crime in the coming battle, Henry anxiously
recounts the measures he has taken to expiate his father's
guilt and appease the soul of the murdered Richard. Henry
falsely claims that his acts of contrition are 'nothing worth'
because his 'penitence comes after all, | Imploring pardon'
(296–8); however, penitence always comes after the act
that is repented. The reason that Henry's public contrition
is hollow is that he is willing to speed Richard's soul to
heaven but unwilling to relinquish the English crown to
Richard's heirs.

'Piece out our imperfections with your thoughts ...' the Prologue instructs the audience, 'For 'tis your thoughts that now must deck our kings' (23–8). In his soliloquy Henry disavows the doctrine of sacred king-ship expounded by Richard II (*Richard II*, III.2.54–7, 193–201). Haunted by his father's crime and by the spectre of political illegitimacy, he reflects on the theatricality of monarchical authority. In a remarkable passage Henry acknowledges that it is ceremony that empowers kings by instilling the custom of obedience in their subjects, 'place, degree, and form, | Creating awe and fear in other men' (IV.1.239–40). Yet that 'idol ceremony' (233), that 'proud dream' (250) inspiring belief becomes substantial. The royal sceptre may be a mere stage property in polit-ical dramas played out on the scale of nations, but its possessor can exact real tears and blood. So long as his orders are obeyed, the king retains the power to end breath with a breath: 'Then every soldier kill his prisoners! | Give the *word* through' (IV.6.37–8; added emphasis). Henry is fully conscious of the 'Twin-born' (IV.1.227) nature of his authority: his dependence on popularity and his consequent need to project greatness to secure his subjects' loyalty and willing obedience.

As the son of a successful rebel, Henry V also knows too well the deadly cost to any occupant of the throne if responsibility and hence blame is heaped 'Upon the King' (IV.1.223). Over the course of the play he is at pains to disclaim his sovereign will. He transfers to the irreligious Canterbury the burden of responsibility for legitimizing his claim to France and sanctioning war (I.2.9–32). The Dauphin's mocking gift of tennis balls is blamed for causing the onset of hostilities and 'his soul', not Henry's, 'Shall stand sore chargèd for the wasteful vengeance | That shall fly with them' (I.2.282–9). The

suggestion that inanimate objects possess greater volition
than a king is nonsense, though the fervency with which
Henry delivers his 'merry message' (299) to the French
ambassadors may mask its strained logic in performance.
Henry's denial of mercy to the Southampton conspirators is their own fault: 'The mercy that was quick in us
but late | By your own counsel is suppressed and killed'
(II.2.79–80). Yet unlike the chronicles, which record that
Henry immediately apprehended and sentenced the
conspirators on learning of their plot, Shakespeare has
Henry delay their public exposure and arrest precisely to
ensure that, by first luring them into counselling against
lenity in the case of the drunkard, he is relieved of blame
for the severity of their punishment. Should he refuse to
deliver up his crown to Henry, the King of France will
be liable for

> . . . the widows' tears, the orphans' cries,
> The dead men's blood, the privèd maidens' groans,
> For husbands, fathers, and betrothèd lovers
> That shall be swallowed in this controversy. (II.4.106–9)

As for the citizens of Harfleur, they too are 'guilty in
defence' (III.3.43), and the disproportionate number of
casualties suffered by the French at Agincourt is ascribed
entirely to God (IV.8.105–11). Contrary to the Tudor
chronicles, in which kings are represented as second only
to God as the agents of historical events, Henry is singu-
larly anxious to deny he plays a vital part in determining
the chronological sequence of cause and effect. He sets
about redeeming his tainted title by seeming to let be,
presenting himself as the selfless agent of a providential
ordering of time. In deposing Richard II, his father also
deposed the doctrine of sacred kingship. Henry V in turn

disclaims his sovereign power so that he can appear to be the chosen agent of divine providence, his blemished title redeemed not by the calculated assertion of his sovereign will or even by popular opinion but by the divine will of God. To accept his providential interpretation, however, we must forget to remember his inveterate role-playing, policy, military and self-discipline.

'WHAT ISH MY NATION?' (III.2.118)

Popularly celebrated as an English hero in Shakespeare's day, Henry V is an artificer of remembrance in Shakespeare's play. As for *Henry V*, it too seems at first glance a quintessentially 'English' history play that intervenes self-reflexively in the processes of remembering and forgetting on which notions of nation depend. And so it does, but in a much more unorthodox manner than might be anticipated given its subject. For among Shakespeare's English histories, *Henry V* is the most preoccupied with the matter of Britain. On the one hand, the words 'England' and 'English' occur more than one hundred times, ensuring that they resonate throughout the play (Schwyzer, *Literature, Nationalism and Memory*, p. 126). The leaders of the French forces repeatedly refer to their opponents as 'the English', and when he urges on his soldiers in battle Henry appeals to their Englishness, a trait he equates with manliness and martial ability. Yet, on the other, the emerging nation, whose former conquests in France under Henry V the Chorus seeks to fashion into a heroic patriotic epic, is elsewhere depicted as conspicuously hybrid, as are their French opponents. We have already noted how the 'strait strossers' of the Irish kern can be detected beneath the

'French hose' worn by Henry's opponents (III.7.51–2). For their part the French mockingly dismiss Henry's soldiers as 'Normans, but bastard Normans, Norman bastards!' (III.5.10), deriding their opponents as the illegitimate offspring of the Norman French who invaded and colonized England in the eleventh century. However, in disparaging their adversaries as ignoble bastards, 'the French-cum-Irish', as one commentator aptly describes them (Altman, '"Vile Participation"', p. 19), inadvertently foreshadow their own defeat at the hands of the invaders by assigning to their opponents the hybrid identity of the Anglo-Normans who invaded and colonized Ireland in the twelfth century. Though he mocks 'the English' as a mongrel people, the Dauphin confesses that

> Our madams mock at us, and plainly say
> Our mettle is bred out, and they will give
> Their bodies to the lust of English youth,
> To new-store France with bastard warriors. (III.5.28–31)

Over-cultivation depletes virility necessitating an injection of 'wild and savage stock' (7) to restore vigour. In a further complication, the prevalent French conception of the English as 'a barbarous people' (4) who nonetheless display extraordinary daring in battle (15–20) closely echoes prevailing English perceptions of the 'wild Irish'. 'Irishness' thus figures in the play as a trait that is both native and alien, immanent and elusive, to be feared for its savagery and admired for its hardiness even as it is mocked.

Meanwhile the outline of a composite British identity, based for the most part on an amalgamation of national stereotypes, is generated by Shakespeare's introduction of a quartet of captains who between them represent the four 'nations' that make up the British isles. Although other characters refer to them by name, the speech-prefixes '*Welch.*', '*Scot.*' and '*Irish.*' used in the first Folio reduce Fluellen, Jamy and Macmorris to their respective national identities, while their speeches and verbal tics further reduce all three to national stereotypes for comic effect (a treatment from which Gower is uniquely exempt). For a fleeting moment the joint entrance of the Scottish and Irish captains appears to confirm contemporary English concerns over Scottish collusion in Ireland, only for Jamy's determination to do 'gud service' (III.2.111) immediately to allay such anxieties. With their discordant voices and disparate mindsets, the interactions among the four captains resemble the workings of Canterbury's beehive whereby 'many things, having full reference | To one consent, may work contrariously, [yet] ... End in one purpose' (I.2.205–13). What they singularly fail to generate is an image of a harmoniously united British 'nation', though their quarrelling and mutual rivalry does put comic pay to residual English fears of a hostile 'pan-Celtic' military alliance (Highley, *Shakespeare, Spenser and the Crisis in Ireland*, p. 146). In place of the threatening spectre of encirclement, the play offers English audiences an alluring fantasy of assimilation in which neighbouring Celtic nations willingly become subsumed within the English (nascent British) imperial effort. The violent imposition of English rule is tactfully displaced from the British isles to France, and resistant Celts mutate into enthusiastic collaborators in the conquest of a neighbouring nation by a king of England.

The use of the Anglicized form of the Welsh name 'Lluellen' suggests that Fluellen is the most assimilated of the Celtic captains, until we reflect that the surname of the fully assimilated 'English' captain, Gower, carries both English and Welsh associations. For English audience members, the readiest link is to the Yorkshire poet John Gower, a contemporary of Geoffrey Chaucer. John Gower appears in *Pericles* (*c.* 1607), which derives its story from Book 8 of Gower's poem *Confessio Amantis* (1390). For Welsh playgoers, Gower is a name associated with the ancient Marcher lordship of Gower in south Wales (Lloyd, *Speak It in Welsh*, pp. 72–3). After its colonization by English speakers, the lordship was divided into English and Welsh Gower, a linguistic division between the southern and northern portions of the region that survives to the present day. The 'English' captain can therefore also be viewed as a fully assimilated Welshman, as can Williams. Williams's speech, like Gower's, is unmarked by putative Welsh traits, yet Williams, like Fluellen, bears an Anglicized version of a (common) Welsh surname, an English 's' substituting for the Welsh prefix '*ap*' ('son of').

The periodic alternation of Fluellen's speech-prefix between '*Flu.*' and '*Welch.*', the former placing him on a par with the consistently individuated Captain Gower and the latter reducing him to a national stereotype on a par with the '*Scot.*' Jamy and the '*Irish.*' Macmorris, reflects the medial position Wales occupied at the close of the sixteenth century as the most politically absorbed of England's Celtic neighbours. Within the Lancastrian tetralogy Fluellen acts as the mirror opposite of Owen Glendower: where the 'irregular and wild Glendower' (*Henry IV, Part I*, I.1.40) leads a Welsh revolt against Henry IV in *Henry IV, Part I*, two plays and a succession later Fluellen is Henry V's most dedicated follower excepting the Chorus. So fervent is Fluellen's commitment to Henry's aggressively expansionist aims that it is

he who beats the dawdling Eastcheapers forward to the
breach at Harfleur, he who subjects Pistol to 'a Welsh
correction' in order to teach the unruly Eastcheaper 'a
good English condition' (V.1.74–5), and he who immod-
estly compares Henry of Monmouth to Alexander the
Great (or 'Pig') of Macedon (IV.7.11–51). Fluellen's
account of the origins of the leek as a Welsh emblem
epitomizes his internalization of the English colonizer's
values. Rather than being the symbol of an autonomous
nation with a distinct culture, the leek becomes 'an
honourable badge of the service' Welshmen performed
for an English king at the battle of Crécy 'in a garden
where leeks did grow' (IV.7.90–99). Fluellen's conception of Welshness as a trait exemplified in military service
to the English crown would be reassuring to English
audiences, especially at a time when the Welsh were
proving particularly resistant to service in Elizabeth's wars
in Ireland (Highley, p. 156).

However, the violent quarrel between Fluellen and
Macmorris destabilizes the prospect of assimilation
fostered by the presence of the four captains in Henry's
army, as it exposes lingering rifts over ethnic and national
identity within the embryonic British nation. For
Macmorris the question of national identity remains
deeply fraught and potentially explosive. When Fluellen
appears to disparage his 'nation' for its lack of learning
Macmorris abruptly interrupts before Fluellen can utter
the familiar racist insults: 'Ish a villain, and a bastard,
and a knave, and a rascal. What ish my nation? Who
talks of my nation?' (III.2.118–20). But determining just
which 'nation' Fluellen is on the point of impugning is
problematic because Macmorris's national identity is
difficult to stabilize. Although the speech-prefix used in
the Folio identifies Macmorris (spelt 'Makmorrice' or

'Mackmorrice') as '*Irish.*', his patronymic (literally 'son of Maurice') conjoins the Gaelic Irish prefix 'Mac' to an Anglicized form of a Norman termination (cf. P. Barton quoted in Hopkins, 'Neighbourhood', p. 16). Distrust of the loyalty of all Irishmen was widespread among the English during the Nine Years War, regardless of whether they were Gaels (whom the English referred to dismissively as 'Macs') or descendants of the twelfth-century Anglo-Norman colonizers known as the Old English or Palesmen, as they suspected many of the latter had 'gone native' after centuries living alongside the 'wild Irish'. Macmorris's hybrid surname neatly encapsulates such fears. As a descendant of the Old English community in Ireland, a population regarded to be more English than Gaelic by the Gaels and more Gaelic than English by New English colonists (Maley, 'Shakespeare, Holinshed and Ireland', pp. 33–4; Highley, p. 145), Macmorris is simultaneously aligned with and excluded from both an Irish and an English national identity. It is therefore unsurprising that Macmorris's urgent question 'What ish my nation?' remains unanswered. Although Gower reputes Macmorris 'a very valiant gentleman' (III.2.64–5) and admonishes both captains that they 'mistake each other' (129), Macmorris's Gaelic-Anglo-Norman identity, cod-Irish accent and matter-of-fact approach to acts of extreme violence ensure that he remains an object of suspicion and savage otherness for English audiences. That is until Henry, having directed his soldiers to 'imitate the action of the tiger' (III.1.6), matches Macmorris's threat to decapitate Fluellen (III.2.128) with a promise to be 'a clipper' and 'cut French crowns' in battle (IV.1.220–22), orders his soldiers to kill their prisoners (IV.6.37) and speaks to Katherine 'plain soldier' (V.2.148–9). So riddled with reputed traits of Irishness is Henry's discourse of war that it is little wonder that Isabel greets the King of England with the anachronistic salutation 'brother Ireland' in the first Folio (see note to V.2.12).

In defiance of history, theatrical convention and audience expectations, the foremost exemplar of hybrid nationality in *Henry V* proves to be the selfsame 'royal Captain' (IV.Chorus.29) the second chorus extols as the model of English greatness (16). Although he Anglicizes his name to 'Harry', and the King of France and the Dauphin both refer to Henry V as 'our brother of England' (II.4.75, 115), 'Harry England' (III.5.48) or simply 'England' (II.4.9 and *passim*), on the two occasions when Henry assigns himself a national identity it is that of a Welshman. When Pistol mistakes 'Harry le Roy' for a Cornishman the disguised king firmly corrects him: 'No, I am a Welshman' (IV.1.49–51). Later Henry reassures Fluellen that he too wears a leek on Wales's national day of celebration, explaining 'For I am Welsh, you know' (IV.7.102–3). Fluellen's conviction that 'All the water in Wye cannot wash [the] Welsh plood' from Henry's body (IV.7.104–5) is characteristically effusive but genealogically unfounded, as although the historical Henry V was born at Monmouth in Wales and was the Prince of Wales before his accession to the English throne, he had no immediate Welsh ancestry (Schwyzer, p. 127). Shakespeare's transfusion of 'Welsh plood' into the English king's body flatters the Tudor dynasty by compounding Henry's identity with that of the Welshman Owain Tudur, who succeeded Henry V as the husband of Katherine and was an ancestor of Elizabeth I. As the Welsh claimed descent from the ancient Britons, Henry's avowals of his Welshness also play a vital role in enabling an English king to become the hero of an embryonic

British nation. Henry's wider purpose is to legitimize his kingly title and rule 'in large and ample empery' (I.2.227) by reviving England's imperial crown. In pursuit of that goal his Welshness, like his Irishness, remains firmly yoked to the harness of an expansive Englishness – 'Cry, "God for Harry, England, and Saint George!"' (III.1.34). In the process the boundaries of England are increasingly blurred, becoming at once more extensive and more permeable. When Rambures misconceives England as an island (III.7.137) he repeats the error of extending England's boundaries to make them coterminal with the island comprising England, Scotland and Wales previously committed by John of Gaunt in his 'sceptred isle' speech in *Richard II* (II.1).

At the close of the play Henry conjures up the vision of 'a boy, half French, half English, that shall go to Constantinople and take the Turk by the beard' (V.2.205–7). In a now familiar strategy of 'busy[ing] giddy minds | With foreign quarrels' (*Henry IV, Part II*, IV.5.213–14), Henry proposes to 'Plant neighbourhood and Christian-like accord' (V.2.345) between the divided kingdoms of France and England by exporting war to the margins of Europe and uniting the two Christian powers in a war against a common Muslim enemy that threatens Europe's borders and its extension eastward. Intermarriages patterned on his betrothal to Katherine are to be encouraged, 'That English may as French, French Englishmen, | Receive each other' (V.2.359–60). The elimination of division through the generation of hybrid national identities emerges not only as a corollary of war but also as the precondition of imperial expansion (Edwards, *Threshold of a Nation*, p. 71). Henry's ability to interpret Katherine's French and speak to her haltingly in her own language is consistent with his

efforts over the preceding *Henry IV* plays to master his
future subjects by mastering their verbal idioms. The
Epilogue abruptly reminds us, however, that rather than
expanding England's borders, enhancing its power and
exporting war to the distant Turk, Henry's invasion of
France and marriage to Katherine rapidly resulted in the
very opposite. Instead of the indomitable warrior he
envisaged as his heir, Henry was succeeded by a son 'in
infant bands crowned King . . . Whose state so many had
the managing | That they lost France, and made his
England bleed' (Epilogue.9–12). Instead of dominating
France, the French wife of Henry VI, Margaret of Anjou,
would dominate the King of England and threaten the
masculine heroic ideal espoused by Henry V and the
Chorus by proving a more formidable warrior than her
husband in the *Henry VI* plays, 'Which oft our stage hath
shown' (13).

INVASION AND POSSESSION

Unlike the *Henry VI* plays to which the Epilogue alludes,
where French women warriors such as Joan of Arc and
Queen Margaret feature prominently, *Henry V* excludes
women from appearing (or even being mentioned as
appearing) on the battlefield, a feature that allies it with
Richard III alone among Shakespeare's English histories
(Howard and Rackin, *Engendering a Nation*, p. 198). The
twin solicitations of the discourses of war in *Henry V*
are to manliness and fraternity, gendered appeals that likewise exclude women. Faced with appalling odds at
Agincourt, Henry invites his soldiers to join in fellowship with him and become a 'band of brothers' (IV.3.60)
by sacrificing their blood in his cause. For its part, the

third chorus portrays willing participation in Henry's campaign as a corollary of manliness. Only those males 'past or not arrived' at their adult strength and virility remain behind in England (21–4). When Henry urges his soldiers to renew their assault on Harfleur he depicts the attack as an opportunity to prove 'That those whom you called fathers did beget you' (III.1.23). Declaring war on France similarly affords Henry the opportunity to show that his forefathers' 'blood and courage' run in his veins (I.2.117–19). The legitimacy of both the king and his male subjects is affirmed by feats of martial courage, as if patrilineal succession did not depend on wives and mothers. Faced with a plethora of such gendered appeals and with only four female speaking roles, none comprising more than 2 per cent of the total lines, it is difficult not to conclude that *Henry V* banishes women to the margins of history. Pistol's parting instruction to his newly married wife Hostess Quickly, formerly sole owner of the Boar's Head tavern, 'Let housewifery appear. Keep close, I thee command' (II.3.58), is characteristic of a play in which none of the women ventures outside the enclosed space of either the tavern or the court, where their identities and duties are domesticated and their public roles curtailed. Although Isabel proposes to add 'a woman's voice' to the peace negotiations, they are not staged (V.2.92–4). Her public utterances conform to contemporary gender conventions where the woman's role is to secure the bonds between men. If women are marginalized as active agents of history and of nation-building in *Henry V*, their bodies nevertheless figure prominently in its discourses of invasion and possession. Set against this is the play's exposure of the limits of a martial ideal of manliness and Henry's reliance on female authority to uphold his right.

Held up as an English exemplar of the heroic masculine ideal by the Chorus, Henry's royal authority is
nonetheless crucially dependent on Frenchwomen.
Canterbury's commentary on the Salic law reminds audiences that the validity of Henry's claim to France relies
on inheritance through the female line. The female in
question, Queen Isabella, daughter of Philip IV of France
and mother to Edward III of England, is never named,
however, and the fact that Henry derives his title to the
French crown from a French female is never broached
again. When the archbishop invites Henry to 'Look back
into your mighty ancestors' (I.2.102) the two 'valiant
dead' (115) he nominates, Edward the Black Prince and
Edward III, are both English and male. This alternative
lineage of male English warriors swiftly supplants the
French female from whom Henry's claim to France
strictly derives. Thus when Exeter delivers Henry's
message bidding the King of France to resign his crown
he makes no mention of Isabella and instead declares that
Henry bases his demand on his lineal descent 'From his
most famed of famous ancestors, | Edward the Third'
(II.4.91–5).

The King of France does not dispute Henry's lineal
ties to Edward III and the Black Prince, nor does he
doubt his power and resolve. However, his ready accept-
ance that Henry 'is a stem | Of that victorious stock'
(62–3) is not entirely complimentary. Where the English
celebrate Crécy as a famous victory, the King of France
associates the battle with the haunting sight of Edward
III, standing on a nearby mountain, smiling to see his
son 'Mangle the work of nature, and deface | The patterns
that by God and by French fathers | Had twenty years
been made' (60–62). From the French perspective
Henry's kinship with the Black Prince, who 'Forage[d]

in blood of French nobility' (I.2.110), allies him with
ungodly acts of bestial savagery. To admit that Henry is
'bred out of that bloody strain' (II.4.51) allows that there
is cause to fear his 'native mightiness' (64), but it also
implies dispraise of his potential barbarism.

The idealization of 'warlike Harry' and his military
exploits in the choruses is further destabilized by the
repeated association of war with sexual aggression
towards women. Henry warns the citizens of Harfleur
that continued resistance will result in the destruction of
their families. The 'reverend heads' of their fathers will
be 'dashed to the walls' (III.3.37) and their 'naked infants
spitted upon pikes' (38), destroying the living bonds on
which the transmission of patrilineality depends.
Motivated by 'licentious wickedness' (22), 'th'enragèd
soldiers in their spoil' (25) shall also expend their aggression on the town's 'fresh fair virgins' (14). The prospective violence targeted at the bodies of young women is
presently sexualized by the English king:

> What is't to me, when you yourselves are cause,
> If your pure maidens fall into the hand
> Of hot and forcing violation?
> . . .
> Take pity of your town and of your people
> Whiles yet my soldiers are in my command,
> . . .
> If not, why, in a moment look to see
> The blind and bloody soldier with foul hand
> Defile the locks of your shrill-shrieking daughters . . .
> (19–35)

Raping young virgins is one of the spoils of war. Having
selected the name of 'soldier' as the one 'that . . . becomes

me best' (5–6) – an identity he will reaffirm in his courtship of Katherine – Henry is implicated in the figure of the invader-as-rapist evoked in his speech. His subsequent instruction to Exeter to 'Use mercy to them all' (54) distinguishes the king's conduct from that of a rapist. Whether that order is sufficient to banish remembrance of his earlier oration urging his soldiers to turn themselves into human battering rams (or erect phalluses) with which to assault the breach in the walls of a feminized Harfleur (III.3.9) remains debatable, however.

The French peers too conceive of invasion as a form of rape, which, if allowed to proceed unopposed, would reduce them to the degrading status of a pimp who stood 'cap in hand' by the chamber-door as a lustful brute raped his 'fairest daughter' (IV.5.12–16). Figuratively, and for women also literally, armed invasion is synonymous with the threat of sexual assault. As previously noted, in characterizing their enemies as 'Norman bastards' Britaine imputes that the English are the descendants of just such a sexual 'contamination' of their foremothers by Norman French invaders in the eleventh century. However, in an important deviation from the rape motif, both he and the Dauphin are concerned that Frenchwomen may willingly 'give | Their bodies to the lust of English youth' (III.5.28–31), having adjudged their 'native lords' (26) to be effeminate cowards. Put plainly, by penetrating the country's borders and its women's bodies the invader impugns the manliness and virility of its male inhabitants whose duty it is to protect the nation's borders and 'their' women's chastity inviolate.

The twin distinctions between forceful possession of and dependence on women, compulsion and consent, are nowhere more blurred or more strenuously maintained rhetorically than in the matter of Henry's betrothal to

Katherine. Henry V ratifies his lineal right to the French crown through the blood-rite of battle, yet his victory is not complete until he secures Katherine as his wife. Marriage to the French princess is vital to Henry's strategy of legitimation, as it enables this dubious claimant to the English throne to reappropriate the female lineage that is the true source of his claim to be the lawful king of France. Possessing Katherine as his wife will be to no purpose, however, if it does not secure Henry's place in the succession to the French crown, hence his rejection of Katherine's hand in marriage when it was offered, together with 'Some petty and unprofitable dukedoms' as dowry, earlier in the play (III.Chorus.29–32). After Agincourt Katherine becomes his 'capital demand' (V.2.96), but in place of the proffered dukedoms he demands that he be proclaimed '*Héritier de France*', the immediate successor to the French throne (V.2.328–34). The marriage, like the peace, must be made on the conqueror's terms.

Henry's possession of Katherine is a metonym for his possession of France, as the King of France is well aware. When Henry reminds the French court that they should be thankful that he has been blinded by love, the French king dismisses Henry's romantic pretence. Rather than being so blinded by infatuation that he 'cannot see many a fair French city for one fair French maid' (V.2.312–13) Henry sees them 'perspectively, the cities turned into a maid' (315–16). The accuracy of this observation is made plain when the King of France seeks to preserve his country's honour in defeat by affirming that, just as his daughter's chastity is intact, so too many French cities remain 'girdled with maiden walls, that war hath never entered' (316–17). Henry's reply is blunt: French cities may keep their 'maiden walls' so long as Katherine ceases to be a maid and becomes his wife, 'so the maiden cities you talk of may wait on her: so the maid that stood in the way for my wish shall show me the way to my will' (320–22). Sexual penetration of Katherine's virginal body in the expectation she shall 'prove a good soldier-breeder' and 'compound a boy . . . that shall . . . take the Turk by the beard' (203–7) and matrimonial possession of her royal genealogy on terms that make Henry next in line to the French crown do not mark Henry's relinquishment of his wider war aims; they are the means by which those war aims are secured – or so he hopes.

The King of France does not ask his daughter whether she is willing to marry the King of England and he agrees to the match offstage while she is onstage with Henry (V.2.326). By contrast, Henry repeatedly asks Katherine 'will you have me?' (231–2, 243), yet his comic-romantic bid for her consent is prefaced by his bald statement that France 'must buy' the peace it seeks and the princess is his 'capital demand' (V.2.70, 96). Consent expressed under compulsion is not consent. Pressed for an answer by her suitor, Katherine eventually responds 'Dat is as it shall please de *Roi mon père*' (V.2.244). The princess frames her conditional consent ('Den it sall also content me', 247) as an act of obedience to her king and father, not as an expression of affection much less love for 'de *ennemi* of *France*' (168–9). Katherine and Henry both know that Agincourt has sealed her fate, a fact that Henry's decision to imitate the bluff manner of Hotspur, court Katherine as 'plain soldier' (V.2.148–9) and rename her English 'Kate' implicitly acknowledges. By addressing Katherine informally by the common English diminutive Henry domesticates the French princess, much as Petruccio asserts his mastery of Katherine Minola in *The Taming of the Shrew* by addressing her as 'plain Kate' in defiance of her wishes (II.1.185). The victor at Agincourt does not need Katherine's consent, yet he persistently seeks it; he is not compelled to extend the prospect of mutual empery, and yet he does. One moment he is the triumphant conqueror speaking unnervingly like Tamburlaine – 'I love France so well that I will not part with a village of it – I will have it all mine' (V.2.172–3); the next he urges Katherine to 'Put off [her] maiden blushes', assume 'the looks of an empress' and receive all that he possesses:

> take me by the hand, and say, 'Harry of England, I am thine': which word thou shalt no sooner bless mine ear withal but I will tell thee aloud, 'England is thine, Ireland is thine, France is thine, and Henry Plantagenet is thine' . . . (V.2.232–8)

The virile conqueror invites the conquered woman to become 'Queen of all' (242), thus does Henry walk a rhetorical tightrope between the fact of compulsion and the semblance of consent and companionate marriage. The gesture is attractive, as is Henry's self-deprecating humour. Within moments, however, the victor at Agincourt betrays his imperiousness when he spurns French custom and insists that Katherine submit, 'patiently, and yielding' (271), to a maiden kiss on the lips, after which she falls silent.

Throughout their encounter Katherine speaks in French or 'broken English' (243), a trait that sets her apart from virtually all of the other speakers in the play. With the exception of the cowardly Le Fer and his translator, the soon-to-be-slaughtered Boy, the men typically speak English regardless of their nationality, as does Isabel, whereas Alice and Katherine typically speak

French. Henry's utterance of a few halting words in French is consistent with his tactful efforts to bridge the differences between himself and his future bride by disclaiming his eloquence. Katherine's language lesson in Act III, scene 4 has the opposite effect: instead of diminishing her marginalization, it intensifies her subjection to a foreign language that strips her of authority. The placement of her lesson immediately after the surrender of Harfleur aligns Katherine's need to learn English (III.4.4–5) with Henry's deepening incursion into France. Her halting acquisition of the conqueror's language takes the form of naming parts of her body, a process that sees Katherine unknowingly translate her chaste body into a bawdy register. Englishing her body doubly debases the French princess, first, by associating her with the brothel-keeping Hostess Quickly, whose comic idiom is the unwitting obscenity, and, second, by figuratively undressing and sexualizing parts of her anatomy in a titillating linguistic striptease conducted in the presence of male playgoers. The sexual connotations of 'Englishing' a woman's body are established in *The Merry Wives of Windsor* when Falstaff boasts that 'to be Englished rightly', what Alice Ford's 'familiar style' towards him denotes is: '"I am Sir John Falstaff's".' Pistol observes that Falstaff has 'translated her will, out of honesty, into English' (I.3.43–4). This sense of Englishing as rendering unchaste may inflect Burgundy's question, 'teach you our Princess English?' (V.2.278), when the sudden re-entrance of the negotiators causes Henry hurriedly to part from kissing Katherine in violation of French decorum. The debasing effects of Katherine's Englishing are apparent when her virginity becomes the subject of coarse sexual banter between Burgundy and Henry conducted in her presence.

In a scene in which Henry is addressed as 'England', France is feminized, peace is personified as a poor naked woman and Katherine is silenced, the relationship between the dynamics of invasion and possession and the martial and sexual mastery of the foreign, feminine and female are all too plain (unless we choose not to note them). It is little wonder, then, that the one unquestionable 'testament of noble-ending love' (IV.6.27) in *Henry V* is not that between Henry and Katherine but that between York and Suffolk, two men 'espoused to death' (26). York's final tender embrace and dying kiss on the lips of Suffolk are loving and unforced. The Epilogue reminds us that Henry's attempt to bring his policy of war to a comic close did not succeed. Peace did not last, the enmity between France and England which he had reignited was not extinguished by his marriage, and his fame did not secure the lineal transmission of either the crown of France or the crown of England to his son. '[T]he world's best garden' (7) was despoiled to no lasting purpose.

PERSPECTIVISM

In *Richard III* Prince Edward asks Buckingham whether Julius Caesar built the Tower of London. Buckingham's matter-of-fact reply, 'He did, my gracious lord, begin that place | Which since succeeding ages have re-edified' (III.1.70–71), does not satisfy the young prince, who presses Buckingham to clarify whether he bases his assertion on written records or on an oral tradition 'reported | Successively from age to age' (72–3). Edward believes 'the truth should live from age to age ... Even to the general all-ending day' (76–8). An idealist, he will soon be dead: his ambitious uncle shall see to it that the proverbial saying 'So wise so young ... do never live long' (III.1.79) holds true by suborning his murder and that of his young brother in the Tower. For Prince Edward history and truth should be unitary and immutable and the spoken word sufficient to ensure that past events are reported accurately to succeeding generations.

The past, however, is not a unified, stable entity that historians, archaeologists, literary scholars and the like can recover wholesale and reconstitute in the form of a single objective narrative. It is endlessly 're-edified' by succeeding ages. On the night before the battle of Agincourt three common soldiers enter into a heated debate with a stranger about the morality of war and the responsibility carried by those who order men into battle. One, suggestively surnamed Williams, mocks the disguised king's intimation that there is anything 'that a poor and a private displeasure can do against a monarch' (IV.1.193–4). Unlike his king, who gives Williams's glove to Fluellen as a prank, Williams keeps his word to challenge whoever bears his gage. When he learns that it was his king with whom he had violently quarrelled Williams defends his conduct: 'had you been as I took you for, I made no offence' (IV.8.54–5) – sight too can prove deceptive. We never learn of the fate of John Bates and Alexander Court. In performance only 'Brother John Bates' (IV.1.84) is addressed by name and the king does not enquire after their identities. Are they among the twenty-five 'other men' deemed not to be 'of name' (IV.8.104–5) listed among the English dead? As _Henry V_ persistently reminds us, there is more than one way of remembering the past and more than one history to be remembered. Like history, Shakespeare's play is multivalent and perspectival. Which version of the play directors choose to stage, which version of events we choose to remember, and which of the many perspectives on Henry and his wars we allow to inform – and challenge – our understanding is ultimately a matter of judgement. However, those seeking a straightforwardly patriotic war play and an uncomplicatedly heroic and pious English national hero should look elsewhere than to the 'long' Folio version of *Henry V* for their entertainment.

Ann Kaegi

The Play in Performance

Performing a play that was written over four centuries ago presents its own set of challenges. Several features of *Henry V* that would have excited the interest of playgoers in Shakespeare's day now distance audiences from his drama. When the play was first staged the 'famous victories' achieved by Henry V in France continued to be memorialized in chronicles, ballads, stage plays and poems, ensuring that the martial exploits of England's warrior king remained the stuff of popular legend. However, for the overwhelming majority of those who encounter *Henry V* in the twenty-first century the once celebrated names of Crécy and Agincourt, Edward III and the Black Prince, not to mention King Harry, have long ceased to be as 'Familiar ... as household words' (IV.3.52). The ancient rivalry between England and France may not be wholly extinguished, but it retains little of its former fervency. The passage of time has also ensured that what had once been a highly topical allusion to the Irish expedition of the Earl of Essex in the fifth chorus (29–35) is now routinely cut in performance. Meantime, as a consequence of changing usage, once familiar words and expressions have fallen out of currency, altering for ever our relationship to the play's language.

While some elements of *Henry V* have lost something of their former immediacy, the capacity of other elements of the play to engage and provoke audiences remains undiminished by time and may even be enhanced as a consequence of wider cultural and historical developments. Several late-twentieth- and early-twenty-first-century productions of *Henry V* on stage and screen have sought to supplement those elements of Shakespeare's play that lend it an arresting contemporaneity by adopting costumes and set designs that evoke more recent military conflicts, such as the Vietnam War, the war over the Falkland/Malvinas islands, the civil wars that destroyed Yugoslavia, the first Gulf War, and the invasions of Afghanistan and Iraq. By providing modern visual equivalents to the verbal intrusion into *Henry V* of the intensifying conflict in Ireland and the lingering fear of a Spanish invasion such 'presentist' productions seek to recapture something of the topical resonance of the original. More importantly, recent military conflicts and the controversies surrounding them have lent those passages that associate warfare variously with greed and deception, rape, massacre and ecological disaster a renewed urgency. The continuing resonance of these speeches is all the more disturbing for the passage of time. Because it was thought to detract from the depiction of Henry V as a heroic figure worthy of emulation and his invasion of France as an ennobling enterprise worthy of celebration, this disquieting material was routinely omitted from productions of *Henry V* until well into the twentieth century. Although contemporary practice varies widely, a rising proportion of productions have opted to retain it. Hopefully this trend signals a greater willingness to confront rather than circumvent the play's many and profound challenges in performance. This section highlights several of those challenges and briefly examines how different performance options may affect key elements of the play.

'THEN BROOK ABRIDGEMENT'
(V.CHORUS.44)

With the publication of modern editions of the first Quarto of *Henry V*, directors have a choice of two distinct versions of the play on which to base their production. As noted in the Introduction (pp. xxv–xxvii), the first Quarto and the first Folio offer not just different but essentially opposing representations of Henry V and his French campaign, so a pick-and-mix approach is best avoided. At around 3,400 lines the first Folio version (1623), on which this edition is based, is one of the longest Shakespearian play texts; at just over 1,620 lines the first Quarto text (1600) is one of the shortest. If a swiftly paced war play that largely favours an idealized interpretation of the warrior king is desired, then the Quarto is the better option. If a more testing theatrical experience is sought, then the Folio text, with its sudden swings from loftiness to lowliness, from grandiose myth-making to chilling realpolitik, supplies the more challenging acoustic, emotional and moral landscape for performers and audiences to navigate. This section on the play in performance is concerned with productions of the Folio text.

With its running time of just under four hours, directors who opt for the Folio version must decide whether and if so how best to make cuts. The existence of the first Quarto (the only version printed in Shakespeare's lifetime) may indicate that even the play's first audiences were thought to lack the stamina (or the stomach) for the 'long' version. Among the longer, and in certain instances more readerly, passages in the Folio text that rarely survive intact are Canterbury's exposition of the Salic law (I.2.33–95), Henry's denunciation of Scroop (II.2.79–144), the once topical and now dated reference to 'the General ... from Ireland coming' (V.Chorus.29–35), Henry's courtship of Katherine, and Burgundy's description of the devastating effects of war on 'Our fertile France' (V.2.23–67) together with his sexually mocking exchange with Henry (277–310).

With the exception of the Essex allusion, the above passages illustrate the care that must be taken in making extensive cuts to the Folio text to quicken the tempo. Tampering with Canterbury's lengthy commentary on the Salic law is particularly hazardous as it sets out the legal justification for Henry's war, while it also subtly draws attention to Henry's tainted title as King of England. Canterbury's assertion that his laboured exposition is 'as clear as is the summer's sun' (I.2.86) usually draws audience laughter; however, trimming the speech to make it clearer presupposes that the legitimacy of Henry's claim to the French crown is meant to appear unambiguous. A large onstage map is sometimes used to clarify Canterbury's contention that the Salic lands (to which the law barring female inheritance applies) lie in Germany not France. His second line of argument consists of citing historical precedents for Henry's claim through the female line, but these precedents are potentially damning as each is characterized by Canterbury as a usurper or the son of a usurper. If the actor emphasizes the words 'deposèd' (65), 'usurped' (69) and 'usurper' (78), their dubiousness and Henry's similarly suspect status as the son of a usurper of the English throne edge into view. If Henry's protracted denunciation of

Scroop is omitted, then the thematic parallel between the king's betrayal by his former bedfellow and his own responsibility for hastening the death of Falstaff is lost. Yet if Henry's long-winded attack on Scroop is not shortened, not only does the opening sequence lose momentum but his sustained reproof may further obscure the political motive for the conspiracy (its likely purpose) and also crowd out the audience's recollection that 'The King hath run bad humours on the knight' (II.1.116), Sir John Falstaff, who had been as a father to him.

In the Quarto text Henry persuades the Governor of Harfleur to surrender with a twelve-line speech and polishes off his courtship of Katherine in less than a third the time it takes in the Folio text. The rapidity of the former makes him appear militarily indomitable while the brevity of the latter fosters the impression that he is romantically irresistible. In the Folio text his assault on Harfleur encounters military setbacks and his love suit meets with linguistic setbacks. Henry eventually wins the French town with words; do his words win over the French princess and could he not 'speak fewer' (IV.1.65)? The analogy between Henry's prospective siege of 'many a fair French city' and his attempted seduction of 'one fair French maid' is made explicit by both Henry and the French king in the Folio text (V.2.311–17). Compressing his courtship is therefore consequential, though possibly less critical than are cuts to Katherine's remarks in French and broken English (the Quarto retains only one) as they establish that her grasp of the conqueror's language is extremely limited. Unlike *The Famous Victories of Henry the fifth*, where Katherine is plainly keen to wed Henry, in Shakespeare the responses of the French princess to 'de *ennemi* of France' (V.2.168–9) are invariably guarded; however, if the actor playing Katherine appears to be won by Henry's torrent of speech, then her efforts to deflect his suit will be interpreted as coyness or coquettishness. Audiences who witness Emma Thompson's Katherine leaning forward to be kissed by Kenneth Branagh's Henry V in close up in his 1989 film are likely to overlook the fact that, textually, Katherine's replies to Henry in the Folio are consistently restrained and noncommittal and are often uncomprehending.

Should Burgundy's framing commentaries on Henry's 'victories' be sacrificed to inject some momentum into the closing sequence? His speech describing the devastation caused by Henry's invasion is a moving indictment of war delivered in the aftermath of Henry's most celebrated victory, while his provocatively cynical sexual banter with Henry imparts a very different gloss to the conqueror's 'courtship' of the French princess (see Introduction, p. lxxiv). Burgundy's contributions to the closing scene challenge audiences to reflect more deeply on the nature of Henry's twin triumphs; if they are omitted, the pace quickens but the play's internal critique of the celebrated history it stages is greatly diminished. The Folio text can 'brook abridgement' but, as these examples demonstrate, cuts to the text need to be done with a scalpel, not an axe.

'ADMIT ME CHORUS TO THIS HISTORY' (PROLOGUE.32)

The hallmark of the Folio text is its extraordinary generic and tonal hybridity and the rapidity with which genre and tone change and often collide. A key source of that hybridity and one of the trickiest elements of the play to accommodate is the Chorus. Stirring, yet at times wildly inaccurate, should the Chorus (absent from the first Quarto along with the Prologue and Epilogue) be kept or jettisoned? And if it is retained, should its speeches be reworked to eliminate the jarring discontinuities between the choric narrative and the ensuing action outlined in the Introduction (pp. xliii–li)? Few decisions will have a greater impact on the tenor of a Folio-based production of *Henry V* than these. David Giles, director of the 1979 BBC television film of *Henry V*, put the case for retaining the Chorus succinctly: 'If you cut the Chorus, you don't do *Henry V*' (quoted in Loehlin, *Shakespeare in Performance: 'Henry V'*, p. 75), or at least not the Folio version. How far, though, should the discontinuities between the choric account and the subsequent action be allowed to undermine the credibility of the heroic legend the Chorus celebrates? Many directors move the announcement by the second chorus of the shift of scene to Southampton to the beginning of Act II, scene 2. Omitting or transposing portions of the other choruses can similarly make them accord with rather than misrepresent the dramatic action. (Laurence Olivier's changes resulted in the creation of ten Chorus speeches in his 1944 film in place of the original six.) Alternatively, Ron Daniels (for the Royal Shakespeare Company in 1997) ensured that as the fourth chorus invited the audience to 'behold | The royal Captain ... Walking from watch to watch' dispensing 'A little touch of Harry in the night' (28–47) Henry could be seen behind a gauze curtain walking among his men precisely as described. Modifying the choruses to eliminate inconsistencies between what the Chorus encourages audiences to anticipate and what happens next presumes that existing discrepancies are errors that should be corrected in performance.

Others note that the Chorus is consistently wrong and

its mis-statements of fact are therefore unlikely to be over-
sights. Rather than reconfigure its speeches to make the
Chorus appear trustworthy, they elect to do the opposite
and draw attention to the discrepancies between the
Chorus's announcements and the subsequent action. The
layout of the Elizabethan public stage, with its openings
flanking and (often) at the centre of the back wall, facil-
itated both continuous action and dramatic juxtapositions
through the use of overlapping entrances and exits. If
Nym and Bardolph enter arguing as the Act II Chorus
is still making his (or her) exit, as happened in Richard
Olivier's 1997 production at the reconstructed Globe
Theatre, the unreliability of the Chorus is vividly
apparent. In theatres where the size or configuration of
the stage makes it difficult for audiences to detect such
overlaps, dumb shows or static tableaux can intensify the
audience's perception of the falsity of the Chorus's
historical account. In his 2003 production in the cavernous
Olivier Theatre, Nicholas Hytner had the Act II Chorus
announce centre stage that 'all the youth of England are
on fire' (1) while Nym, seated upstage in a 'pub', used a
television remote to flick idly between a broadcast by
Henry, an interview with Canterbury and assorted
sporting fixtures until, visibly bored by the offerings, he
switched the set off as the Chorus affirmed 'now sits expectation in the air' (8). Another option is to sharpen the
rivalry between the heroic and anti-heroic voices in the
play. In Giles's television film the camera pulls back to
reveal the Chorus unknowingly standing nose to nose
with Bardolph; startled, the Chorus hastily retreats. Terry
Hands went a step further in his 1975 RSC production
and had Bardolph and Nym interrupt the Chorus as he
spoke of 'English Mercuries' (7), forcing him to give way
to their anti-heroic ribaldry with a resigned shrug; only

after their departure did the Chorus reappear to announce the shift of scene. Perhaps the Chorus is merely indulging the habit of 'remember[ing], with advantages' (IV.3.50) to which we are all susceptible. By having a different cast member speak each chorus Richard Olivier transformed the choric narrative into a collaborative account that recorded how key participants wished to be remembered (a device previously adopted in a 1957 production at the Library Theatre, Manchester).

Harry's observation that 'Old men forget' (IV.3.49) provides another explanation for the Chorus's faulty memory. Just how old *is* the Chorus? Advancing age might account for the sense of loss and nostalgic yearning that pervades the choruses; alternatively, youth – earnest, eager, unbloodied – might explain their zealous idealization of Henry V and war and reinforce the contrast with the prematurely knowing Boy, particularly if the same actor plays both parts. When *Henry V* is performed as part of a sequence of histories there is scope for inventive doubling across the series. John Woodvine, who had played Falstaff, reappeared as the Chorus in Michael Bogdanov's touring production of the *Richard II* to *Henry V* sequence (English Shakespeare Company, 1986–9), deftly fulfilling the pledge in the Epilogue to *Henry IV, Part II* to 'continue the story, with Sir John in it' (27) while accentuating the contrast between Falstaff's loyalty to Hal and Hal's public spurning of the 'fat knight with the great-belly doublet' (IV.7.46). And what about a female Chorus? The scarcity of female roles in *Henry V* can be slightly allayed by casting women in non-speaking roles or transformed by having an all-female cast, an option some theatre companies resorted to during the two world wars. It can also be mitigated by having a female Chorus, a practice that was widely adopted from the mid nineteenth century until the 1930s and shows signs of a moderate comeback. Formerly women Choruses personified an abstraction such as Britannia or Clio, the Muse of history. In 1872 Mrs Charles Calvert spoke the Prologue as 'Rumour' from *Henry IV, Part II*, accoutred with a golden horn. More unusually, a cross-dressed Sybil Thorndike reversed the practice of female impersonation on the all-male stage of Shakespeare's day by performing Chorus as an Elizabethan boy (at the Lyric, Hammersmith, 1927–8), suggesting how a woman too might double the roles of Chorus and Boy. The growing numbers of women in a greater range of employment allows for a wider variety of depictions. With half-moon reading specs perched on her nose, Penny Downie's hero-worshipping Chorus in Hytner's modern-dress production was characterized by one reviewer as 'an insinuating spin-doctor in high heels' (*Observer*, 18 May 2003) and by another as 'sounding like a cross between a condescending *Newsnight* compere and a literature don lecturing to fairly thick students' (*Evening Standard*, 14 May 2003).

Costuming can clarify the relationship of the Chorus to the play. The Chorus's fondness for rhetorical flourishes can be mocked or indulged by portraying him or her as a flamboyant figure in dandyish modern or Elizabethan dress (as in Laurence Olivier's 1944 film or Peter Hall and John Barton's production in 1964). Is the Chorus a detached observer or an actual or vicarious participant in the drama? Portraying the Chorus as Britannia, Clio, 'Time' (complete with scythe and hourglass) like the choric figure in *The Winter's Tale* (William Macready in 1839 and Samuel Phelps in 1852) or Shakespeare (as happened in the wartime Shakespeare Birthday Celebrations in April 1943) lends the Chorus considerable authority. Such depictions also emphasize the Chorus's detachment from the dramatic action, as does the option of having the Chorus wear modern dress while the other actors wear period costume or vice versa. Modern dress enables the insinuating Chorus to appear as a disarming intermediary between the audience and the play. Branagh wanted the Chorus in his film to be an 'everyman' figure. While the rest of the cast wear medieval garb, Derek Jacobi as Chorus wears a modern, nondescript overcoat and a red scarf wrapped loosely around his neck, his anachronistic and slightly 'actorly' appearance serving as a constant reminder both of the filmic dimension and of his (and our) historical remove from the events being portrayed – that is until he appears with a grimy face and grazed forehead bearing visible marks of battle! Costuming the Chorus in military attire further blurs the distinction between the roles of participant and observer. An anachronistically overcoated Chorus reappeared in Mathew Warchus's 1994 RSC version, but the addition of a Remembrance Day poppy and campaign ribbons, complemented by his upright military bearing, conveyed that the elderly Chorus was a war veteran, a fellowship in arms that was reinforced when he assisted Henry to his feet during the battle for Agincourt.

Young or old, male or female, modern or period dress, what matters is that the Chorus is understood by directors to be engaged in a struggle to fashion remembrance. What directors decide to do with the Chorus can tip the balance in the contest to control whose story is told and how the past is remembered that lies at the heart of the Folio version. If the choruses are left in place and no attempt is made to mask the glaring inconsistencies between what the Chorus reports and the ensuing action, a production based on the Folio text will feature acute shifts in tone, from epic to comic, from hyperbolic verse to plain-speaking prose, and in historical remembrance from the promotion of a legend to its abrupt demystification. The first Quarto provides a precedent for those who wish to dispense with the services of the Chorus, Prologue and Epilogue. If the director's aim is to represent Henry V and his victory at Agincourt as a model of greatness, then performance history suggests that the choruses will need to be selectively edited, transposed or dropped. If the intent is to explore in collaboration with the audience how such martial legends are 'perfected' and the harsh truths they obscure, then the choruses are best kept in place.

'FOUR OR FIVE MOST VILE AND RAGGED FOILS' (IV.CHORUS.50)

If the Chorus's speeches are preserved, directors face the daunting prospect of beginning the performance with a prologue that anticipates that the 'unworthy scaffold' (10) of the commercial theatre (or film set) will inevitably debase 'So great an object' (11) as 'warlike Harry' (5) and his memorable triumph at Agincourt. As for the actors or 'ciphers to this great account' (17), the fourth chorus glumly predicts that they will 'much disgrace, | With four or five most vile and ragged foils, | Right ill-disposed in brawl ridiculous, | The name of Agincourt' (IV. Chorus.49–52). The intrusively non-naturalistic Chorus reminds audiences that what they are witnessing is a play, that the people on stage are actors and that the theatre has limited powers of representation. How best to respond? Olivier and Branagh both opted to emphasize this quality of self-reflexivity at the outset of their respective *Henry V* films, Branagh by having the Chorus speak straight to camera as he leads the viewer through a film studio on to the sound stage and 'into' the film, and Olivier by first transporting viewers across Elizabethan London to the Globe Theatre where a performance of *The Chronicle History of King Henry the Fift*' is about to begin. Our first glimpse of Henry V is of the actor clearing his throat backstage as he awaits his cue. In Hands's 1975 RSC production actors milled about the stage in rehearsal clothes as audience members found their seats and only relinquished their everyday outfits after the French Ambassador arrived in 'period' costume with the Chorus remaining in 'rehearsal' clothes throughout. Such devices foreground the performance medium and its conventions and may prompt audiences to consider the extent to which Henry's authority (and legendary stature) is similarly a theatrical and rhetorical construction.

Directors who try to rebut the Chorus by exploiting all available resources to create realist or stylized spectacle accord the audience a lesser role than it is allocated by the Chorus. The Prologue shifts responsibility for ensuring Henry V and his famous victories assume epic stature decisively away from the 'wooden O' (13) of the theatre and the 'crookèd figure' (15) of the actor to the audience's 'imaginary forces' (18). However, many directors are reluctant to entrust such a crucial task of 'imaginary puissance' (25) to the audience and are disinclined to restrain the impulse to confect a 'swelling scene' (4) on stage or screen, since it obliges them to jettison treasured assumptions about what a play about Henry V and Agincourt should look like. Despite the Chorus's apologetic insistence that the performance doesn't remotely resemble the majestic scenes it urges us to imagine, lavish spectacle, pageantry and vast numbers of supernumeraries were characteristic features of eighteenth- and

nineteenth-century productions. As Olivier's and
Branagh's films attest, Harfleur and Agincourt are still
prone to becoming occasions for elaborate military spectacle in modern productions. Having adopted a 'found
space aesthetic' that entailed stripping the Olivier stage
back to its architectural frame, Hytner broke with that
aesthetic to incorporate realist military spectacles: instead
of audiences imagining horses 'Printing their proud hoofs
i'th'receiving earth' (Prologue.27), two military Land
Rovers, complete with mounted machine guns, were
driven on and off the stage during battle sequences accompanied by smoke and the sound of modern ordnance,
while actors dressed in military fatigues and bearing realistic weapons used actual military tactics to move across
the stage. It is not a lack of extras and realistic weaponry,
however, that risks making Agincourt appear a 'brawl
ridiculous' but rather Shakespeare's audacious decision
to limit the depiction of the celebrated battle to an
encounter between two misapprehending cowards and a
scene of French confusion (Act IV, scenes 4 and 5), and
to restrict the display of Henry's generalship once combat
has commenced to an order to kill defenceless prisoners
(IV.6.37) and a renewed threat to 'cut the throats of those
we have' (IV.7.61) when he spies French horsemen on a
nearby hill. Staging this version as distinct from the legend
requires few resources except courage.

On the subject of courage, the most controversial
material in the Folio text continues to test the mettle of
directors. Ron Daniels (RSC, 1997) and Nicholas Hytner
(National Theatre, 2003) are among a minority of directors to preserve Henry's cruellest threats to the citizens
of Harfleur in Act III, scene 3, for example. Most directors, from Kemble in the eighteenth century through to
Branagh in the twentieth, have tended to make heavy cuts

similar to those in the Quarto (which omits lines 11–41) to prevent Henry's graphic threats from tarnishing his heroic and pious image. However, unlike the historical sources, which report that Henry V sacked Harfleur, in Shakespeare Henry's threatening speech is exposed as a ruse moments after the town surrenders and can be played up as such. Michael Pennington (ESC, 1986–9) whistled with amazement when his gambit succeeded; Branagh 'closes his eyes in exhaustion and relief' in his film version (*Beginning*, p. 60); and both drew attention to the sickness spreading through Henry's army (III.3.55–6) by betraying signs of illness as the scene ended, giving the lie to the terrifying vision of 'th'enragèd soldiers in their spoil' (25) Henry had evoked in his speech.

If Henry's famous rallying speech at Harfleur and his most savage menaces are retained (both are absent from the Quarto) to whom should they be directed? The carrying on of scaling-ladders (III.1.0) suggests that in Shakespeare's theatre the attack on the breach was directed at the back wall of the stage, with the Governor appearing on its balcony. The audience would then view the attack from the conqueror's (and the Eastcheapers') perspective. Daniels and Hytner opted to have Henry address both his battle oration urging his soldiers to advance 'Once more unto the breach' (III.1.1) and his speech threatening total war to the audience, with the soldiers in Hytner's production 'entering' Harfleur by advancing up the aisles, making Henry's terror tactics all the more palpable. The audience thus experienced the attack on Harfleur from the dual perspectives of the town's attackers and its defenders, significantly complicating their response to Henry's 'victory'.

Unlike Henry's speech threatening the citizens of Harfleur with total war, the execution of Bardolph is not a bluff. By substituting Bardolph for the unnamed soldier recorded in the sources and by making it plain that Henry could yet intervene to save his former companion, who is still alive but 'like to be executed' by Exeter (III.6.97–8), Shakespeare generates what can be a defining moment in the characterization of the king – and of Pistol. Henry's tactical calculation that 'when lenity and cruelty play for a kingdom, the gentler gamester is the soonest winner' (109–10) puts productions that emphasize the king's heroism and piety under acute strain. David Gwilliam (BBC, 1979) brought out the hollowness of Henry's espousals of fellowship and bravely risked audience sympathy by coldly pronouncing Bardolph's death sentence, 'We would have all such offenders so cut off' (104–5), after a considered pause from polishing his boots. By contrast, Alan Howard (RSC, 1975) portrayed Henry's seemingly impersonal response to Bardolph's offstage execution as a painful emotional ordeal for the king, as does a tearful Branagh as he watches Bardolph hanged in his film version. Instead of emphasizing Henry's pain, Bogdanov (ESC, 1986–9) and Michael Boyd (RSC, 2007) both emphasized Pistol's desperate efforts to save his friend, with Pistol braving sniper and mortar fire in Boyd's production in a fruitless attempt to persuade Fluellen to intervene on Bardolph's behalf. Pistol's steadfast fellowship sharply contrasted with Henry's ruthlessness and increasing isolation in these versions.

Those who wish to endorse Henry's attribution of the historic victory at Agincourt to divine intervention will be strongly tempted to follow Olivier and Branagh in omitting Henry's command to kill the French prisoners (IV.6.37). If it is kept, should the audience witness the massacre? 'Give the word through' (38) implies the killing occurs offstage, a pragmatic solution that avoids the need to drag off several bodies. Boyd solved the staging problem by using smoke, sound and lighting effects to create the impression the French prisoners were being burnt alive in a pit beneath the stage. In the Quarto Pistol (present but silent until now) responds to Henry's order with his catchphrase, 'Couple gorge'. Productions that adopt the Quarto line typically have Pistol kill Le Fer on stage, often under compulsion as Pistol's hopes of profiting from Henry's wars die with his captive. Having Fluellen reprise his role at the breach and compel Pistol's compliance foregrounds the increasingly bitter relationship between the two. Kevin Kline displayed a willingness to sacrifice audience sympathy rare among performers of the title role by personally cutting Le Fer's throat when he played Henry V in the 1984 Central Park production. Warchus too took the unusual step of involving the king in the killing by having Henry physically force Pistol's sword across Le Fer's throat (RSC, 1994). Another consideration is what, if any, causal relation Henry's order should have to the French raid on the boys guarding the luggage wagons. Gower wrongly assumes that Henry's command was in revenge for the cowardly French raid when, textually, it precedes it (IV.7.5–10). By reversing the dramatic sequence to make Gower's misconstruction appear correct Hands glossed over Henry's most chilling act of pragmatism in the play. The widespread practice of showing the killing of the boys in dumb show, as in Adrian Noble's 1984 RSC version, or of bearing the body of the Boy on stage may prompt audiences to forget the actual sequence of events, particularly if the killing of the French prisoners is not shown. If both massacres are accorded equal prominence, the horror of war 'That makes such waste in brief mortality' (I.2.28) is impressed on the audience as the battle of Agincourt staggers to a gruesome and unseemly close.

Less gruesome episodes, such as Henry's quarrel with Bates and Williams and its aftermath, can be defining moments in a production, particularly as their quarrel centres on the king's moral responsibilities towards his subjects when he wages war. Does Williams accept Henry's offer of the glove filled with crowns, or does he dare to reject it? If the latter, the king would presumably need to respond, yet neither speaks to the other after it is offered. If he accepts the gift of crowns, does he do so happily, relieved to extricate himself from the quarrel and its hazards? Or does Williams accept the glove grudgingly because he must, since 'to disobey were against all proportion of subjection' (IV.1.141–2). And does he continue to refuse Fluellen's offer of a shilling to mend his shoes because he can express his anger openly to the Welsh captain whereas he could not spurn the king, or are they too reconciled?

How the opposing parties to the conflict in France are portrayed can significantly sway audience sympathies for or against war, Henry and the French. Speakers on both sides, not least Henry himself, emphasize the starkly contrasting appearance of the two forces. The Chorus could hardly be characterized as unbiased, but its appraisal of the French as 'Proud ... secure ... confident and over-lusty' (IV.Chorus.17–18) before Agincourt is fair. The same Chorus describes Henry's army as a 'ruined band' (29) whose 'lank-lean cheeks and war-worn coats' (26) lend them the appearance of 'So many horrid ghosts' (28), as if the dead of the preceding history plays had been conjured back to life for one last battle. In the early nineteenth century when Napoleon threatened invasion productions pandered to jingoist anti-French sentiment by depicting the French as effete dandies. Just as costuming and set design can reinforce a derogatory national stereotype, they can also be used to reverse or unseat it. Rather than staging Act II, scene 4 as a formal council scene, Bogdanov's production showed the French court in their first appearance enjoying a summer luncheon: the men, dressed in white linen and seated downstage on white garden chairs, sipped wine as they evaluated the English threat while the women picnicked upstage, until Exeter brusquely strode across their white picnic blanket in his dark diplomat's suit and red sash to deliver Henry's imperialist threat of 'Bloody constraint' (II.4.97), abruptly shattering the Impressionist idyll. So striking and persistent were the contrasts between dignified French civility and xenophobic British warmongering (a banner proclaiming 'Fuck the French' was draped over the balcony as Henry embarked from Southampton) that one reviewer confessed it was 'the first version I've ever seen where you wanted the French to win' (*Guardian*, 23 March 1987). Whereas the entrances of both the English and French forces were occasions for historical pageantry on the Victorian stage, spectacle tends to be reserved for the French in modern productions in keeping with the preoccupation of the French peers with the accoutrements of their status: their noble lineages, their horses (and mistresses) and their armour. The vertical axis can be exploited to emphasize French hubris, as in Noble's production, where Henry's mud-splattered army entered at stage level while the French descended before Agincourt 'godlike, on golden tea-trays' (*Times Literary Supplement*, 13 April 1984), resplendent in their glistening armour, and Boyd's, where the French peers and their herald routinely appeared on trapezes, the exaggeratedly long tails of the peers' embroidered frock coats trailing beneath their languid forms until defeat at Agincourt brought them to ground. Costuming the French in historically outmoded dress and Henry's army in modern dress can illuminate why the devotion of the French peers to an outmoded medieval chivalric code results not only in their defeat at Agincourt but also in the disproportionate losses suffered by France.

Although historical pageantry is rare in modern productions, those that retain the play's most brutal episodes and utterances sometimes neuter much of their force by using vivid tableau staging and choreographed movements of military banners and soldiers to project warfare as having a savage beauty. More commonly, evocations of modern warfare – the muddy slaughter of the First World War, the hooding of prisoners and their handcuffing with plastic ties, the machine-gunning of opponents – are used to deglamorize war for a public familiar with television images of recent conflicts. Williams's vivid reminder of 'all those legs, and arms, and heads, chopped off in a battle' (IV.1.131–2) distils this sense of the dehumanizing brutality of armed conflict. Some productions, such as Noble's, combine elements of the two. Even when war is deglamorized, Henry and his victory are frequently still valorized by portraying the king as a remorseful and self-doubting insomniac who is struggling selflessly to cope with the burden of responsibility he has inherited with the crown.

'THIS STAR OF ENGLAND'
(EPILOGUE.6)

With over forty speaking roles the Folio text is ideally suited to ensemble performance. Directors operating on a limited budget must give careful consideration to the doubling (or more) of parts, a practice that provides actors the opportunity to demonstrate their versatility and audiences the added pleasure of detecting contrasts and connections between roles, such as those discussed in relation to the Chorus. *Henry V* can also serve as a potential 'star vehicle'. The title role provides the opportunity to be both an action hero (though more in word than in deed) and briefly a romantic lead. As Henry V speaks about a third of all lines (in both versions), nearly four times as many as any other speaker, the leading actor can dominate the production. Aged just twenty-four, Kenneth Branagh made his name in the part in Noble's 1984 RSC production, while Laurence Olivier's film version broke box office records and established the veteran British stage actor as a film star in the United States. To serve as a star vehicle the play requires judicious trimming and rejigging. As noted above, Henry's order to kill the French prisoners and his later threat to cut the throats of those that survive are hurdles that some actors shy from. If the production is merely a vehicle for the leading actor then the smaller parts suffer, but the play's performance history shows that roles such as Quickly, Pistol, Fluellen, Exeter, Montjoy, the Boy, Bates and Williams can make a significant impact with the right casting and directorial care. Even the virtually silent Alexander Court has made a lasting impression in productions where he appears to be visibly suffering from post-traumatic stress.

Since the rise of Stanislavskian 'method' acting, with its emphasis on character psychology and motivation, one limitation of the title role is that Henry V has only one, interrupted soliloquy, most of which is given over to a complaint about the burdens of office and a meditation on ceremony until, in a postscript, we glimpse

Henry's anxious 'sense of reckoning' for his father's crimes against Richard II (IV.1.282–98). The contrast to *Julius Caesar* and *Hamlet*, one possibly written within months and the other within a year of *Henry V*, is striking – Henry V is no Brutus much less a brooding Hamlet. Although the role of Henry V does not obviously lend itself to meditative introspection, this has not deterred some actors from seeking to project just such qualities on to the king. Despite the paucity of soliloquies, Kenneth Branagh discerned a 'sense of Hamletian doubt' running through the part (*Beginning*, p. 137). One method of portraying Henry V as a ruler beset by inner conflicts is to place particular emphasis on moments of moral crisis in the play, such as Henry's blunt query to Canterbury, 'May I with right and conscience make this claim?' (I.2.96), Scroop's intimate act of betrayal, the hanging of Bardolph, the quarrel with Williams and, of course, the divided soliloquy on the night before Agincourt. Alan Howard portrayed Henry V as a youthful and inexperienced king struggling with his conscience and the burdens of kingship in Hands's 1975 RSC production by expanding on Henry's preoccupation in his soliloquy with the responsibility placed 'Upon the King' (IV.1.223) at every opportunity afforded by the text. This approach is often adopted when *Henry V* is performed as part of a historical cycle that includes the two parts of *Henry IV*. When the actor playing the role of Henry V also plays the role of Hal he is able to depict the political maturation of the prince and his (possibly reluctant) adaptation to and adoption of his political responsibilities as heir to the throne. That said, Hal's speech in *Henry IV, Part I* when he sets out his political strategy (I.2.192–214) shows a prince whose immaturity is more apparent than real. Is Henry V a calculating Machiavel intent on distracting attention from his dubious claim to the English crown by following his father's advice to 'busy giddy minds | With foreign quarrels' (*Henry IV, Part II*, IV.5.213–14), or is he 'the mirror of all Christian kings' (II.Chorus.6) and the heroic 'model to [England's] inward greatness' (16) celebrated by the Chorus?

These are among the many questions each production of *Henry V* must tackle and for which the play supplies an array of performance options. The challenges the Folio version of *Henry V* presents to performers and audiences are frequently daunting, and the temptation may be to eliminate contradiction, smooth sharp swings in genre and tone, cut complexity, and underplay or remove controversial material. There is always the first Quarto version for those so inclined. But as Shakespeare appears to have had the courage to include these unsettling traits in a play about a celebrated national hero written at a time of war, avoiding the challenges of his heterodox drama seems both cowardly and uninventive.

Ann Kaegi

Further Reading

EDITIONS AND SOURCES

There are a good range of editions of *Henry V* available in the major Shakespeare series, including two modern editions of the first Quarto (Q1) and a parallel text edition of the first Folio version (F). J. H. Walter's Arden edition (Second Series, 1954) was the first comprehensively edited text of the play and as such provides the template for most modern editions. (It is also the most 'pro-Henry' of the lot.) The most recent Folio-based editions of *Henry V* include the Oxford edition by Gary Taylor (1984), the New Cambridge edition by Andrew Gurr (Second Series, 1992) and T. W. Craik's edition in the Arden Third Series (1995). Their introductions are very different, but each provides an informative commentary on the play, its context and sources, date of composition, and critical and performance histories. Reading all three would be a good groundwork exercise for any student of the play. Taylor's Oxford edition follows on from his *Three Studies in the Text of 'Henry V'* (1979), where he argues that Q1 is a somewhat garbled record of how the play was adapted and abridged for performance, 'probably in the provinces' (p. 39), by a reduced company of eleven players. He nonetheless makes a case in his introduction for adopting a textual variant from Q1, which has Pistol pronounce his catchphrase, 'Couple gorge', at the end of Act IV, scene 6 after Henry gives his order to kill the French prisoners, and incorporates several other significant Quarto variants in his Folio-based edition. Appendix F provides a helpful list of passages not included in Q1. Craik is especially strong on Shakespeare's extensive borrowings from Holinshed's *Chronicle* (see below), which he reproduces in the notes beneath the passages in *Henry V* to which they relate. This procedure illuminates Shakespeare's heavy reliance on Holinshed and how the playwright went about adapting (or simply pilfering) source material. Another feature of Craik's edition likely to appeal in the classroom is its inclusion of a reduced photographic facsimile of the British Library's copy of Q1 in an appendix, though the size and quality of the reproduction can make for difficult reading at times. Andrew Gurr is presently in the unique position of having edited both the F (1992) and Q1 (2000) versions of *Henry V*. Printed eight years apart, Gurr's two editions are meant to complement each other, yet they clearly chart an important shift in textual scholarship on the so-called 'bad' quartos. Prior to Graham Holderness and Brian Loughrey's edition of Q1 in the Shakespearean Originals: First Editions series (1993) all editions of *Henry V* since 1623 had been based on F, as Q1 had long been regarded as one of the 'Stolne and surreptitious copies' of Shakespeare's plays to which Heminges and Condell refer in their preface to the first Folio. In a dramatic departure from this long-held view, Gurr argues in the introduction to his edition of Q1 that the Quarto text 'offers the best evidence we have of what routinely happened to the scripts that the Shakespeare company bought from their resident playwright' (p. ix). Where Gurr affirms the merits of Q1 as a record of how Shakespeare's scripts were radically altered for performance, Holderness and Loughrey argue that Q1 is worthy of critical attention and performance in its own right 'as a vigorous and powerful instance of Elizabethan comic-historical drama' (p. 13). Their approach is 'to essay comparisons between Quarto and Folio on the assumption of textual multiplicity and equivalence, as distinct from the tradition of interpretation predicated on the Quarto's self-evident inferiority' (pp. 22–3). A facsimile of Q1 can be found in *Shakespeare's Plays in Quarto*, edited by Michael Allen and Kenneth Muir (1981). In addition to the Folio-based editions of *Henry V* already discussed, F can also be accessed in a parallel text edition, *Henry V/The Life of Henry the Fift*, edited by Nick de Somogyi (2001), in The Shakespeare Folios series, which prints the text of the 1623 Folio on the right-hand page and a modernized version on the facing page.

The best guide to Shakespeare's sources remains Geoffrey Bullough's eight-volume compendium *Narrative and Dramatic Sources of Shakespeare* (1957–75). Volume IV (1962) provides substantial extracts from the major sources for *Henry V*, including a key dramatic source for *Henry V* and the preceding *Henry IV* plays, *The Famous Victories of Henry the fifth: Containing the Honourable Battell of Agin-court. Famous Victories* can also be found in *The Oldcastle Controversy* (1991) by Peter Corbin and Douglas Sedge. Anne Barton, in 'The King Disguised: Shakespeare's *Henry V* and the Comical History' (in *The Triple Bond: Plays, Mainly Shakespearean, in Performance* (1975), ed. Joseph G. Price, pp. 92–117), challenges Bullough's suggestion that the episode in which Henry dons Erpingham's cloak and moves among his troops in disguise is modelled on a passage in Tacitus' *Annals*.

Instead she proposes several historical romances if not as sources then as analogues for the encounter between the disguised king and three common soldiers. Shakespeare's principal historical source for the plays of the second tetralogy was the second edition of the multiply authored, multi-volume prose history commonly referred to as Raphael Holinshed's *Chronicles of England, Scotland, and Ireland* (1587). This vast work is available in a six-volume edition published in 1807–8. Alternatively, the Everyman edition (no. 800) compiled by Allardyce and Josephine Nicoll offers a single-volume abridgement that, on the whole, lives up to its title, *Holinshed's Chronicle, As Used in Shakespeare's Plays* (1927; repr. 1978). If neither is available a third, more selective compilation, *Shakespeare's Holinshed: An Edition of Holinshed's Chronicles, 1587; Source of Shakespeare's History Plays, King Lear, Cymbeline, and Macbeth* (1968), edited by Richard Hosley, provides much of the core material. Annabel Patterson's *Reading Holinshed's 'Chronicles'* (1994) reappraises Holinshed's *Chronicles* as 'an archive for cultural history . . . from which we might reconstruct the *conditions* of playwrighting' (p. xiii) in Shakespeare's time. The other chronicle history on which Shakespeare habitually relied, Edward Hall's *Union of the Two Noble and Illustre Families of Lancaster and York* (1548), is available as a Scolar Press reprint (1970).

BIBLIOGRAPHIES, ANTHOLOGIES AND COLLECTIONS

Richard Dutton provides a helpful survey of twentieth-century criticism of the second tetralogy in *Shakespeare: A Bibliographical Guide* (1990), edited by Stanley Wells.

Unfortunately, it was compiled before the ground shift in views on the first Quarto of *Henry V* had made itself felt, and it also unavoidably omits more recent work on the play's engagement with questions of national identity and the matter of Britain. *'Henry V': An Annotated Bibliography*, compiled by Joseph Candido and Charles R. Forker, is a valuable resource, but as it was published in 1983 it too has obvious limitations. Seventeenth- and eighteenth-century commentaries on *Henry V* can be found scattered across the six volumes of *Shakespeare: The Critical Heritage* (1974–81), edited by Brian Vickers. Useful collections of essays include *Shakespeare's Histories* (2004; ed. Emma Smith); *A Companion to Shakespeare's Works, Volume II: The Histories* (2003; ed. Richard Dutton and Jean E. Howard); *The Cambridge Companion to Shakespeare's History Plays* (2002; ed. Michael Hattaway); *Shakespeare's History Plays: Richard II to Henry V* (1992; ed. Graham Holderness); *William Shakespeare's 'Henry V'* (1988; ed. Harold Bloom); *Shakespeare: 'Henry V'* (1969; ed. Michael Quinn); *Twentieth-Century Interpretations of 'Henry V'* (1968; ed. Ronald Berman); and the journal *Shakespeare Survey 6* (1953) and *38* (1985).

TEXTUAL ISSUES

In recent years the status of the first Quarto of *Henry V* and its relationship to the first Folio version on which this edition and most other modern editions of the play are based have been the subject of renewed debate. At just over 1,620 lines, Q1 (1600) is half the length of F (1623), which at nearly 3,400 lines is one of Shakespeare's longest plays. Three influential theories have been advanced to explain the striking disparity between these two early versions of *Henry V*. The theory that Q1 represents an unauthorized 'bad' or 'pirated' text is set out by Alfred W. Pollard, in *Shakespeare Folios and Quartos: A Study in the Bibliography of Shakespeare's Plays 1594–1685* (1909), especially pp. 64–80. The theory that it is the product of a flawed attempt at 'memorial reconstruction' by two or more actors who had participated in performances of the 'long' version derives from W. W. Greg's *Shakespeare's 'Merry Wives of Windsor', 1602* (1910). It is most fully developed in relation to *Henry V* by George Ian Duthie, in 'The Quarto of Shakespeare's *Henry V*' (in *Papers Mainly Shakespearian* (1964), ed. Duthie). The favourite contenders for the role of 'memorial reporter' are the actors playing Exeter, Gower, the Governor of Harfleur and Scroop. The theory that it is a pared down acting version used by a reduced company of actors touring in the provinces has been elaborated most fully by Gary Taylor, in *Three Studies in the Text of 'Henry V'* (published with *Modernizing Shakespeare's Spelling* (1979) by Stanley Wells, pp. 37–164). This theory presupposes that the 'long' versions of the plays were performed substantially uncut in the London theatres. Kathleen Irace, in 'Reconstruction and Adaptation in Q *Henry V*' (in *Studies in Bibliography* 44 (1991), pp. 228–53), advocates elements of the second and third theories, arguing that the manuscript from which Q1 derives is a memorial reconstruction and was devised 'as a promptbook for use in performances outside London' (p. 249). Andrew Gurr, in *The First Quarto of 'King Henry V'* (2000), and Lukas Erne, in *Shakespeare as Literary Dramatist* (2003), have recently rejected all three theories. Gurr argues that Q1 represents 'a version closely based on the Shakespeare company's own performance script of the play, a text made for or from its first performances in 1599 ... a text set from an authorised playhouse manuscript' (p. ix). Erne makes a similar claim, affirming that 'the authoritative performance script is what the first quarto imperfectly recovers' (p. 209). Far from being an unauthorized or 'pirated' version to be regarded with suspicion, Gurr characterizes Q1 as 'probably the best surviving example of a Shakespeare play-script as it was first performed by the company that bought it' (p. 2), a company for which Shakespeare acted and of which he was also a principal shareholder, having purchased a second share in the Lord Chamberlain's Men in 1599, the year in which *Henry V* was probably written. (Warren D. Smith, in 'The *Henry V* Choruses in the First Folio' (*Journal of English and Germanic Philology* 53 (1954), pp. 38–57), and David Bevington, in *Tudor Drama and Politics: A Critical Approach to Topical Meaning* (1968), argue for composition in 1600, but their arguments have attracted few adherents.) Annabel Patterson, in 'Back by Popular Demand: The Two Versions of *Henry V*' (in *Shakespeare and the Popular Voice* (1989), pp. 71–92), argues that political developments, specifically the alarming deterioration in the already strained relations between Elizabeth and Essex after his unauthorized return from Ireland in September 1599, may account for the omission of the Chorus from Q1, as the thinly veiled reference to Essex in the fifth chorus and the Chorus's idolization of a popular military hero throughout may have been judged too dangerous to publish. The very fact that Q1 was rushed into print in August 1600 (a unique contraction of the usual two-to-three-year gap between the date a play was written by Shakespeare and first performed and the date a version came into print) may represent a 'tactical retreat' by the playing company in the very month Essex was to appear before the Privy Council to defend his conduct in Ireland.

Where most commentators characterize Q1 as more
orthodox in its depiction of Henry V and his French
campaign, Leah S. Marcus, in *Puzzling Shakespeare: Local
Reading and Its Discontents* (1988), and Graham
Holderness, in 'Writing and Fighting: *Henry V*' (in his
Textual Shakespeare (2003), pp. 213–37), argue respectively that Q1 plebeianizes and carnivalizes the king. Q1
is not lesser or more orthodox; it is generically distinct.
As Holderness puts it: 'The Henry of the Quarto is
presented not as an epic hero or an awe-inspiring histor-
ical character, but as a "gentle gamester"' (p. 26). The
validity of the theory of 'memorial reconstruction' and
its application to the so-called 'bad' quartos, including
Q1 of *Henry V*, has also been challenged by Paul
Werstine, in 'A Century of "Bad"' Shakespeare Quartos'
(*Shakespeare Quarterly*, 50 (1999), pp. 310–33), and Laurie
Maguire, in *Shakespearean Suspect Texts: The 'Bad'
Quartos and Their Contexts* (1996).

CRITICISM

No other Shakespeare play has divided modern critics as
sharply as *Henry V* nor has any other Shakespearian character provoked such polarized responses as the victor at
Agincourt. The case for Henry V as a Christian epic hero
is put most famously by J. H. Walter in the introduction
to his 1954 edition. John Dover Wilson also sturdily
defends Henry V against his detractors in his introduction to his Cambridge edition (1947). The first person to
publish the countervailing view of Henry as a warmongering tyrant appears to have been William Hazlitt
in 1817, who memorably characterizes Henry V as 'a
very amiable monster' (p. 170) in his *Characters of*

Shakespear[e]'s Plays (1949 edn). Dissatisfaction with the play, or more precisely with the 'long' Folio version, predates Hazlitt's attack on its hero (as the printing of the first Quarto in 1600 and a history of heavy revisions to the Folio text in performance from the time of its revival in the eighteenth century arguably attest). Writing half a century before Hazlitt, Samuel Johnson expressed bafflement that in the courtship scene 'Shakespeare now gives the king nearly such a character as he made him formerly ridicule in Percy'. To Johnson it appeared 'that the poet's matter failed him in the fifth act'. Although he had attempted 'to fill it up with whatever he could get', not even a writer as skilled as Shakespeare could 'paint upon vacuity'. As for the coarse sexual banter between Burgundy and Henry, 'the merriment is very gross, and the sentiments are very worthless' (*Notes to the Edition of Shakespeare's Plays*, quoted in *Samuel Johnson on Shakespeare*, ed. H. R. Woodhuysen (1989), p. 210). Unlike Johnson, it was not the abrupt shift from heroic drama to romantic comedy in the last act that concerned Hazlitt but rather Shakespeare's concerted effort (as he saw it) 'to apologize for the actions of the king', not least as Henry V 'seemed to have no idea of any rule of right or wrong, but brute force, glossed over with a little religious hypocrisy' (p. 168). Hazlitt never entertains the possibility that the play was designed to complicate, question or qualify a celebrated national legend.

The first essay to claim 'the play is ironic' was written by Gerald Gould in the aftermath of the First World War. The ironic interpretation of *Henry V* proposed by Gould in his ground-breaking essay 'A new reading of *Henry V*' (in *The English Review* 128 (1919), pp. 42–55; repr. abridged as 'Irony and Satire in *Henry V*' in *Shakespeare: 'Henry V'. A Casebook* (1969), ed. Michael

Quinn, pp. 81–94) has since become one of the dominant critical views of the play. Gould's ironic interpretation sharpens into a cynical view of Henry as 'too close
for comfort to Machiavelli's ideal prince' in H. C.
Goddard's *The Meaning of Shakespeare* (1951; vol. 1, p.
267), written in the aftermath of the Second World War.
The appraisal of Henry V as a Machiavellian tyrant,
ruthless, cunning and hypocritical, a master of verbal
forms of deception, has been elaborated and variously
embellished by a host of subsequent commentators,
among them Andrew Gurr, in '*Henry V* and the Bees'
Commonwealth' (*Shakespeare Survey 30* (1977), pp. 61–
72), a particularly subtle variation on the standard
approach; and Vicki Sullivan, in 'Princes to Act: Henry
V as the Machiavellian Prince of Appearance'
(*Shakespeare's Political Pageant: Essays in Literature and
Politics* (1996), ed. Joseph Alulis and Vickie Sullivan).

Other commentators, such as Una Ellis-Fermor, in
'Shakespeare's Political Plays' (*The Frontiers of Drama*
(1945; 2nd edn, 1948)), and Derek Traversi, in *Shakespeare:
From 'Richard II' to 'Henry V'* (1957), are more equivocal. Ellis-Fermor supports the view that Henry V epitomizes Shakespeare's idea of the statesman-king. Henry
V is 'the perfect public man' (p. 45); however, his political accomplishment is at the expense of the inner or
'private' person: 'It is in vain that we look for the person-
ality of Henry behind the king; there is nothing else there
. . . There is no Henry, only a king' (pp. 45–6). According
to Ellis-Fermor, this is why 'generations of Shakespeare's
readers have found little to love in this play' (p. 46).
Shakespeare's Henry V is 'a dead man walking' and
'Shakespeare himself . . . begins to recoil' from the figure
of the 'statesman-king' he had constructed across the
Henriad with such care (p. 47). For Traversi, '*Henry V*

represents ... a step in the realization of themes only fully developed in the tragedies' (p. 187). Henry's 'increasing awareness of his isolation' (p. 188), the elements of 'harshness and inhumanity' (p. 194) that accompany his exhibitions of self-control, and the notorious throat-cutting order are examples of 'the tougher strain of disillusioned realism that emerges from the play' (p. 194). In a seminal essay, 'Rabbits, Ducks and *Henry V*' (*Shakespeare Quarterly* 28 (1977), pp. 279–96; repr. as 'Either/Or: Responding to *Henry V*' in *Shakespeare and the Problem of Meaning* (1981)), Norman Rabkin compares Shakespeare's play to a gestalt sketch that can be perceived to be in the shape of either a rabbit or a duck with equal plausibility. For Rabkin, *Henry V* is a rabbit-duck, meaning that it can be interpreted by the audience as a heroic sequel to *Henry IV, Part I* that celebrates the victor at Agincourt as a 'mirror of all Christian kings' (II. Chorus.6) or as a sequel to the more troubling *Henry IV, Part II* that exposes the ruthlessness and hypocrisy of a Machiavellian opportunist. Its 'ultimate power', he argues, 'is precisely the fact that it points in two opposite directions, virtually daring us to choose one of the two opposed interpretations it requires of us' (p. 279). Where Rabkin argues that the opposing responses to *Henry V* tell us something about the play and about Shakespeare's own deep ambivalence, James Black, in 'Shakespeare's *Henry V* and the Dreams of History' (*English Studies in Canada* 1 (1975), pp. 13–30), and Alexander Leggatt, in *Shakespeare's Political Drama: The History Plays and the Roman Plays* (1988), argue that the critical and performance history of *Henry V* exposes, as no other Shakespearian drama, 'the biases of its interpreters' (p. 114).

Whether or not the critical divisions over *Henry V*

prompt commentators to reflect on their own interpretative practices, *Henry V* is a conspicuously self-reflexive drama. The self-conscious theatricality of the play and the self-conscious mastery of rhetoric exhibited by Hal-Henry-Harry across the *Henriad* are the subject of metadramatic studies by James L. Calderwood, *Metadrama in Shakespeare's Henriad* (1979); Joseph A. Porter, *The Drama of Speech Acts: Shakespeare's Lancastrian Tetralogy* (1979); John W. Blanpied, *Time and the Artist in Shakespeare's English Histories* (1983); and Kent T. van den Berg, *Playhouse and Cosmos: Shakespearean Theatre as Metaphor* (1985). Calderwood argues that 'in *Henry V* . . . the divinely guaranteed truths of Richard's reign and the ubiquitous lies of [Henry IV's] are succeeded by rhetoric, the language of conquest' (p. 7). However, where Calderwood finds that in Shakespeare 'Political affairs . . . become metaphors for arts' (p. 4), new historicist and cultural materialist critics argue the reverse. In his widely anthologized essay 'Invisible Bullets: Renaissance Authority and Its Subversion, *Henry IV* and *Henry V*' (*Political Shakespeare: New Essays in Cultural Materialism* (1985; 2nd edn, 1994), ed. Jonathan Dollimore and Alan Sinfield, pp. 18–47; repr. in revised form in *Shakespearean Negotiations: The Circulation of Social Energy in Renaissance England* (1988)), new historicist Stephen Greenblatt contends that 'Theatricality . . . is not set over against power but is one of power's essential modes' (p. 46). Although the play awakens 'subversive doubts' (p. 62), Greenblatt questions whether '*Henry V* can be successfully performed as subversive' (p. 63). 'The ideal king must be in large part the invention of the audience'; however, Greenblatt's totalizing assumption that all audience members will be 'induced to make up the difference, to invest in the illusion of magnificence'

(p. 63) is disputed by Jonathan Dollimore and Alan Sinfield, in 'History and Ideology: The Instance of *Henry V*' (*Alternative Shakespeares* (1985), ed. John Drakakis, pp. 206–27), and by Graham Bradshaw, who also takes issue with Dollimore and Sinfield's cultural materialist approach, in 'Is Shakespeare Evil?' and 'Being Oneself: New Historicists, Cultural Materialists, and *Henry V*' (*Misrepresentations: Shakespeare and the Materialists* (1993), pp. 1–33, 34–124). Other late-twentieth-century ideological readings include Leonard Tennenhouse, 'Strategies of State and Political Plays: *A Midsummer Night's Dream, Henry IV, Henry V, Henry VIII*' (*Political Shakespeare*, pp. 109–28); Gunter Walch, '*Henry V* as Working-House of Ideology' (*Shakespeare Survey 40* (1988), pp. 63–8); Robert Weimann, 'Bifold Authority in Shakespeare's Theatre' (*Shakespeare Quarterly* 39 (1988), pp. 401–17); and Graham Holderness, *Shakespeare Recycled: The Making of Historical Drama* (1992) and '*Henry V*' (*Shakespeare: The Histories* (2000), pp. 136–55). Joel B. Altman, in '"Vile Participation": The Amplification of Violence in the Theatre of *Henry V*' (*Shakespeare Quarterly* 42 (1991), pp. 1–32), argues that these recent ideological readings 'exult [ideological] process at the expense of playwrighting', while formalists are hesitant to relate 'the play of significations in *Henry V* . . . to the shifting contours of the times' in which Shakespeare wrote. Both approaches tend 'to anaesthetize and immobilize . . . *Henry V*, arguably the most active dramatic experience Shakespeare ever offered his audience' (p. 2). In their place Altman provides an 'essentially rhetorical' reading of the play that explains 'the play's power in terms of its crafted interaction with the needs of its players and its first audiences' (p. 3). Describing *Henry V* as 'perhaps, Shakespeare's most conspicuous achievement in the reasoning *in utramque partem*' (p. 137), Paula Pugliatti, in *Shakespeare the Historian* (1996), relates the play's ambivalence to the rhetorical practice, central to the educational system of Shakespeare's day, of arguing on opposing sides of a question (*in utramque partem*). P. K. Ayers, in '"Fellows of Infinite Tongue": Henry V and the King's English' (*Studies in English Literature* 34 (1994), pp. 253–77), too favours a rhetorical approach and takes Henry's courtship of Katherine, specifically his spurious denial that he is one of 'these fellows of infinite tongue' (V.2.154–5), as the starting point for his investigation of 'the complex web of relationships between language and power' (p. 254) in *Henry V* and in the two parts of *Henry IV*.

Although numerous utterances in *Henry V* foreground the issue of gender, feminist studies of *Henry V* are comparatively thin on the ground, presumably because of the paucity of female roles in the play and in the second tetralogy as a whole. Lance Wilcox, in 'Katherine of France as Victim and Bride' (*Shakespeare Studies* 17 (1985), pp. 61–76), was the first to devote considered attention to the play's rape motif. Karen Newman, in 'Englishing the Other: "le tiers exclu" and Shakespeare's *Henry V*' (*Fashioning Femininity and English Renaissance Drama* (1991)), notes how 'the expansionist aims of the nation state are worked out on and through the woman's body' (p. 101) and includes a discussion of the Englishing of Katherine as a strategy of mastery. Peter Erickson, in 'Fathers, Sons, and Brothers in *Henry V*' (*Patriarchal Structures in Shakespeare's Drama* (1985; repr. in *William Shakespeare's 'Henry V'* (1988), ed. Harold Bloom, pp. 111–33)), traces the father–son motif and the damaging effect the martial definition of masculinity adopted by Henry V has on the play's comic denouement. Erickson's contention that 'The second tetralogy . . . avoids the threat to male rule that formidable women present in the first tetralogy by restricting women to the periphery' (p. 130) is endorsed by Jean E. Howard and Phyllis Rackin in *Engendering a Nation: A Feminist Account of Shakespeare's English Histories* (1997). In *Stages of History: Shakespeare's English Chronicles* (1990), Rackin emphasizes the resemblance between Henry V and Elizabeth I and explores Henry's reliance on women to legitimize his authority. In 'History and Ideology, Masculinity and Miscegenation: The Instance of *Henry V*' by Alan Sinfield with Jonathan Dollimore (*Faultlines: Cultural Materialism and the Politics of Dissident Reading* (1992) by Alan Sinfield, pp. 109–42; a revised, retitled and extended version of their essay in *Alternative Shakespeares* cited above), the authors argue that '[s]exualities and genders constitute a further ground of disturbance in the England of *Henry V*' (p. 127). '[B]anishment of the feminine and the female, even as these are conceived of by the masculine and the patriarchal, cannot easily be achieved' (p. 129): 'the state cannot be secured against female influence' (p. 139).

MILITARY CONTEXT

The battle between the genders tends not to be at the forefront of studies of Elizabethan militarism. Paul A. Jorgensen's landmark study *Shakespeare's Military World* (1956) remains an important guide to Shakespeare's knowledge of and extensive borrowings from sixteenth-century 'art of war' literature. J. Hale focuses on military character types in his essay 'Shakespeare and Warfare' (in *William Shakespeare: His World, His Work, His Influence*, ed. J. Andrews, 3 vols. (1985)). The field has since been enriched by two studies that depart from this earlier, characterological approach. In *Shakespeare's Theatre of War* (1998) Nick de Somogyi reads 'the Elizabethan plays of Shakespeare and his contemporaries in the light of contemporary writings which deal overtly with the waging, reporting, and social context of war' (p. 4). The twin aims of his study are to establish 'the aptness of the stage to the representation of war' (p. 4) and 'the currency of war among the audiences and players of London between 1585 and 1604' (p. 7), issues that bear directly on *Henry V* and its choruses. Nina Taunton is more concerned with the discourse of war as distinct from Somogyi's preoccupation with the theatricality of war in late-sixteenth-century England in *1590s Drama and Militarism: Portrayals of War in Marlowe, Chapman and Shakespeare's 'Henry V'* (2001). A limitation of her Foucauldian approach is that it tends to predetermine the ideological 'anxieties' found to be circulating in the war manuals and plays under examination. A compensatory strength of the book is its consideration of the challenge posed to the dominant, virulently masculinist conception of war by the historical presence of women in the military camp and on the battlefield, 'Officially excluded yet indubitably there' (p. 217). John Sutherland, in 'Henry V, War Criminal?' (*Henry V, War Criminal? And Other Shakespeare Puzzles* (2000) by John Sutherland and Cedric Watts), considers the twin possibilities that Henry's query after the battle of Agincourt, 'What prisoners *of good sort* are taken' (IV.8.74), means either that he was disobeyed at the height of the battle or that 'only the unregarded ordinary prisoners of war have been put to the sword', those of gentle rank having been retained for their ransom after giving their *parole* (p. 116). *Elizabeth I: War and Politics, 1588–1603* (1992) by the historian Wallace T. MacCaffrey provides an excellent account of the wider historical context of 1590s militarism and the factors that contributed to the eruption of open and sustained war in Ireland late in Elizabeth's reign.

NATION

Some of the best work on *Henry V* in recent years has been concerned with notions of nationhood and with the broader issue of how national identities are constituted in the play and over the history of its production. *Threshold of a Nation* (1979), Philip Edwards's ground-breaking study on the inter-relationship between imperialism and drama in the period, opened up this rich field of research. Subsequent studies have explored the play's engagement with Wales, Ireland and its treatment of the matter of Britain. Critics who have examined the preoccupation with Wales and Welsh identity in *Henry V* and in Shakespeare's English histories more generally include Lisa Hopkins, 'Welshness in Shakespeare's English Histories' (*Shakespeare's English History Plays: Performance, Translation and Adaptation in Britain and Abroad* (2004), ed. Ton Hoenselaars); Terence Hawkes, 'Bryn Glas' (*Shakespeare in the Present* (2002)); Patricia Parker, 'Uncertain Unions: Welsh Leeks in *Henry V*' (*British Identities and English Renaissance Literature* (2002), ed. David Baker and Willy Maley); and Megan S. Lloyd, *Speak It in Welsh: Wales and the Welsh Language in Shakespeare* (2007). David Cairns and Shaun Richards, in 'What Ish My Nation?' (in *Writing Ireland: Colonialism, Nationalism and Culture* (1988)), drew attention to a neglected aspect of Shakespearian drama that has since become a focus of scholarly interest. *Shakespeare and Ireland: History, Politics, Culture* (1997), edited by Mark

Thornton Burnett and Ramona Wray, includes impor-
tant essays on *Henry V* and Ireland by Lisa Hopkins,
'Neighbourhood in *Henry V*'; Willy Maley, 'Shakespeare,
Holinshed and Ireland: Resources and Con-texts'; and
Andrew Murphy, '"Tish ill done: *Henry the Fift* and the
Politics of Editing'. The subject of David J. Baker's article
'"Wildehirissheman": Colonialist Representation in
Shakespeare's *Henry V*' (*English Literary Renaissance* 22
(1993), pp. 37–61) is aptly summarized in the title (see
also 'Imagining Britain: William Shakespeare's *Henry V*'
in his *Between Nations: Shakespeare, Spenser, Marvell, and
the Question of Britain* (1997)). Michael Neill, in 'Broken
English and Broken Irish: Nation, Language, and the
Optic of Power in Shakespeare's Histories' (*Shakespeare
Quarterly* 45 (1994), pp. 1–32; repr. in his *Putting History
to the Question: Power, Politics, and Society in English
Renaissance Drama* (2000)), discusses the disruptive
presence of the English enterprise in Ireland in
Shakespeare's history plays within a wider theatrical
context in which 'Ireland can seem to constitute ... one
of the great and unexplained lacunae in the drama of the
period' (p. 11). In '"If the Cause be not good": *Henry V*
and Essex's Irish Campaign' (in his *Shakespeare, Spenser,
and the Crisis in Ireland* (1997)), Christopher Highley
argues that 'In *Henry V*, Shakespeare's misgivings about
Essex together with an awareness of burgeoning public
alarm at the war in Ireland produce a sceptical counter-
discourse about English expansionism within the British
Isles' (pp. 135–6). Philip Schwyzer sets out the case for
regarding *Henry V* as a play 'drenched in the now-familiar
language of British nationalism' (p. 128) with admirable
clarity in his chapter '"I am Welsh, you know": The
Nation in *Henry V*' (*Literature, Nationalism, and Memory
in Early Modern England and Wales* (2004)). Much

of Graham Holderness's '"What ish my nation?":
Shakespeare and National Identities' (*Textual Practice* 5
(1991), pp. 74–93; repr. in *Shakespeare's Histories* (2004),
ed. Emma Smith) is devoted to an examination of the
relationship between Laurence Olivier's and especially
Kenneth Branagh's iconic film adaptations of *Henry V*
and the patriotic and nationalist ideologies of 1940s and
1980s Britain respectively.

THE PLAY IN PERFORMANCE

A wide variety of resources are available to those inter-
ested in the performance history of *Henry V. Shakespeare
in Performance: Henry V* (1996) by James N. Loehlin and
King Henry V (2002) by Emma Smith are both excellent.
Anthony Brennan's *Henry V* (1992) includes a solid
chapter on its stage history. In his chapter on *Henry V* in
Shakespeare's Histories: Plays for the Stage (1964) Arthur
Colby Sprague appraises key trends in its performance
history from its revival in the eighteenth century through
to the early twentieth century, making his personal pref-
erences plain throughout. Several modern productions
benefit from publications that record aspects of the
production process by theatre and film professionals. *The
Royal Shakespeare Company's Production of 'Henry V' for
the Centenary Season at The Royal Shakespeare Theatre*
(1976) by Sally Beauman incorporates production photos,
costume sketches and numerous interviews with those
involved in the 1975 RSC production (dir. Terry Hands).
Written in the style of a diary, *English Shakespeare
Company: The Story of 'The Wars of the Roses', 1986–
1989* (1990) offers Michael Bogdanov's and Michael
Pennington's account of their touring production of the

two tetralogies. In his early autobiography, *Beginning* (1989), Kenneth Branagh comments extensively on the 1984 RSC production (dir. Adrian Noble), and on his own 1989 film version of *Henry V*, in both of which he played the title role. '*Henry V' at the National: A Rehearsal Diary* (2003), compiled by Peter Reynolds and Lee White, includes several photographs in its forty-four-page glimpse into the rehearsal process for the 2003 production (dir. Nicholas Hytner). The screenplay for Laurence Olivier's 1944 film can be accessed in *Henry V by William Shakespeare* (1984) in the Classic Film Scripts series. Branagh's *Henry V by William Shakespeare: A Screen Adaptation* (1989) includes a brief introduction by the actor-director together with an annotated version of the final edited film script (as distinct from the original screenplay) and numerous production stills. Other useful publications include Harry Geduld's *Filmguide to Henry V* (1976) on Olivier's 1944 film adaptation; Kenneth Branagh's essay on 'Henry V' in *Players of Shakespeare 2* (ed. Russell Jackson and Robert Smallwood; 1988); and Adrian Lester's on 'King Henry V' in *Players of Shakespeare 6* (ed. Robert Smallwood; 2004).

Laurence Olivier's film adaptation, *Henry V* (1944), Kenneth Branagh's 1989 film version and David Giles's 1979 BBC television film are all available on both video and DVD. *The Wars of the Roses: Henry V* is a video recording of a live performance of the English Shakespeare Company's touring production, directed by Michael Bogdanov (1997). The original soundtrack of Kenneth Branagh's film is also available, as is a sound recording of the unabridged New Cambridge Shakespeare text.

THE LIFE OF
HENRY THE FIFTH

The Characters in the Play

CHORUS

Archbishop of CANTERBURY
Bishop of ELY

KING HENRY the Fifth, King of England, claimant to
the French throne
Duke of GLOUCESTER ⎫
Duke of BEDFORD ⎬ his brothers
Duke of Clarence ⎭
Duke of EXETER, his uncle
Duke of YORK, his cousin
Earl of SALISBURY
Earl of WESTMORLAND
Earl of WARWICK
Earl of Huntingdon

BARDOLPH ⎫
NYM ⎬ formerly companions of Sir John Falstaff
PISTOL ⎭
Nell, HOSTESS of an Eastcheap tavern, formerly
Mistress Quickly, now Pistol's wife
BOY, formerly Falstaff's Page

Henry, Lord SCROOP of Masham ⎫
Richard, Earl of CAMBRIDGE ⎬ conspirators
Sir Thomas GREY ⎭

Sir Thomas ERPINGHAM ⎫
Captain FLUELLEN   ⎬
Capain GOWER   ⎬ officers in Henry's army
Captain JAMY   ⎬
Captain MACMORRIS   ⎭
John BATES   ⎫
Alexander COURT   ⎬ soldiers in Henry's army
Michael WILLIAMS   ⎭
English HERALDS

Charles the Sixth, the FRENCH KING
QUEEN ISABEL, the Queen of France
Lewis, the DAUPHIN, their son and heir
Princess KATHERINE, their daughter
ALICE, Katherine's lady-in-waiting

The CONSTABLE of France, Charles Delabreth
Duke of Berri   ⎫
Duke of BRITAINE   ⎬
Duke of Brabant   ⎬
Duke of ORLEANS   ⎬ French noblemen at Agincourt
Lord RAMBURES   ⎬
Lord GRANDPRÉ   ⎬
Duke of BOURBON   ⎭

French AMBASSADORS to England
GOVERNOR of Harfleur
MONTJOY, a French Herald
Monsieur le Fer, a FRENCH SOLDIER
Duke of BURGUNDY
French MESSENGERS

Attendants, lords, soldiers, and citizens

Prologue

Flourish. Enter Chorus

CHORUS

O for a Muse of fire, that would ascend
The brightest heaven of invention,
A kingdom for a stage, princes to act,
And monarchs to behold the swelling scene!
Then should the warlike Harry, like himself,
Assume the port of Mars, and at his heels,
Leashed in like hounds, should famine, sword, and fire
Crouch for employment. But pardon, gentles all,
The flat unraisèd spirits that hath dared
On this unworthy scaffold to bring forth   10
So great an object. Can this cockpit hold
The vasty fields of France? Or may we cram
Within this wooden O the very casques
That did affright the air at Agincourt?
O, pardon! since a crookèd figure may
Attest in little place a million,
And let us, ciphers to this great account,
On your imaginary forces work.
Suppose within the girdle of these walls
Are now confined two mighty monarchies,   20
Whose high uprearèd and abutting fronts
The perilous narrow ocean parts asunder.

Piece out our imperfections with your thoughts:
Into a thousand parts divide one man,
And make imaginary puissance.
Think, when we talk of horses, that you see them
Printing their proud hoofs i'th'receiving earth;
For 'tis your thoughts that now must deck our kings,
Carry them here and there, jumping o'er times,
30 Turning th'accomplishment of many years
Into an hour-glass: for the which supply,
Admit me Chorus to this history,
Who Prologue-like your humble patience pray,
Gently to hear, kindly to judge, our play.   *Exit*

I.I   *Enter the Archbishop of Canterbury and the*
             Bishop of Ely

CANTERBURY

My lord, I'll tell you. That self bill is urged
Which in th'eleventh year of the last King's reign
Was like, and had indeed against us passed,
But that the scambling and unquiet time
Did push it out of farther question.

ELY

But how, my lord, shall we resist it now?

CANTERBURY

It must be thought on. If it pass against us,
We lose the better half of our possession;
For all the temporal lands which men devout
10 By testament have given to the Church
Would they strip from us; being valued thus –
As much as would maintain, to the King's honour,
Full fifteen earls, and fifteen hundred knights,
Six thousand and two hundred good esquires;
And, to relief of lazars and weak age,

Of indigent faint souls past corporal toil,
A hundred almshouses right well supplied;
And, to the coffers of the King beside,
A thousand pounds by th'year. Thus runs the bill.

ELY
This would drink deep.

CANTERBURY   'Twould drink the cup and all.   20

ELY
But what prevention?

CANTERBURY
The King is full of grace and fair regard.

ELY
And a true lover of the holy Church.

CANTERBURY
The courses of his youth promised it not.
The breath no sooner left his father's body
But that his wildness, mortified in him,
Seemed to die too. Yea, at that very moment,
Consideration like an angel came
And whipped th'offending Adam out of him,
Leaving his body as a paradise   30
T'envelop and contain celestial spirits.
Never was such a sudden scholar made;
Never came reformation in a flood
With such a heady currance scouring faults;
Nor never Hydra-headed wilfulness
So soon did lose his seat, and all at once,
As in this King.

ELY   We are blessèd in the change.

CANTERBURY
Hear him but reason in divinity,
And all-admiring, with an inward wish,
You would desire the King were made a prelate.   40
Hear him debate of commonwealth affairs,

You would say it hath been all in all his study.
List his discourse of war, and you shall hear
A fearful battle rendered you in music.
Turn him to any cause of policy,
The Gordian knot of it he will unloose,
Familiar as his garter; that, when he speaks,
The air, a chartered libertine, is still,
And the mute wonder lurketh in men's ears
50   To steal his sweet and honeyed sentences.
So that the art and practic part of life
Must be the mistress to this theoric –
Which is a wonder how his grace should glean it,
Since his addiction was to courses vain,
His companies unlettered, rude, and shallow,
His hours filled up with riots, banquets, sports,
And never noted in him any study,
Any retirement, any sequestration,
From open haunts and popularity.

ELY

60   The strawberry grows underneath the nettle,
And wholesome berries thrive and ripen best
Neighboured by fruit of baser quality:
And so the Prince obscured his contemplation
Under the veil of wildness, which, no doubt,
Grew like the summer grass, fastest by night,
Unseen, yet crescive in his faculty.

CANTERBURY

It must be so, for miracles are ceased;
And therefore we must needs admit the means
How things are perfected.

ELY   But, my good lord,
70   How now for mitigation of this bill
Urged by the Commons? Doth his majesty
Incline to it, or no?

CANTERBURY   He seems indifferent,
     Or rather swaying more upon our part
     Than cherishing th'exhibiters against us;
     For I have made an offer to his majesty –
     Upon our spiritual Convocation,
     And in regard of causes now in hand,
     Which I have opened to his grace at large
     As touching France – to give a greater sum
     Than ever at one time the clergy yet   80
     Did to his predecessors part withal.
ELY
     How did this offer seem received, my lord?
CANTERBURY
     With good acceptance of his majesty,
     Save that there was not time enough to hear,
     As I perceived his grace would fain have done,
     The severals and unhidden passages
     Of his true titles to some certain dukedoms,
     And generally to the crown and seat of France,
     Derived from Edward, his great-grandfather.
ELY
     What was th'impediment that broke this off?   90
CANTERBURY
     The French ambassador upon that instant
     Craved audience, and the hour, I think, is come
     To give him hearing. Is it four o'clock?
ELY
     It is.
CANTERBURY
     Then go we in to know his embassy;
     Which I could with a ready guess declare
     Before the Frenchman speak a word of it.
ELY
     I'll wait upon you, and I long to hear it.   *Exeunt*

I.2   *Enter the King, Gloucester, Bedford, Clarence,*
            Exeter, Warwick, Westmorland, and attendants

KING HENRY
   Where is my gracious Lord of Canterbury?

EXETER
   Not here in presence.

KING HENRY   Send for him, good uncle.

WESTMORLAND
   Shall we call in th'ambassador, my liege?

KING HENRY
   Not yet, my cousin; we would be resolved,
   Before we hear him, of some things of weight
   That task our thoughts, concerning us and France.
            Enter the Archbishop of Canterbury and the Bishop of
            Ely

CANTERBURY
   God and His angels guard your sacred throne,
   And make you long become it!

KING HENRY   Sure, we thank you.
   My learnèd lord, we pray you to proceed,
10   And justly and religiously unfold
   Why the law Salic that they have in France
   Or should or should not bar us in our claim.
   And God forbid, my dear and faithful lord,
   That you should fashion, wrest, or bow your reading,
   Or nicely charge your understanding soul
   With opening titles miscreate, whose right
   Suits not in native colours with the truth;
   For God doth know how many now in health
   Shall drop their blood in approbation
20   Of what your reverence shall incite us to.
   Therefore take heed how you impawn our person,
   How you awake our sleeping sword of war.
   We charge you in the name of God, take heed;

For never two such kingdoms did contend
Without much fall of blood, whose guiltless drops
Are every one a woe, a sore complaint
'Gainst him whose wrongs gives edge unto the swords
That makes such waste in brief mortality.
Under this conjuration speak, my lord,
For we will hear, note, and believe in heart   30
That what you speak is in your conscience washed
As pure as sin with baptism.

CANTERBURY

Then hear me, gracious sovereign, and you peers,
That owe yourselves, your lives, and services
To this imperial throne. There is no bar
To make against your highness' claim to France
But this, which they produce from Pharamond:
'*In terram Salicam mulieres ne succedant*' –
'No woman shall succeed in Salic land';
Which Salic land the French unjustly gloze   40
To be the realm of France, and Pharamond
The founder of this law and female bar.
Yet their own authors faithfully affirm
That the land Salic is in Germany,
Between the floods of Sala and of Elbe;
Where Charles the Great, having subdued the Saxons,
There left behind and settled certain French,
Who, holding in disdain the German women
For some dishonest manners of their life,
Established then this law: to wit, no female   50
Should be inheritrix in Salic land;
Which Salic, as I said, 'twixt Elbe and Sala,
Is at this day in Germany called Meisen.
Then doth it well appear the Salic law
Was not devisèd for the realm of France;
Nor did the French possess the Salic land

Until four hundred one-and-twenty years
After defunction of King Pharamond,
Idly supposed the founder of this law,
60   Who died within the year of our redemption
Four hundred twenty-six; and Charles the Great
Subdued the Saxons, and did seat the French
Beyond the river Sala, in the year
Eight hundred five. Besides, their writers say,
King Pepin, which deposèd Childeric,
Did, as heir general, being descended
Of Blithild, which was daughter to King Clothair,
Make claim and title to the crown of France.
Hugh Capet also – who usurped the crown
70   Of Charles the Duke of Lorraine, sole heir male
Of the true line and stock of Charles the Great –
To find his title with some shows of truth,
Though in pure truth it was corrupt and naught,
Conveyed himself as th'heir to th'Lady Lingare,
Daughter to Charlemain, who was the son
To Lewis the Emperor, and Lewis the son
Of Charles the Great. Also King Lewis the Tenth,
Who was sole heir to the usurper Capet,
Could not keep quiet in his conscience,
80   Wearing the crown of France, till satisfied
That fair Queen Isabel, his grandmother,
Was lineal of the Lady Ermengare,
Daughter to Charles the foresaid Duke of Lorraine;
By the which marriage the line of Charles the Great
Was re-united to the crown of France.
So that, as clear as is the summer's sun,
King Pepin's title, and Hugh Capet's claim,
King Lewis his satisfaction, all appear
To hold in right and title of the female;
90   So do the kings of France unto this day,

Howbeit they would hold up this Salic law
To bar your highness claiming from the female,
And rather choose to hide them in a net
Than amply to imbare their crookèd titles
Usurped from you and your progenitors.

KING HENRY

May I with right and conscience make this claim?

CANTERBURY

The sin upon my head, dread sovereign!
For in the Book of Numbers is it writ,
When the man dies, let the inheritance
Descend unto the daughter. Gracious lord,   100
Stand for your own, unwind your bloody flag,
Look back into your mighty ancestors.
Go, my dread lord, to your great-grandsire's tomb,
From whom you claim; invoke his warlike spirit,
And your great-uncle's, Edward the Black Prince,
Who on the French ground played a tragedy,
Making defeat on the full power of France,
Whiles his most mighty father on a hill
Stood smiling to behold his lion's whelp
Forage in blood of French nobility.   110
O noble English, that could entertain
With half their forces the full pride of France,
And let another half stand laughing by,
All out of work and cold for action!

ELY

Awake remembrance of these valiant dead,
And with your puissant arm renew their feats.
You are their heir, you sit upon their throne,
The blood and courage that renownèd them
Runs in your veins; and my thrice-puissant liege
Is in the very May-morn of his youth,   120
Ripe for exploits and mighty enterprises.

EXETER

    Your brother kings and monarchs of the earth
    Do all expect that you should rouse yourself,
    As did the former lions of your blood.

WESTMORLAND

    They know your grace hath cause and means and
        might –
    So hath your highness. Never King of England
    Had nobles richer and more loyal subjects,
    Whose hearts have left their bodies here in England
    And lie pavilioned in the fields of France.

CANTERBURY

130   O, let their bodies follow, my dear liege,
    With blood and sword and fire to win your right!
    In aid whereof we of the spiritualty
    Will raise your highness such a mighty sum
    As never did the clergy at one time
    Bring in to any of your ancestors.

KING HENRY

    We must not only arm t'invade the French
    But lay down our proportions to defend
    Against the Scot, who will make road upon us
    With all advantages.

CANTERBURY

140   They of those marches, gracious sovereign,
    Shall be a wall sufficient to defend
    Our inland from the pilfering borderers.

KING HENRY

    We do not mean the coursing snatchers only,
    But fear the main intendment of the Scot,
    Who hath been still a giddy neighbour to us;
    For you shall read that my great-grandfather
    Never went with his forces into France
    But that the Scot on his unfurnished kingdom

Came pouring, like the tide into a breach,
With ample and brim fullness of his force,   150
Galling the gleanèd land with hot assays,
Girding with grievous siege castles and towns;
That England, being empty of defence,
Hath shook and trembled at th'ill neighbourhood.

CANTERBURY
She hath been then more feared than harmed, my liege;
For hear her but exampled by herself:
When all her chivalry hath been in France,
And she a mourning widow of her nobles,
She hath herself not only well defended
But taken and impounded as a stray   160
The King of Scots, whom she did send to France
To fill King Edward's fame with prisoner kings,
And make her chronicle as rich with praise
As is the ooze and bottom of the sea
With sunken wrack and sumless treasuries.

ELY
But there's a saying very old and true:
    'If that you will France win,
    Then with Scotland first begin.'
For once the eagle England being in prey,
To her unguarded nest the weasel Scot   170
Comes sneaking, and so sucks her princely eggs,
Playing the mouse in absence of the cat,
To 'tame and havoc more than she can eat.

EXETER
It follows then the cat must stay at home;
Yet that is but a crushed necessity,
Since we have locks to safeguard necessaries,
And pretty traps to catch the petty thieves.
While that the armèd hand doth fight abroad,
Th'advisèd head defends itself at home;

180   For government, though high, and low, and lower,
        Put into parts, doth keep in one consent,
        Congreeing in a full and natural close,
        Like music.
    CANTERBURY True: therefore doth heaven divide
        The state of man in divers functions,
        Setting endeavour in continual motion;
        To which is fixèd as an aim or butt
        Obedience; for so work the honey-bees,
        Creatures that by a rule in nature teach
        The act of order to a peopled kingdom.
190   They have a king, and officers of sorts,
        Where some, like magistrates, correct at home;
        Others, like merchants, venture trade abroad;
        Others, like soldiers, armèd in their stings,
        Make boot upon the summer's velvet buds;
        Which pillage they with merry march bring home
        To the tent-royal of their emperor;
        Who, busied in his majesty, surveys
        The singing masons building roofs of gold,
        The civil citizens kneading up the honey,
200   The poor mechanic porters crowding in
        Their heavy burdens at his narrow gate,
        The sad-eyed justice, with his surly hum,
        Delivering o'er to executors pale
        The lazy yawning drone. I this infer,
        That many things, having full reference
        To one consent, may work contrariously,
        As many arrows loosèd several ways
        Come to one mark,
        As many several ways meet in one town,
210   As many fresh streams meet in one salt sea,
        As many lines close in the dial's centre;
        So may a thousand actions, once afoot,

End in one purpose, and be all well borne
Without defeat. Therefore to France, my liege!
Divide your happy England into four;
Whereof take you one quarter into France,
And you withal shall make all Gallia shake.
If we, with thrice such powers left at home,
Cannot defend our own doors from the dog,
Let us be worried, and our nation lose   220
The name of hardiness and policy.

KING HENRY

Call in the messengers sent from the Dauphin.

Exeunt some attendants

Now are we well resolved, and by God's help
And yours, the noble sinews of our power,
France being ours, we'll bend it to our awe,
Or break it all to pieces. Or there we'll sit,
Ruling in large and ample empery
O'er France and all her almost kingly dukedoms,
Or lay these bones in an unworthy urn,
Tombless, with no remembrance over them.   230
Either our history shall with full mouth
Speak freely of our acts, or else our grave,
Like Turkish mute, shall have a tongueless mouth,
Not worshipped with a waxen epitaph.

Enter Ambassadors of France

Now are we well prepared to know the pleasure
Of our fair cousin Dauphin; for we hear
Your greeting is from him, not from the King.

AMBASSADOR

May't please your majesty to give us leave
Freely to render what we have in charge,
Or shall we sparingly show you far off   240
The Dauphin's meaning and our embassy?

KING HENRY
    We are no tyrant, but a Christian king,
    Unto whose grace our passion is as subject
    As is our wretches fettered in our prisons:
    Therefore with frank and with uncurbèd plainness
    Tell us the Dauphin's mind.

AMBASSADOR   Thus then, in few:
    Your highness, lately sending into France,
    Did claim some certain dukedoms, in the right
    Of your great predecessor, King Edward the Third.
250   In answer of which claim, the Prince our master
    Says that you savour too much of your youth,
    And bids you be advised there's naught in France
    That can be with a nimble galliard won;
    You cannot revel into dukedoms there.
    He therefore sends you, meeter for your spirit,
    This tun of treasure; and, in lieu of this,
    Desires you let the dukedoms that you claim
    Hear no more of you. This the Dauphin speaks.

KING HENRY
    What treasure, uncle?

EXETER   Tennis-balls, my liege.

KING HENRY
260   We are glad the Dauphin is so pleasant with us.
    His present, and your pains, we thank you for.
    When we have matched our rackets to these balls,
    We will in France, by God's grace, play a set
    Shall strike his father's crown into the hazard.
    Tell him he hath made a match with such a wrangler
    That all the courts of France will be disturbed
    With chases. And we understand him well,
    How he comes o'er us with our wilder days,
    Not measuring what use we made of them.
270   We never valued this poor seat of England,

And therefore, living hence, did give ourself
To barbarous licence; as 'tis ever common
That men are merriest when they are from home.
But tell the Dauphin I will keep my state,
Be like a king, and show my sail of greatness,
When I do rouse me in my throne of France.
For that I have laid by my majesty,
And plodded like a man for working-days;
But I will rise there with so full a glory
That I will dazzle all the eyes of France,   280
Yea, strike the Dauphin blind to look on us.
And tell the pleasant Prince this mock of his
Hath turned his balls to gun-stones, and his soul
Shall stand sore chargèd for the wasteful vengeance
That shall fly with them: for many a thousand widows
Shall this his mock mock out of their dear husbands;
Mock mothers from their sons, mock castles down;
And some are yet ungotten and unborn
That shall have cause to curse the Dauphin's scorn.
But this lies all within the will of God,   290
To whom I do appeal, and in whose name,
Tell you the Dauphin, I am coming on,
To venge me as I may, and to put forth
My rightful hand in a well-hallowed cause.
So get you hence in peace; and tell the Dauphin
His jest will savour but of shallow wit
When thousands weep more than did laugh at it.
Convey them with safe conduct. Fare you well.
                              Exeunt Ambassadors

EXETER
    This was a merry message.
KING HENRY
    We hope to make the sender blush at it.   300
    Therefore, my lords, omit no happy hour

That may give furtherance to our expedition;
For we have now no thought in us but France,
Save those to God, that run before our business.
Therefore let our proportions for these wars
Be soon collected, and all things thought upon
That may with reasonable swiftness add
More feathers to our wings; for, God before,
We'll chide this Dauphin at his father's door.
310   Therefore let every man now task his thought
That this fair action may on foot be brought. *Exeunt*

*

II   *Flourish. Enter Chorus*
      CHORUS
            Now all the youth of England are on fire,
            And silken dalliance in the wardrobe lies.
            Now thrive the armourers, and honour's thought
            Reigns solely in the breast of every man.
            They sell the pasture now to buy the horse,
            Following the mirror of all Christian kings
            With wingèd heels, as English Mercuries.
            For now sits expectation in the air,
            And hides a sword from hilts unto the point
10   With crowns imperial, crowns and coronets,
            Promised to Harry and his followers.
            The French, advised by good intelligence
            Of this most dreadful preparation,
            Shake in their fear, and with pale policy
            Seek to divert the English purposes.
            O England! model to thy inward greatness,
            Like little body with a mighty heart,
            What mightst thou do, that honour would thee do,

Were all thy children kind and natural!
But see, thy fault France hath in thee found out,   20
A nest of hollow bosoms, which he fills
With treacherous crowns; and three corrupted men —
One, Richard Earl of Cambridge, and the second,
Henry Lord Scroop of Masham, and the third,
Sir Thomas Grey, knight, of Northumberland —
Have, for the gilt of France — O guilt indeed! —
Confirmed conspiracy with fearful France;
And by their hands this grace of kings must die,
If hell and treason hold their promises,
Ere he take ship for France, and in Southampton.   30
Linger your patience on, and we'll digest
Th'abuse of distance, force a play.
The sum is paid; the traitors are agreed;
The King is set from London; and the scene
Is now transported, gentles, to Southampton.
There is the playhouse now, there must you sit,
And thence to France shall we convey you safe
And bring you back, charming the narrow seas
To give you gentle pass; for, if we may,
We'll not offend one stomach with our play.   40
But till the King come forth, and not till then,
Unto Southampton do we shift our scene.   *Exit*

Enter Corporal Nym and Lieutenant Bardolph   II.I

BARDOLPH Well met, Corporal Nym.

NYM Good morrow, Lieutenant Bardolph.

BARDOLPH What, are Ancient Pistol and you friends yet?

NYM For my part, I care not. I say little; but when time
    shall serve, there shall be smiles — but that shall be as it
    may. I dare not fight, but I will wink and hold out mine
    iron. It is a simple one, but what though? It will toast

cheese, and it will endure cold as another man's sword
will – and there's an end.

10 BARDOLPH I will bestow a breakfast to make you friends,
and we'll be all three sworn brothers to France. Let't
be so, good Corporal Nym.

NYM Faith, I will live so long as I may, that's the certain
of it; and when I cannot live any longer, I will do as I
may. That is my rest, that is the rendezvous of it.

BARDOLPH It is certain, Corporal, that he is married to
Nell Quickly, and certainly she did you wrong, for you
were troth-plight to her.

NYM I cannot tell; things must be as they may. Men may
20 sleep, and they may have their throats about them at
that time, and some say knives have edges: it must be as
it may – though patience be a tired mare, yet she will
plod – there must be conclusions – well, I cannot tell.

Enter Pistol and Hostess Quickly

BARDOLPH Here comes Ancient Pistol and his wife. Good
Corporal, be patient here.

NYM How now, mine host Pistol?

PISTOL
Base tike, call'st thou me host?
Now by this hand I swear I scorn the term;
Nor shall my Nell keep lodgers.

30 HOSTESS No, by my troth, not long; for we cannot lodge
and board a dozen or fourteen gentlewomen that live
honestly by the prick of their needles but it will be
thought we keep a bawdy-house straight.

Nym draws his sword

O well-a-day, Lady, if he be not drawn now! We shall
see wilful adultery and murder committed.

BARDOLPH Good Lieutenant! Good Corporal! Offer
nothing here.

NYM Pish!

PISTOL

Pish for thee, Iceland dog! thou prick-eared cur of
Iceland!

HOSTESS Good Corporal Nym, show thy valour, and put   40
up your sword.

NYM Will you shog off? I would have you *solus*.

He sheathes his sword

PISTOL

'*Solus*', egregious dog? O viper vile!
The '*solus*' in thy most mervailous face!
The '*solus*' in thy teeth and in thy throat,
And in thy hateful lungs, yea, in thy maw, perdy!
And, which is worse, within thy nasty mouth!
I do retort the '*solus*' in thy bowels,
For I can take, and Pistol's cock is up,
And flashing fire will follow.   50

NYM I am not Barbason; you cannot conjure me. I have
an humour to knock you indifferently well. If you grow
foul with me, Pistol, I will scour you with my rapier,
as I may, in fair terms. If you would walk off, I would
prick your guts a little, in good terms, as I may, and
that's the humour of it.

PISTOL

O braggart vile, and damnèd furious wight!
The grave doth gape, and doting death is near:
Therefore exhale!

They both draw

BARDOLPH Hear me, hear me what I say! He that strikes   60
the first stroke, I'll run him up to the hilts, as I am a
soldier.

He draws

PISTOL

An oath of mickle might, and fury shall abate.

Pistol and Nym sheathe their swords

Give me thy fist, thy forefoot to me give;
Thy spirits are most tall.

NYM I will cut thy throat one time or other, in fair terms,
that is the humour of it.

PISTOL
    '*Couple a gorge!*'
    That is the word. I thee defy again!
70 O hound of Crete, think'st thou my spouse to get?
    No, to the spital go,
    And from the powdering tub of infamy
    Fetch forth the lazar kite of Cressid's kind,
    Doll Tearsheet she by name, and her espouse.
    I have, and I will hold, the quondam Quickly
    For the only she; and – *pauca*, there's enough.
    Go to!

    Enter the Boy

BOY Mine host Pistol, you must come to my master – and
you, Hostess: he is very sick, and would to bed. Good
80 Bardolph, put thy face between his sheets, and do the
office of a warming-pan. Faith, he's very ill.

BARDOLPH Away, you rogue!

HOSTESS By my troth, he'll yield the crow a pudding one
of these days; the King has killed his heart. Good
husband, come home presently.   *Exit with Boy*

BARDOLPH Come, shall I make you two friends? We must
to France together: why the devil should we keep knives
to cut one another's throats?

PISTOL
    Let floods o'erswell, and fiends for food howl on!

90 NYM You'll pay me the eight shillings I won of you at
betting?

PISTOL
    Base is the slave that pays!

NYM That now I will have; that's the humour of it.

PISTOL

As manhood shall compound. Push home!

They draw

BARDOLPH By this sword, he that makes the first thrust,
I'll kill him! By this sword, I will.

PISTOL

Sword is an oath, and oaths must have their course.

He sheathes his sword

BARDOLPH Corporal Nym, an thou wilt be friends, be
friends: an thou wilt not, why then be enemies with me
too. Prithee put up.   100

NYM I shall have my eight shillings I won of you at betting?

PISTOL

A noble shalt thou have, and present pay;
And liquor likewise will I give to thee,
And friendship shall combine, and brotherhood.
I'll live by Nym, and Nym shall live by me.
Is not this just? For I shall sutler be
Unto the camp, and profits will accrue.
Give me thy hand.

Nym sheathes his sword

NYM I shall have my noble?

PISTOL

In cash most justly paid.   110

NYM Well then, that's the humour of 't.

Enter Hostess

HOSTESS As ever you came of women, come in quickly
to Sir John. Ah, poor heart! he is so shaked of a burning
quotidian tertian that it is most lamentable to behold.
Sweet men, come to him.

NYM The King hath run bad humours on the knight, that's
the even of it.

PISTOL

Nym, thou hast spoke the right;

His heart is fracted and corroborate.

120   NYM The King is a good king, but it must be as it may: he
      passes some humours and careers.

PISTOL
      Let us condole the knight; for, lambkins, we will live.

                                                        Exeunt

II.2   *Enter Exeter, Bedford, and Westmorland*

BEDFORD
      Fore God, his grace is bold to trust these traitors.

EXETER
      They shall be apprehended by and by.

WESTMORLAND
      How smooth and even they do bear themselves!
      As if allegiance in their bosoms sat,
      Crownèd with faith and constant loyalty.

BEDFORD
      The King hath note of all that they intend,
      By interception which they dream not of.

EXETER
      Nay, but the man that was his bedfellow,
      Whom he hath dulled and cloyed with gracious
            favours –

10   That he should, for a foreign purse, so sell
      His sovereign's life to death and treachery!
            *Sound trumpets. Enter the King, Scroop, Cambridge,
            Grey, and attendants*

KING HENRY
      Now sits the wind fair, and we will aboard.
      My Lord of Cambridge, and my kind Lord of Masham,
      And you, my gentle knight, give me your thoughts.
      Think you not that the powers we bear with us
      Will cut their passage through the force of France,

Doing the execution and the act
For which we have in head assembled them?

SCROOP

No doubt, my liege, if each man do his best.

KING HENRY

I doubt not that, since we are well persuaded   20
We carry not a heart with us from hence
That grows not in a fair consent with ours,
Nor leave not one behind that doth not wish
Success and conquest to attend on us.

CAMBRIDGE

Never was monarch better feared and loved
Than is your majesty. There's not, I think, a subject
That sits in heart-grief and uneasiness
Under the sweet shade of your government.

GREY

True: those that were your father's enemies
Have steeped their galls in honey, and do serve you   30
With hearts create of duty and of zeal.

KING HENRY

We therefore have great cause of thankfulness,
And shall forget the office of our hand
Sooner than quittance of desert and merit
According to the weight and worthiness.

SCROOP

So service shall with steelèd sinews toil,
And labour shall refresh itself with hope
To do your grace incessant services.

KING HENRY

We judge no less. Uncle of Exeter,
Enlarge the man committed yesterday   40
That railed against our person. We consider
It was excess of wine that set him on,
And on his more advice we pardon him.

SCROOP

    That's mercy, but too much security.

    Let him be punished, sovereign, lest example

    Breed, by his sufferance, more of such a kind.

KING HENRY

    O, let us yet be merciful.

CAMBRIDGE

    So may your highness, and yet punish too.

GREY

    Sir,

50   You show great mercy if you give him life

    After the taste of much correction.

KING HENRY

    Alas, your too much love and care of me

    Are heavy orisons 'gainst this poor wretch!

    If little faults, proceeding on distemper,

    Shall not be winked at, how shall we stretch our eye

    When capital crimes, chewed, swallowed, and digested,

    Appear before us? We'll yet enlarge that man,

    Though Cambridge, Scroop, and Grey, in their dear
        care

    And tender preservation of our person

60   Would have him punished. And now to our French
        causes:

    Who are the late commissioners?

CAMBRIDGE

    I one, my lord.

    Your highness bade me ask for it today.

SCROOP

    So did you me, my liege.

GREY

    And I, my royal sovereign.

KING HENRY

    Then, Richard Earl of Cambridge, there is yours;

There yours, Lord Scroop of Masham; and, sir knight,
Grey of Northumberland, this same is yours.
Read them, and know I know your worthiness.
My Lord of Westmorland, and uncle Exeter,   70
We will aboard tonight. – Why, how now, gentlemen?
What see you in those papers, that you lose
So much complexion? Look ye, how they change!
Their cheeks are paper. – Why, what read you there
That have so cowarded and chased your blood
Out of appearance?

CAMBRIDGE   I do confess my fault,
And do submit me to your highness' mercy.

GREY, SCROOP
To which we all appeal.

KING HENRY
The mercy that was quick in us but late
By your own counsel is suppressed and killed.   80
You must not dare, for shame, to talk of mercy,
For your own reasons turn into your bosoms
As dogs upon their masters, worrying you.
See you, my Princes, and my noble peers,
These English monsters! My Lord of Cambridge here –
You know how apt our love was to accord
To furnish him with all appertinents
Belonging to his honour; and this man
Hath, for a few light crowns, lightly conspired,
And sworn unto the practices of France,   90
To kill us here in Hampton: to the which
This knight, no less for bounty bound to us
Than Cambridge is, hath likewise sworn. But O,
What shall I say to thee, Lord Scroop, thou cruel,
Ingrateful, savage, and inhuman creature?
Thou that didst bear the key of all my counsels,
That knew'st the very bottom of my soul,

That almost mightst have coined me into gold,
Wouldst thou have practised on me, for thy use?
May it be possible that foreign hire
Could out of thee extract one spark of evil
That might annoy my finger? 'Tis so strange
That, though the truth of it stands off as gross
As black and white, my eye will scarcely see it.
Treason and murder ever kept together,
As two yoke-devils sworn to either's purpose,
Working so grossly in a natural cause
That admiration did not whoop at them.
But thou, 'gainst all proportion, didst bring in
Wonder to wait on treason and on murder:
And whatsoever cunning fiend it was
That wrought upon thee so preposterously
Hath got the voice in hell for excellence.
All other devils that suggest by treasons
Do botch and bungle up damnation
With patches, colours, and with forms, being fetched
From glistering semblances of piety;
But he that tempered thee bade thee stand up,
Gave thee no instance why thou shouldst do treason,
Unless to dub thee with the name of traitor.
If that same demon that hath gulled thee thus
Should with his lion gait walk the whole world,
He might return to vasty Tartar back,
And tell the legions, 'I can never win
A soul so easy as that Englishman's.'
O, how hast thou with jealousy infected
The sweetness of affiance! Show men dutiful?
Why, so didst thou. Seem they grave and learnèd?
Why, so didst thou. Come they of noble family?
Why, so didst thou. Seem they religious?
Why, so didst thou. Or are they spare in diet,

Free from gross passion or of mirth or anger,
Constant in spirit, not swerving with the blood,
Garnished and decked in modest complement,
Not working with the eye without the ear,
And but in purgèd judgement trusting neither?
Such and so finely bolted didst thou seem:
And thus thy fall hath left a kind of blot
To mark the full-fraught man and best endued
With some suspicion. I will weep for thee;   140
For this revolt of thine, methinks, is like
Another fall of man. Their faults are open.
Arrest them to the answer of the law;
And God acquit them of their practices!

EXETER I arrest thee of high treason, by the name of
Richard Earl of Cambridge.
I arrest thee of high treason, by the name of Henry
Lord Scroop of Masham.
I arrest thee of high treason, by the name of Thomas
Grey, knight, of Northumberland.   150

SCROOP
Our purposes God justly hath discovered,
And I repent my fault more than my death,
Which I beseech your highness to forgive,
Although my body pay the price of it.

CAMBRIDGE
For me, the gold of France did not seduce,
Although I did admit it as a motive
The sooner to effect what I intended.
But God be thankèd for prevention,
Which I in sufferance heartily will rejoice,
Beseeching God and you to pardon me.   160

GREY
Never did faithful subject more rejoice
At the discovery of most dangerous treason

Than I do at this hour joy o'er myself,
Prevented from a damnèd enterprise.
My fault, but not my body, pardon, sovereign.

KING HENRY

God quit you in His mercy! Hear your sentence.
You have conspired against our royal person,
Joined with an enemy proclaimed, and from his coffers
Received the golden earnest of our death;
170 Wherein you would have sold your King to slaughter,
His princes and his peers to servitude,
His subjects to oppression and contempt,
And his whole kingdom into desolation.
Touching our person seek we no revenge,
But we our kingdom's safety must so tender,
Whose ruin you have sought, that to her laws
We do deliver you. Get you therefore hence,
Poor miserable wretches, to your death;
The taste whereof God of His mercy give
180 You patience to endure, and true repentance
Of all your dear offences. Bear them hence.

          Exeunt Cambridge, Scroop, and Grey, guarded
Now, lords, for France; the enterprise whereof
Shall be to you, as us, like glorious.
We doubt not of a fair and lucky war,
Since God so graciously hath brought to light
This dangerous treason lurking in our way
To hinder our beginnings. We doubt not now
But every rub is smoothèd on our way.
Then forth, dear countrymen! Let us deliver
190 Our puissance into the hand of God,
Putting it straight in expedition.
Cheerly to sea! The signs of war advance!
No King of England if not King of France!

                                        Flourish. Exeunt

Enter Pistol, Hostess, Nym, Bardolph, and Boy   II.3

HOSTESS Prithee, honey-sweet husband, let me bring thee
to Staines.

PISTOL

No, for my manly heart doth earn.
Bardolph, be blithe! Nym, rouse thy vaunting veins!
Boy, bristle thy courage up! For Falstaff, he is dead,
And we must earn therefor.

BARDOLPH Would I were with him, wheresome'er he is,
either in heaven or in hell!

HOSTESS Nay, sure, he's not in hell: he's in Arthur's
bosom, if ever man went to Arthur's bosom. 'A made   10
a finer end, and went away an it had been any christom
child; 'a parted e'en just between twelve and one, e'en
at the turning o'th'tide; for after I saw him fumble with
the sheets, and play with flowers, and smile upon his
fingers' ends, I knew there was but one way; for his
nose was as sharp as a pen, and 'a babbled of green
fields. 'How now, Sir John?' quoth I, 'What, man, be
o'good cheer!' So 'a cried out, 'God, God, God!' three
or four times. Now I, to comfort him, bid him 'a should
not think of God – I hoped there was no need to   20
trouble himself with any such thoughts yet. So 'a bade
me lay more clothes on his feet; I put my hand into the
bed, and felt them, and they were as cold as any stone;
then I felt to his knees, and so up'ard and up'ard, and
all was as cold as any stone.

NYM They say he cried out of sack.

HOSTESS Ay, that 'a did.

BARDOLPH And of women.

HOSTESS Nay, that 'a did not.

BOY Yes, that 'a did, and said they were devils incarnate.   30

HOSTESS 'A could never abide carnation, 'twas a colour
he never liked.

BOY 'A said once, the devil would have him about women.

HOSTESS 'A did in some sort, indeed, handle women; but
then he was rheumatic, and talked of the Whore of
Babylon.

BOY Do you not remember, 'a saw a flea stick upon Bardolph's nose, and 'a said it was a black soul burning in
hell?

40 BARDOLPH Well, the fuel is gone that maintained that
fire – that's all the riches I got in his service.

NYM Shall we shog? The King will be gone from Southampton.

PISTOL

Come, let's away. My love, give me thy lips.
Look to my chattels and my movables.
Let senses rule. The word is 'Pitch and pay!'
Trust none;
For oaths are straws, men's faiths are wafer-cakes,
And Holdfast is the only dog, my duck.
50 Therefore, *Caveto* be thy counsellor.
Go, clear thy crystals. Yoke-fellows in arms,
Let us to France, like horse-leeches, my boys,
To suck, to suck, the very blood to suck!

BOY And that's but unwholesome food, they say.

PISTOL

Touch her soft mouth, and march.

BARDOLPH Farewell, Hostess.

He kisses her

NYM I cannot kiss, that is the humour of it; but adieu.

PISTOL

Let housewifery appear. Keep close, I thee command.

HOSTESS Farewell! Adieu!   *Exeunt*

Flourish. Enter the French King, the Dauphin, the   II.4
Dukes of Berri and Britaine, the Constable and others

FRENCH KING
Thus comes the English with full power upon us,
And more than carefully it us concerns
To answer royally in our defences.
Therefore the Dukes of Berri and of Britaine,
Of Brabant and of Orleans, shall make forth,
And you, Prince Dauphin, with all swift dispatch,
To line and new repair our towns of war
With men of courage and with means defendant;
For England his approaches makes as fierce
As waters to the sucking of a gulf.   10
It fits us then to be as provident
As fear may teach us, out of late examples
Left by the fatal and neglected English
Upon our fields.

DAUPHIN   My most redoubted father,
It is most meet we arm us 'gainst the foe;
For peace itself should not so dull a kingdom,
Though war nor no known quarrel were in question,
But that defences, musters, preparations,
Should be maintained, assembled, and collected,
As were a war in expectation.   20
Therefore, I say, 'tis meet we all go forth
To view the sick and feeble parts of France:
And let us do it with no show of fear –
No, with no more than if we heard that England
Were busied with a Whitsun morris-dance;
For, my good liege, she is so idly kinged,
Her sceptre so fantastically borne
By a vain, giddy, shallow, humorous youth,
That fear attends her not.

CONSTABLE   O, peace, Prince Dauphin!

30   You are too much mistaken in this King.
        Question your grace the late ambassadors,
        With what great state he heard their embassy,
        How well supplied with noble counsellors,
        How modest in exception, and withal
        How terrible in constant resolution,
        And you shall find his vanities forespent
        Were but the outside of the Roman Brutus,
        Covering discretion with a coat of folly;
        As gardeners do with ordure hide those roots
40   That shall first spring and be most delicate.

DAUPHIN
        Well, 'tis not so, my Lord High Constable;
        But though we think it so, it is no matter.
        In cases of defence, 'tis best to weigh
        The enemy more mighty than he seems.
        So the proportions of defence are filled;
        Which of a weak and niggardly projection
        Doth like a miser spoil his coat with scanting
        A little cloth.

FRENCH KING Think we King Harry strong;
        And, Princes, look you strongly arm to meet him.
50   The kindred of him hath been fleshed upon us,
        And he is bred out of that bloody strain
        That haunted us in our familiar paths.
        Witness our too much memorable shame
        When Crécy battle fatally was struck,
        And all our princes captived by the hand
        Of that black name, Edward, Black Prince of Wales;
        Whiles that his mountain sire, on mountain standing,
        Up in the air, crowned with the golden sun,
        Saw his heroical seed, and smiled to see him,
60   Mangle the work of nature, and deface
        The patterns that by God and by French fathers

Had twenty years been made. This is a stem
Of that victorious stock; and let us fear
The native mightiness and fate of him.
    Enter a Messenger

MESSENGER

Ambassadors from Harry King of England
Do crave admittance to your majesty.

FRENCH KING

We'll give them present audience. Go and bring them.
                    Exeunt Messenger and certain lords
You see this chase is hotly followed, friends.

DAUPHIN

Turn head, and stop pursuit, for coward dogs
Most spend their mouths when what they seem to
    threaten   70
Runs far before them. Good my sovereign,
Take up the English short, and let them know
Of what a monarchy you are the head.
Self-love, my liege, is not so vile a sin
As self-neglecting.
    Enter lords, with Exeter and train

FRENCH KING   From our brother of England?

EXETER

From him; and thus he greets your majesty:
He wills you, in the name of God Almighty,
That you divest yourself, and lay apart
The borrowed glories that by gift of heaven,
By law of nature and of nations, 'longs   80
To him and to his heirs – namely, the crown,
And all wide-stretchèd honours that pertain
By custom and the ordinance of times
Unto the crown of France. That you may know
'Tis no sinister nor no awkward claim
Picked from the worm-holes of long-vanished days,

Nor from the dust of old oblivion raked,
He sends you this most memorable line,
In every branch truly demonstrative,
90   Willing you overlook this pedigree;
And when you find him evenly derived
From his most famed of famous ancestors,
Edward the Third, he bids you then resign
Your crown and kingdom, indirectly held
From him, the native and true challenger.

FRENCH KING
Or else what follows?

EXETER
Bloody constraint; for if you hide the crown
Even in your hearts, there will he rake for it.
Therefore in fierce tempest is he coming,
100   In thunder and in earthquake, like a Jove,
That, if requiring fail, he will compel;
And bids you, in the bowels of the Lord,
Deliver up the crown, and to take mercy
On the poor souls for whom this hungry war
Opens his vasty jaws; and on your head
Turning the widows' tears, the orphans' cries,
The dead men's blood, the privèd maidens' groans,
For husbands, fathers, and betrothèd lovers
That shall be swallowed in this controversy.
110   This is his claim, his threatening, and my message –
Unless the Dauphin be in presence here,
To whom expressly I bring greeting too.

FRENCH KING
For us, we will consider of this further.
Tomorrow shall you bear our full intent
Back to our brother of England.

DAUPHIN   For the Dauphin,
I stand here for him. What to him from England?

EXETER

 Scorn and defiance, slight regard, contempt,
 And anything that may not misbecome
 The mighty sender, doth he prize you at.
 Thus says my King: an if your father's highness 120
 Do not, in grant of all demands at large,
 Sweeten the bitter mock you sent his majesty,
 He'll call you to so hot an answer of it
 That caves and womby vaultages of France
 Shall chide your trespass, and return your mock
 In second accent of his ordinance.

DAUPHIN

 Say, if my father render fair return,
 It is against my will, for I desire
 Nothing but odds with England. To that end,
 As matching to his youth and vanity, 130
 I did present him with the Paris balls.

EXETER

 He'll make your Paris Louvre shake for it,
 Were it the mistress court of mighty Europe:
 And, be assured, you'll find a difference,
 As we his subjects have in wonder found,
 Between the promise of his greener days
 And these he masters now. Now he weighs time
 Even to the utmost grain; that you shall read
 In your own losses, if he stay in France.

FRENCH KING

 Tomorrow shall you know our mind at full. 140
  Flourish

EXETER

 Dispatch us with all speed, lest that our King
 Come here himself to question our delay,
 For he is footed in this land already.

FRENCH KING
>You shall be soon dispatched with fair conditions.
>A night is but small breath and little pause
>To answer matters of this consequence.   *Exeunt*

*

III   *Flourish. Enter Chorus*

CHORUS
>Thus with imagined wing our swift scene flies
>In motion of no less celerity
>Than that of thought. Suppose that you have seen
>The well-appointed King at Hampton pier
>Embark his royalty, and his brave fleet
>With silken streamers the young Phoebus fanning.
>Play with your fancies, and in them behold
>Upon the hempen tackle ship-boys climbing;
>Hear the shrill whistle which doth order give
>To sounds confused; behold the threaden sails,
>Borne with th'invisible and creeping wind,
>Draw the huge bottoms through the furrowed sea,
>Breasting the lofty surge. O, do but think
>You stand upon the rivage and behold
>A city on th'inconstant billows dancing;
>For so appears this fleet majestical,
>Holding due course to Harfleur. Follow, follow!
>Grapple your minds to sternage of this navy,
>And leave your England, as dead midnight still,
>Guarded with grandsires, babies, and old women,
>Either past or not arrived to pith and puissance.
>For who is he whose chin is but enriched
>With one appearing hair that will not follow
>These culled and choice-drawn cavaliers to France?

10

20

Work, work your thoughts, and therein see a siege:
Behold the ordnance on their carriages,
With fatal mouths gaping on girded Harfleur.
Suppose th'ambassador from the French comes back;
Tells Harry that the King doth offer him
Katherine his daughter, and with her, to dowry,   30
Some petty and unprofitable dukedoms.
The offer likes not; and the nimble gunner
With linstock now the devilish cannon touches,
   Alarum, and chambers go off
And down goes all before them. Still be kind,
And eke out our performance with your mind.   *Exit*

   Alarum. Enter the King, Exeter, Bedford, Gloucester,   III.I
   other lords, and soldiers with scaling-ladders

KING HENRY
Once more unto the breach, dear friends, once more,
Or close the wall up with our English dead!
In peace there's nothing so becomes a man
As modest stillness and humility:
But when the blast of war blows in our ears,
Then imitate the action of the tiger;
Stiffen the sinews, conjure up the blood,
Disguise fair nature with hard-favoured rage;
Then lend the eye a terrible aspect;
Let it pry through the portage of the head   10
Like the brass cannon; let the brow o'erwhelm it
As fearfully as doth a gallèd rock
O'erhang and jutty his confounded base,
Swilled with the wild and wasteful ocean.
Now set the teeth, and stretch the nostril wide,
Hold hard the breath, and bend up every spirit
To his full height! On, on, you noblest English,

Whose blood is fet from fathers of war-proof! –
Fathers that, like so many Alexanders,
20   Have in these parts from morn till even fought,
And sheathed their swords for lack of argument.
Dishonour not your mothers; now attest
That those whom you called fathers did beget you!
Be copy now to men of grosser blood,
And teach them how to war. And you, good yeomen,
Whose limbs were made in England, show us here
The mettle of your pasture; let us swear
That you are worth your breeding – which I doubt not;
For there is none of you so mean and base
30   That hath not noble lustre in your eyes.
I see you stand like greyhounds in the slips,
Straining upon the start. The game's afoot!
Follow your spirit, and upon this charge
Cry, 'God for Harry, England, and Saint George!'

Exeunt. Alarum, and chambers go off

III.2   *Enter Nym, Bardolph, Pistol, and Boy*

BARDOLPH On, on, on, on, on! To the breach, to the
breach!

NYM Pray thee, Corporal, stay – the knocks are too hot,
and, for mine own part, I have not a case of lives. The
humour of it is too hot, that is the very plainsong of it.

PISTOL
The plainsong is most just; for humours do abound.
Knocks go and come; God's vassals drop and die;
                    And sword and shield,
                    In bloody field,
10   Doth win immortal fame.

BOY Would I were in an alehouse in London! I would
give all my fame for a pot of ale, and safety.

PISTOL And I:

>   If wishes would prevail with me,
>   My purpose should not fail with me,
>   But thither would I hie.

BOY   As duly,
>   But not as truly,
>   As bird doth sing on bough.

Enter Fluellen

FLUELLEN Up to the breach, you dogs! Avaunt, you   20
cullions!

He drives them forward

PISTOL

Be merciful, great Duke, to men of mould!
Abate thy rage, abate thy manly rage,
Abate thy rage, great Duke!
Good bawcock, bate thy rage! Use lenity, sweet chuck!

NYM These be good humours! Your honour wins bad
humours.   *Exeunt all but the Boy*

BOY As young as I am, I have observed these three
swashers. I am boy to them all three, but all they three,
though they would serve me, could not be man to me;   30
for indeed three such antics do not amount to a man.
For Bardolph, he is white-livered and red-faced; by
the means whereof 'a faces it out, but fights not. For
Pistol, he hath a killing tongue, and a quiet sword; by
the means whereof 'a breaks words, and keeps whole
weapons. For Nym, he hath heard that men of few
words are the best men; and therefore he scorns to say
his prayers, lest 'a should be thought a coward; but his
few bad words are matched with as few good deeds, for
'a never broke any man's head but his own, and that   40
was against a post, when he was drunk. They will steal
anything, and call it purchase. Bardolph stole a lute-
case, bore it twelve leagues, and sold it for three half-

pence. Nym and Bardolph are sworn brothers in filching,
and in Calais they stole a fire-shovel – I knew by that
piece of service the men would carry coals. They would
have me as familiar with men's pockets as their gloves
or their handkerchers: which makes much against my
manhood, if I should take from another's pocket to
put into mine; for it is plain pocketing up of wrongs. I
must leave them, and seek some better service. Their
villainy goes against my weak stomach, and therefore
I must cast it up.   *Exit*

Enter Fluellen, Gower following

GOWER Captain Fluellen, you must come presently to the
mines. The Duke of Gloucester would speak with you.

FLUELLEN To the mines? Tell you the Duke, it is not so
good to come to the mines, for, look you, the mines is
not according to the disciplines of the war. The concavities of it is not sufficient; for, look you, th'athversary,
you may discuss unto the Duke, look you, is digt himself four yard under the countermines. By Cheshu, I
think 'a will plow up all, if there is not better directions.

GOWER The Duke of Gloucester, to whom the order of the
siege is given, is altogether directed by an Irishman, a
very valiant gentleman, i'faith.

FLUELLEN It is Captain Macmorris, is it not?

GOWER I think it be.

FLUELLEN By Cheshu, he is an ass, as in the world; I
will verify as much in his beard. He has no more
directions in the true disciplines of the wars, look you,
of the Roman disciplines, than is a puppy-dog.

Enter Captain Macmorris and Captain Jamy

GOWER Here 'a comes, and the Scots captain, Captain
Jamy, with him.

FLUELLEN Captain Jamy is a marvellous falorous gentleman, that is certain, and of great expedition and

knowledge in th'aunchient wars, upon my particular
knowledge of his directions. By Cheshu, he will maintain
his argument as well as any military man in the world, in
the disciplines of the pristine wars of the Romans.

JAMY I say gud-day, Captain Fluellen.   80

FLUELLEN Good-e'en to your worship, good Captain
James.

GOWER How now, Captain Macmorris, have you quit the
mines? Have the pioneers given o'er?

MACMORRIS By Chrish, la, 'tish ill done! The work ish
give over, the trompet sound the retreat. By my hand
I swear, and my father's soul, the work ish ill done: it
ish give over. I would have blowed up the town, so
Chrish save me, la, in an hour. O, 'tish ill done, 'tish ill
done – by my hand, 'tish ill done!   90

FLUELLEN Captain Macmorris, I beseech you now, will
you voutsafe me, look you, a few disputations with you,
as partly touching or concerning the disciplines of the
war, the Roman wars, in the way of argument, look you,
and friendly communication? – partly to satisfy my
opinion, and partly for the satisfaction, look you, of my
mind – as touching the direction of the military discipline, that is the point.

JAMY It sall be vary gud, gud feith, gud captens bath, and
I sall quit you with gud leve, as I may pick occasion: that 100
sall I, marry.

MACMORRIS It is no time to discourse, so Chrish save me!
The day is hot, and the weather, and the wars, and the
King, and the Dukes – it is no time to discourse, the
town is beseeched, and the trumpet call us to the breach,
and we talk, and, be Chrish, do nothing; 'tis shame for us
all: so God sa' me, 'tis shame to stand still, it is shame, by
my hand – and there is throats to be cut, and works to be
done, and there ish nothing done, so Chrish sa' me, la!

110 JAMY By the mess, ere theise eyes of mine take themselves to slomber, ay'll de gud service, or ay'll lig
i'th'grund for it, ay, or go to death! And ay'll pay't as
valorously as I may, that sall I surely do, that is the
breff and the long. Marry, I wad full fain hear some
question 'tween you tway.

FLUELLEN Captain Macmorris, I think, look you, under
your correction, there is not many of your nation –

MACMORRIS Of my nation? What ish my nation? Ish a
villain, and a bastard, and a knave, and a rascal. What
120 ish my nation? Who talks of my nation?

FLUELLEN Look you, if you take the matter otherwise
than is meant, Captain Macmorris, peradventure I shall
think you do not use me with that affability as in dis-
cretion you ought to use me, look you, being as good a
man as yourself, both in the disciplines of war, and in
the derivation of my birth, and in other particularities.

MACMORRIS I do not know you so good a man as myself.
So Chrish save me, I will cut off your head.

GOWER Gentlemen both, you will mistake each other.

130 JAMY Ah, that's a foul fault!

A parley is sounded

GOWER The town sounds a parley.

FLUELLEN Captain Macmorris, when there is more
better opportunity to be required, look you, I will be
so bold as to tell you, I know the disciplines of war; and
there is an end.   *Exeunt*

III.3   *Some citizens of Harfleur appear on the walls. Enter*
             the King and all his train before the gates

KING HENRY
        How yet resolves the Governor of the town?
        This is the latest parle we will admit:

Therefore to our best mercy give yourselves,
Or, like to men proud of destruction,
Defy us to our worst; for, as I am a soldier,
A name that in my thoughts becomes me best,
If I begin the battery once again,
I will not leave the half-achievèd Harfleur
Till in her ashes she lie burièd.
The gates of mercy shall be all shut up,   10
And the fleshed soldier, rough and hard of heart,
In liberty of bloody hand shall range
With conscience wide as hell, mowing like grass
Your fresh fair virgins, and your flowering infants.
What is it then to me, if impious war,
Arrayed in flames, like to the prince of fiends,
Do, with his smirched complexion, all fell feats
Enlinked to waste and desolation?
What is't to me, when you yourselves are cause,
If your pure maidens fall into the hand   20
Of hot and forcing violation?
What rein can hold licentious wickedness
When down the hill he holds his fierce career?
We may as bootless spend our vain command
Upon th'enragèd soldiers in their spoil
As send precepts to the leviathan
To come ashore. Therefore, you men of Harfleur,
Take pity of your town and of your people
Whiles yet my soldiers are in my command,
Whiles yet the cool and temperate wind of grace   30
O'erblows the filthy and contagious clouds
Of heady murder, spoil, and villainy.
If not, why, in a moment look to see
The blind and bloody soldier with foul hand
Defile the locks of your shrill-shrieking daughters;
Your fathers taken by the silver beards,

And their most reverend heads dashed to the walls;
Your naked infants spitted upon pikes,
Whiles the mad mothers with their howls confused
40   Do break the clouds, as did the wives of Jewry
At Herod's bloody-hunting slaughtermen.
What say you? Will you yield, and this avoid?
Or, guilty in defence, be thus destroyed?

    Enter the Governor on the wall

GOVERNOR
Our expectation hath this day an end.
The Dauphin, whom of succours we entreated,
Returns us that his powers are yet not ready
To raise so great a siege. Therefore, great King,
We yield our town and lives to thy soft mercy.
Enter our gates, dispose of us and ours,
50   For we no longer are defensible.

KING HENRY
Open your gates.   *Exit Governor*
               Come, uncle Exeter,
Go you and enter Harfleur; there remain,
And fortify it strongly 'gainst the French.
Use mercy to them all. For us, dear uncle,
The winter coming on, and sickness growing
Upon our soldiers, we will retire to Calais.
Tonight in Harfleur will we be your guest;
Tomorrow for the march are we addressed.

    Flourish, and enter the town

III.4   *Enter Katherine and Alice, an old gentlewoman*
KATHERINE Alice, tu as été en Angleterre, et tu parles
bien le langage.
ALICE Un peu, madame.

KATHERINE Je te prie, m'enseignez–il faut que j'apprenne
  à parler. Comment appelez-vous la main en anglais?

ALICE La main? Elle est appelée de hand.

KATHERINE De hand. Et les doigts?

ALICE Les doigts? Ma foi, j'oublie les doigts, mais je me
  souviendrai. Les doigts? Je pense qu'ils sont appelés
  de fingres; oui, de fingres.   10

KATHERINE La main, de hand; les doigts, de fingres. Je
  pense que je suis le bon écolier; j'ai gagné deux mots
  d'anglais vitement. Comment appelez-vous les ongles?

ALICE Les ongles? Nous les appelons de nailès.

KATHERINE De nailès. Écoutez: dites-moi si je parle
  bien – de hand, de fingres, et de nailès.

ALICE C'est bien dit, madame. Il est fort bon anglais.

KATHERINE Dites-moi l'anglais pour le bras.

ALICE De arm, madame.

KATHERINE Et le coude?   20

ALICE D'elbow.

KATHERINE D'elbow. Je m'en fais la répétition de tous
  les mots que vous m'avez appris dès à présent.

ALICE Il est trop difficile, madame, comme je pense.

KATHERINE Excusez-moi, Alice; écoutez – d'hand, de
  fingre, de nailès, d'arma, de bilbow.

ALICE D'elbow, madame.

KATHERINE O Seigneur Dieu, je m'en oublie! D'elbow.
  Comment appelez-vous le col?

ALICE De nick, madame.   30

KATHERINE De nick. Et le menton?

ALICE De chin.

KATHERINE De sin. Le col, de nick; le menton, de sin.

ALICE Oui. Sauf votre honneur, en vérité, vous prononcez
  les mots aussi droit que les natifs d'Angleterre.

KATHERINE Je ne doute point d'apprendre, par la grace
  de Dieu, et en peu de temps.

ALICE N'avez-vous pas déjà oublié ce que je vous ai
enseigné?

40 KATHERINE Non, je réciterai à vous promptement: d'hand,
de fingre, de mailès –

ALICE De nailès, madame.

KATHERINE De nailès, de arm, de ilbow –

ALICE Sauf votre honneur, d'elbow.

KATHERINE Ainsi dis-je: d'elbow, de nick, et de sin.
Comment appelez-vous le pied et la robe?

ALICE Le foot, madame, et le count.

KATHERINE Le foot, et le count? O Seigneur Dieu! Ils
sont mots de son mauvais, corruptible, gros, et impu-
50 dique, et non pour les dames d'honneur d'user. Je ne
voudrais prononcer ces mots devant les seigneurs de
France pour tout le monde. Foh! Le foot et le count!
Néanmoins, je réciterai une autre fois ma leçon ensemble: d'hand, de fingre, de nailès, d'arm, d'elbow, de
nick, de sin, de foot, le count.

ALICE Excellent, madame!

KATHERINE C'est assez pour une fois. Allons-nous à
dîner.   *Exeunt*

III.5   *Enter the King of France, the Dauphin, the Duke of*
             Britaine, the Constable of France, and others

FRENCH KING
    'Tis certain he hath passed the River Somme.

CONSTABLE
    And if he be not fought withal, my lord,
    Let us not live in France: let us quit all,
    And give our vineyards to a barbarous people.

DAUPHIN
    O Dieu vivant! Shall a few sprays of us,
    The emptying of our fathers' luxury,

Our scions, put in wild and savage stock,
Spirt up so suddenly into the clouds,
And overlook their grafters?

BRITAINE

Normans, but bastard Normans, Norman bastards!   10
Mort Dieu! Ma vie! If they march along
Unfought withal, but I will sell my dukedom
To buy a slobbery and a dirty farm
In that nook-shotten isle of Albion.

CONSTABLE

Dieu de batailles! Where have they this mettle?
Is not their climate foggy, raw, and dull,
On whom, as in despite, the sun looks pale,
Killing their fruit with frowns? Can sodden water,
A drench for sur-reined jades, their barley broth,
Decoct their cold blood to such valiant heat?   20
And shall our quick blood, spirited with wine,
Seem frosty? O, for honour of our land,
Let us not hang like roping icicles
Upon our houses' thatch, whiles a more frosty people
Sweat drops of gallant youth in our rich fields! –
Lest poor we call them in their native lords.

DAUPHIN

By faith and honour,
Our madams mock at us, and plainly say
Our mettle is bred out, and they will give
Their bodies to the lust of English youth,   30
To new-store France with bastard warriors.

BRITAINE

They bid us to the English dancing-schools,
And teach lavoltas high and swift corantos,
Saying our grace is only in our heels,
And that we are most lofty runaways.

FRENCH KING

 Where is Montjoy the Herald? Speed him hence,
 Let him greet England with our sharp defiance.
 Up, Princes, and with spirit of honour edged,
 More sharper than your swords, hie to the field!
40 Charles Delabreth, High Constable of France,
 You Dukes of Orleans, Bourbon, and of Berri,
 Alençon, Brabant, Bar, and Burgundy,
 Jaques Chatillon, Rambures, Vaudemont,
 Beaumont, Grandpré, Roussi, and Faulconbridge,
 Foix, Lestrake, Bouciqualt, and Charolois,
 High Dukes, great Princes, Barons, Lords, and Knights,
 For your great seats, now quit you of great shames.
 Bar Harry England, that sweeps through our land
 With pennons painted in the blood of Harfleur!
50 Rush on his host, as doth the melted snow
 Upon the valleys, whose low vassal seat
 The Alps doth spit and void his rheum upon!
 Go down upon him, you have power enough,
 And in a captive chariot into Rouen
 Bring him our prisoner.

CONSTABLE   This becomes the great.

 Sorry am I his numbers are so few,
 His soldiers sick, and famished in their march;
 For I am sure, when he shall see our army,
 He'll drop his heart into the sink of fear,
60 And for achievement offer us his ransom.

FRENCH KING

 Therefore, Lord Constable, haste on Montjoy,
 And let him say to England that we send
 To know what willing ransom he will give.
 Prince Dauphin, you shall stay with us in Rouen.

DAUPHIN

 Not so, I do beseech your majesty.

FRENCH KING

Be patient, for you shall remain with us.

Now forth, Lord Constable, and Princes all,

And quickly bring us word of England's fall. *Exeunt*

Enter Captains, English and Welsh (Gower and   III.6
Fluellen)

GOWER How now, Captain Fluellen? Come you from the
bridge?

FLUELLEN I assure you, there is very excellent services
committed at the bridge.

GOWER Is the Duke of Exeter safe?

FLUELLEN The Duke of Exeter is as magnanimous as
Agamemnon, and a man that I love and honour with my
soul, and my heart, and my duty, and my live, and my
living, and my uttermost power. He is not – God be
praised and blessed! – any hurt in the world, but keeps   10
the bridge most valiantly, with excellent discipline.
There is an aunchient lieutenant there at the pridge, I
think in my very conscience he is as valiant a man as
Mark Antony, and he is a man of no estimation in the
world, but I did see him do as gallant service.

GOWER What do you call him?

FLUELLEN He is called Aunchient Pistol.

GOWER I know him not.

Enter Pistol

FLUELLEN Here is the man.

PISTOL

Captain, I thee beseech to do me favours.   20

The Duke of Exeter doth love thee well.

FLUELLEN Ay, I praise God, and I have merited some love
at his hands.

PISTOL

    Bardolph, a soldier firm and sound of heart,
    And of buxom valour, hath, by cruel fate,
    And giddy Fortune's furious fickle wheel,
    That goddess blind,
    That stands upon the rolling restless stone –

FLUELLEN By your patience, Aunchient Pistol: Fortune
30   is painted blind, with a muffler afore her eyes, to signify
    to you that Fortune is blind; and she is painted also
    with a wheel, to signify to you, which is the moral of it,
    that she is turning, and inconstant, and mutability, and
    variation; and her foot, look you, is fixed upon a
    spherical stone, which rolls, and rolls, and rolls. In
    good truth, the poet makes a most excellent description
    of it: Fortune is an excellent moral.

PISTOL

    Fortune is Bardolph's foe, and frowns on him;
    For he hath stolen a pax, and hangèd must 'a be –
40   A damnèd death!
    Let gallows gape for dog; let man go free,
    And let not hemp his windpipe suffocate.
    But Exeter hath give the doom of death
    For pax of little price.
    Therefore go speak – the Duke will hear they voice;
    And let not Bardolph's vital thread be cut
    With edge of penny cord and vile reproach.
    Speak, Captain, for his life, and I will thee requite.

FLUELLEN Aunchient Pistol, I do partly understand your
50   meaning.

PISTOL

    Why then, rejoice therefor!

FLUELLEN Certainly, Aunchient, it is not a thing to
    rejoice at, for if, look you, he were my brother, I would
    desire the Duke to use his good pleasure, and put him to
    execution; for discipline ought to be used.

PISTOL

Die and be damned! and *figo* for thy friendship.

FLUELLEN It is well.

PISTOL

The fig of Spain!   *Exit*

FLUELLEN Very good.

GOWER Why, this is an arrant counterfeit rascal, I   60
remember him now – a bawd, a cutpurse.

FLUELLEN I'll assure you, 'a uttered as prave words at
the pridge as you shall see in a summer's day. But it is
very well; what he has spoke to me, that is well, I
warrant you, when time is serve.

GOWER Why, 'tis a gull, a fool, a rogue, that now and then
goes to the wars, to grace himself at his return into
London under the form of a soldier. And such fellows
are perfect in the great commanders' names, and they
will learn you by rote where services were done: at such   70
and such a sconce, at such a breach, at such a convoy;
who came off bravely, who was shot, who disgraced,
what terms the enemy stood on; and this they con
perfectly in the phrase of war, which they trick up with
new-tuned oaths: and what a beard of the general's
cut and a horrid suit of the camp will do among foaming
bottles and ale-washed wits is wonderful to be thought
on. But you must learn to know such slanders of the
age, or else you may be marvellously mistook.

FLUELLEN I tell you what, Captain Gower; I do perceive   80
he is not the man that he would gladly make show to
the world he is. If I find a hole in his coat, I will tell
him my mind. (*Drum within*) Hark you, the King is
coming, and I must speak with him from the pridge.

> *Drum and colours. Enter the King and his poor*
> *soldiers, with Gloucester*

God pless your majesty!

KING HENRY
  How now, Fluellen, cam'st thou from the bridge?

FLUELLEN Ay, so please your majesty. The Duke of
  Exeter has very gallantly maintained the pridge. The
  French is gone off, look you, and there is gallant and
90 most prave passages. Marry, th'athversary was have
  possession of the pridge, but he is enforced to retire,
  and the Duke of Exeter is master of the pridge. I can
  tell your majesty, the Duke is a prave man.

KING HENRY What men have you lost, Fluellen?

FLUELLEN The perdition of th'athversary hath been very
  great, reasonable great. Marry, for my part, I think the
  Duke hath lost never a man, but one that is like to be
  executed for robbing a church, one Bardolph, if your
  majesty know the man: his face is all bubukles, and
100 whelks, and knobs, and flames o'fire; and his lips blows
  at his nose, and it is like a coal of fire, sometimes plue,
  and sometimes red; but his nose is executed, and his
  fire's out.

KING HENRY We would have all such offenders so cut
  off: and we give express charge, that in our marches
  through the country there be nothing compelled from
  the villages, nothing taken but paid for, none of the
  French upbraided or abused in disdainful language;
  for when lenity and cruelty play for a kingdom, the
110 gentler gamester is the soonest winner.

    Tucket. Enter Montjoy

MONTJOY You know me by my habit.

KING HENRY Well then, I know thee: what shall I know
  of thee?

MONTJOY My master's mind.

KING HENRY Unfold it.

MONTJOY Thus says my King: 'Say thou to Harry of
  England, Though we seemed dead, we did but sleep.

Advantage is a better soldier than rashness. Tell him
we could have rebuked him at Harfleur, but that we
thought not good to bruise an injury till it were full   120
ripe. Now we speak upon our cue, and our voice is
imperial: England shall repent his folly, see his weakness,
and admire our sufferance. Bid him therefore consider
of his ransom, which must proportion the losses we
have borne, the subjects we have lost, the disgrace we
have digested; which in weight to re-answer, his pettiness would bow under. For our losses, his exchequer is
too poor; for th'effusion of our blood, the muster of his
kingdom too faint a number; and for our disgrace, his
own person kneeling at our feet but a weak and worth-   130
less satisfaction. To this add defiance: and tell him for
conclusion, he hath betrayed his followers, whose
condemnation is pronounced.' So far my King and
master; so much my office.

KING HENRY

What is thy name? I know thy quality.

MONTJOY Montjoy.

KING HENRY

Thou dost thy office fairly. Turn thee back,
And tell thy King I do not seek him now,
But could be willing to march on to Calais
Without impeachment: for, to say the sooth,   140
Though 'tis no wisdom to confess so much
Unto an enemy of craft and vantage,
My people are with sickness much enfeebled,
My numbers lessened, and those few I have
Almost no better than so many French;
Who when they were in health, I tell thee, Herald,
I thought upon one pair of English legs
Did march three Frenchmen. Yet forgive me, God,
That I do brag thus! This your air of France

150 Hath blown that vice in me – I must repent.
Go, therefore, tell thy master here I am;
My ransom is this frail and worthless trunk;
My army but a weak and sickly guard:
Yet, God before, tell him we will come on,
Though France himself, and such another neighbour,
Stand in our way. There's for thy labour, Montjoy.
Go bid thy master well advise himself:
If we may pass, we will; if we be hindered,
We shall your tawny ground with your red blood
160 Discolour: and so, Montjoy, fare you well.
The sum of all our answer is but this:
We would not seek a battle as we are,
Nor, as we are, we say we will not shun it.
So tell your master.

MONTJOY
I shall deliver so. Thanks to your highness.   *Exit*

GLOUCESTER
I hope they will not come upon us now.

KING HENRY
We are in God's hand, brother, not in theirs.
March to the bridge; it now draws toward night.
Beyond the river we'll encamp ourselves,
170 And on tomorrow bid them march away.   *Exeunt*

III.7   *Enter the Constable of France, the Lord Rambures,*
               Orleans, Dauphin, with others

CONSTABLE Tut! I have the best armour of the world.
     Would it were day!

ORLEANS You have an excellent armour; but let my horse
     have his due.

CONSTABLE It is the best horse of Europe.

ORLEANS Will it never be morning?

DAUPHIN My Lord of Orleans, and my Lord High
    Constable, you talk of horse and armour?

ORLEANS You are as well provided of both as any prince
    in the world.   10

DAUPHIN What a long night is this! I will not change my
    horse with any that treads but on four pasterns. *Ça, ha!*
    He bounds from the earth as if his entrails were hairs –
    le cheval volant, the Pegasus, *cheʒ les narines de feu!*
    When I bestride him, I soar, I am a hawk. He trots the
    air; the earth sings when he touches it; the basest horn
    of his hoof is more musical than the pipe of Hermes.

ORLEANS He's of the colour of the nutmeg.

DAUPHIN And of the heat of the ginger. It is a beast for
    Perseus: he is pure air and fire; and the dull elements of   20
    earth and water never appear in him, but only in
    patient stillness while his rider mounts him. He is
    indeed a horse, and all other jades you may call beasts.

CONSTABLE Indeed, my lord, it is a most absolute and
    excellent horse.

DAUPHIN It is the prince of palfreys; his neigh is like the
    bidding of a monarch, and his countenance enforces
    homage.

ORLEANS No more, cousin.

DAUPHIN Nay, the man hath no wit that cannot, from the   30
    rising of the lark to the lodging of the lamb, vary
    deserved praise on my palfrey. It is a theme as fluent as
    the sea: turn the sands into eloquent tongues, and my
    horse is argument for them all. 'Tis a subject for a
    sovereign to reason on, and for a sovereign's sovereign
    to ride on; and for the world, familiar to us and un-
    known, to lay apart their particular functions and
    wonder at him. I once writ a sonnet in his praise, and
    began thus: 'Wonder of nature –'.

ORLEANS I have heard a sonnet begin so to one's mistress.   40

DAUPHIN Then did they imitate that which I composed
to my courser, for my horse is my mistress.

ORLEANS Your mistress bears well.

DAUPHIN Me well, which is the prescript praise and
perfection of a good and particular mistress.

CONSTABLE Nay, for methought yesterday your mistress
shrewdly shook your back.

DAUPHIN So perhaps did yours.

CONSTABLE Mine was not bridled.

50 DAUPHIN O, then belike she was old and gentle, and you
rode like a kern of Ireland, your French hose off, and in
your strait strossers.

CONSTABLE You have good judgement in horsemanship.

DAUPHIN Be warned by me, then: they that ride so, and
ride not warily, fall into foul bogs. I had rather have my
horse to my mistress.

CONSTABLE I had as lief have my mistress a jade.

DAUPHIN I tell thee, Constable, my mistress wears his
own hair.

60 CONSTABLE I could make as true a boast as that, if I had
a sow to my mistress.

DAUPHIN '*Le chien est retourné à son propre vomissement,
et la truie lavée au bourbier*': thou mak'st use of anything.

CONSTABLE Yet do I not use my horse for my mistress, or
any such proverb so little kin to the purpose.

RAMBURES My Lord Constable, the armour that I saw
in your tent tonight – are those stars or suns upon it?

CONSTABLE Stars, my lord.

DAUPHIN Some of them will fall tomorrow, I hope.

70 CONSTABLE And yet my sky shall not want.

DAUPHIN That may be, for you bear a many super-
fluously, and 'twere more honour some were away.

CONSTABLE E'en as your horse bears your praises,
who would trot as well were some of your brags dis-
mounted.

DAUPHIN Would I were able to load him with his desert!
  Will it never be day? I will trot tomorrow a mile, and
  my way shall be paved with English faces.

CONSTABLE I will not say so, for fear I should be faced
  out of my way; but I would it were morning, for I   80
  would fain be about the ears of the English.

RAMBURES Who will go to hazard with me for twenty
  prisoners?

CONSTABLE You must first go yourself to hazard ere you
  have them.

DAUPHIN 'Tis midnight: I'll go arm myself.   *Exit*

ORLEANS The Dauphin longs for morning.

RAMBURES He longs to eat the English.

CONSTABLE I think he will eat all he kills.

ORLEANS By the white hand of my lady, he's a gallant 90
  prince.

CONSTABLE Swear by her foot, that she may tread out
  the oath.

ORLEANS He is simply the most active gentleman of
  France.

CONSTABLE Doing is activity, and he will still be doing.

ORLEANS He never did harm, that I heard of.

CONSTABLE Nor will do none tomorrow: he will keep that
  good name still.

ORLEANS I know him to be valiant.   100

CONSTABLE I was told that, by one that knows him better
  than you.

ORLEANS What's he?

CONSTABLE Marry, he told me so himself, and he said he
  cared not who knew it.

ORLEANS He needs not; it is no hidden virtue in him.

CONSTABLE By my faith, sir, but it is; never anybody
  saw it but his lackey. 'Tis a hooded valour, and when it
  appears it will bate.

110 ORLEANS Ill will never said well.

CONSTABLE I will cap that proverb with 'There is flattery in friendship.'

ORLEANS And I will take up that with 'Give the devil his due!'

CONSTABLE Well placed! There stands your friend for the devil. Have at the very eye of that proverb with 'A pox of the devil!'

ORLEANS You are the better at proverbs by how much 'A fool's bolt is soon shot.'

120 CONSTABLE You have shot over.

ORLEANS 'Tis not the first time you were overshot.

Enter a Messenger

MESSENGER My Lord High Constable, the English lie within fifteen hundred paces of your tents.

CONSTABLE Who hath measured the ground?

MESSENGER The Lord Grandpré.

CONSTABLE A valiant and most expert gentleman. Would it were day! Alas, poor Harry of England! He longs not for the dawning as we do.

ORLEANS What a wretched and peevish fellow is this King
130 of England, to mope with his fat-brained followers so far out of his knowledge.

CONSTABLE If the English had any apprehension, they would run away.

ORLEANS That they lack; for if their heads had any intellectual armour, they could never wear such heavy head-pieces.

RAMBURES That island of England breeds very valiant creatures: their mastiffs are of unmatchable courage.

ORLEANS Foolish curs, that run winking into the mouth
140 of a Russian bear, and have their heads crushed like rotten apples! You may as well say that's a valiant flea that dare eat his breakfast on the lip of a lion.

CONSTABLE Just, just: and the men do sympathize with the mastiffs in robustious and rough coming on, leaving their wits with their wives; and then, give them great meals of beef, and iron and steel; they will eat like wolves, and fight like devils.

ORLEANS Ay, but these English are shrewdly out of beef.

CONSTABLE Then shall we find tomorrow they have only stomachs to eat, and none to fight. Now is it time to   150 arm. Come, shall we about it?

ORLEANS
It is now two o'clock: but, let me see – by ten
We shall have each a hundred Englishmen.   *Exeunt*

*

Flourish. Enter Chorus   **IV**

CHORUS
Now entertain conjecture of a time
When creeping murmur and the poring dark
Fills the wide vessel of the universe.
From camp to camp, through the foul womb of night,
The hum of either army stilly sounds,
That the fixed sentinels almost receive
The secret whispers of each other's watch.
Fire answers fire, and through their paly flames
Each battle sees the other's umbered face.
Steed threatens steed, in high and boastful neighs,   10
Piercing the night's dull ear; and from the tents
The armourers, accomplishing the knights,
With busy hammers closing rivets up,
Give dreadful note of preparation.
The country cocks do crow, the clocks do toll,
And the third hour of drowsy morning name.

Proud of their numbers, and secure in soul,
The confident and over-lusty French
Do the low-rated English play at dice,
20   And chide the cripple tardy-gaited night
Who like a foul and ugly witch doth limp
So tediously away. The poor condemnèd English,
Like sacrifices, by their watchful fires
Sit patiently, and inly ruminate
The morning's danger; and their gesture sad,
Investing lank-lean cheeks and war-worn coats,
Presenteth them unto the gazing moon
So many horrid ghosts. O now, who will behold
The royal Captain of this ruined band
30   Walking from watch to watch, from tent to tent,
Let him cry, 'Praise and glory on his head!'
For forth he goes and visits all his host,
Bids them good morrow with a modest smile,
And calls them brothers, friends, and countrymen.
Upon his royal face there is no note
How dread an army hath enrounded him,
Nor doth he dedicate one jot of colour
Unto the weary and all-watchèd night,
But freshly looks, and overbears attaint
40   With cheerful semblance and sweet majesty;
That every wretch, pining and pale before,
Beholding him, plucks comfort from his looks.
A largess universal, like the sun,
His liberal eye doth give to every one,
Thawing cold fear, that mean and gentle all
Behold, as may unworthiness define,
A little touch of Harry in the night.
And so our scene must to the battle fly;
Where – O for pity! – we shall much disgrace,
50   With four or five most vile and ragged foils,

Right ill-disposed in brawl ridiculous,
The name of Agincourt. Yet sit and see,
Minding true things by what their mockeries be. *Exit*

    Enter the King, Bedford, and Gloucester   **IV.I**
KING HENRY
    Gloucester, 'tis true that we are in great danger:
    The greater therefore should our courage be.
    Good morrow, brother Bedford. God Almighty!
    There is some soul of goodness in things evil,
    Would men observingly distil it out;
    For our bad neighbour makes us early stirrers,
    Which is both healthful, and good husbandry.
    Besides, they are our outward consciences,
    And preachers to us all, admonishing
    That we should dress us fairly for our end.   10
    Thus may we gather honey from the weed,
    And make a moral of the devil himself.
    Enter Erpingham
    Good morrow, old Sir Thomas Erpingham!
    A good soft pillow for that good white head
    Were better than a churlish turf of France.
ERPINGHAM
    Not so, my liege – this lodging likes me better,
    Since I may say, 'Now lie I like a king.'
KING HENRY
    'Tis good for men to love their present pains
    Upon example: so the spirit is eased;
    And when the mind is quickened, out of doubt   20
    The organs, though defunct and dead before,
    Break up their drowsy grave and newly move
    With casted slough and fresh legerity.
    Lend me thy cloak, Sir Thomas. Brothers both,

Commend me to the princes in our camp;
Do my good morrow to them, and anon
Desire them all to my pavilion.

GLOUCESTER We shall, my liege.

ERPINGHAM
Shall I attend your grace?

KING HENRY   No, my good knight.
30 Go with my brothers to my lords of England.
I and my bosom must debate awhile,
And then I would no other company.

ERPINGHAM
The Lord in heaven bless thee, noble Harry!
                                    Exeunt all but the King

KING HENRY
God-a-mercy, old heart, thou speak'st cheerfully.
    Enter Pistol

PISTOL
    Qui va là?

KING HENRY A friend.

PISTOL
Discuss unto me, art thou officer,
Or art thou base, common, and popular?

KING HENRY I am a gentleman of a company.

PISTOL
40 Trail'st thou the puissant pike?

KING HENRY Even so. What are you?

PISTOL
As good a gentleman as the Emperor.

KING HENRY Then you are a better than the King.

PISTOL
The King's a bawcock, and a heart of gold,
A lad of life, an imp of fame;
Of parents good, of fist most valiant.
I kiss his dirty shoe, and from heartstring

I love the lovely bully. What is thy name?
KING HENRY Harry le Roy.
PISTOL
    Le Roy? A Cornish name. Art thou of Cornish crew? 50
KING HENRY No, I am a Welshman.
PISTOL
    Know'st thou Fluellen?
KING HENRY Yes.
PISTOL
    Tell him I'll knock his leek about his pate
    Upon Saint Davy's day.
KING HENRY Do not you wear your dagger in your cap
    that day, lest he knock that about yours.
PISTOL
    Art thou his friend?
KING HENRY And his kinsman too.
PISTOL
    The *figo* for thee then!   60
KING HENRY I thank you. God be with you!
PISTOL
    My name is Pistol called.   *Exit*
KING HENRY It sorts well with your fierceness.
        Enter Fluellen and Gower
GOWER Captain Fluellen!
FLUELLEN So! In the name of Jesu Christ, speak fewer.
    It is the greatest admiration in the universal world,
    when the true and aunchient prerogatifes and laws of
    the wars is not kept. If you would take the pains but to
    examine the wars of Pompey the Great, you shall find,
    I warrant you, that there is no tiddle-taddle nor pibble- 70
    pabble in Pompey's camp. I warrant you, you shall
    find the ceremonies of the wars, and the cares of it, and
    the forms of it, and the sobriety of it, and the modesty
    of it, to be otherwise.

GOWER Why, the enemy is loud, you hear him all night.

FLUELLEN If the enemy is an ass, and a fool, and a
prating coxcomb, is it meet, think you, that we should
also, look you, be an ass, and a fool, and a prating coxcomb? In your own conscience now?

80 GOWER I will speak lower.

FLUELLEN I pray you and beseech you that you will.

Exeunt Gower and Fluellen

KING HENRY

Though it appear a little out of fashion,

There is much care and valour in this Welshman.

Enter three soldiers, John Bates, Alexander Court,
and Michael Williams

COURT Brother John Bates, is not that the morning which
breaks yonder?

BATES I think it be; but we have no great cause to desire
the approach of day.

WILLIAMS We see yonder the beginning of the day, but I
think we shall never see the end of it. Who goes there?

90 KING HENRY A friend.

WILLIAMS Under what captain serve you?

KING HENRY Under Sir Thomas Erpingham.

WILLIAMS A good old commander, and a most kind
gentleman. I pray you, what thinks he of our estate?

KING HENRY Even as men wrecked upon a sand, that
look to be washed off the next tide.

BATES He hath not told his thought to the King?

KING HENRY No, nor it is not meet he should. For
though I speak it to you, I think the King is but a man,
100 as I am: the violet smells to him as it doth to me; the
element shows to him as it doth to me; all his senses have
but human conditions. His ceremonies laid by, in his
nakedness he appears but a man; and though his
affections are higher mounted than ours, yet when they

stoop, they stoop with the like wing. Therefore, when
he sees reason of fears, as we do, his fears, out of doubt,
be of the same relish as ours are: yet, in reason, no
man should possess him with any appearance of fear,
lest he, by showing it, should dishearten his army.

BATES He may show what outward courage he will, but I   110
believe, as cold a night as 'tis, he could wish himself in
Thames up to the neck; and so I would he were, and
I by him, at all adventures, so we were quit here.

KING HENRY By my troth, I will speak my conscience of
the King: I think he would not wish himself anywhere
but where he is.

BATES Then I would he were here alone; so should he be
sure to be ransomed, and a many poor men's lives
saved.

KING HENRY I dare say you love him not so ill to wish   120
him here alone, howsoever you speak this to feel other
men's minds. Methinks I could not die anywhere so
contented as in the King's company, his cause being
just and his quarrel honourable.

WILLIAMS That's more than we know.

BATES Ay, or more than we should seek after; for we know
enough if we know we are the King's subjects. If his
cause be wrong, our obedience to the King wipes the
crime of it out of us.

WILLIAMS But if the cause be not good, the King himself   130
hath a heavy reckoning to make, when all those legs,
and arms, and heads, chopped off in a battle, shall join
together at the latter day, and cry all, 'We died at such
a place'; some swearing, some crying for a surgeon,
some upon their wives left poor behind them, some upon
the debts they owe, some upon their children rawly left.
I am afeard there are few die well that die in a battle,
for how can they charitably dispose of anything when

blood is their argument? Now, if these men do not die
140 well, it will be a black matter for the King that led them
to it, who to disobey were against all proportion of
subjection.

KING HENRY So, if a son that is by his father sent about
merchandise do sinfully miscarry upon the sea, the
imputation of his wickedness, by your rule, should be
imposed upon his father that sent him; or if a servant,
under his master's command, transporting a sum of
money, be assailed by robbers, and die in many irreconciled iniquities, you may call the business of the master
150 the author of the servant's damnation. But this is not so.
The King is not bound to answer the particular endings
of his soldiers, the father of his son, nor the master of
his servant; for they purpose not their death when they
purpose their services. Besides, there is no king, be
his cause never so spotless, if it come to the arbitrement
of swords, can try it out with all unspotted soldiers.
Some, peradventure, have on them the guilt of premeditated and contrived murder; some, of beguiling
virgins with the broken seals of perjury; some, making
160 the wars their bulwark, that have before gored the
gentle bosom of peace with pillage and robbery. Now,
if these men have defeated the law, and outrun native
punishment, though they can outstrip men they have no
wings to fly from God. War is His beadle, war is His
vengeance; so that here men are punished for before-
breach of the King's laws, in now the King's quarrel.
Where they feared the death, they have borne life away;
and where they would be safe, they perish. Then if
they die unprovided, no more is the King guilty of their
170 damnation than he was before guilty of those impieties
for the which they are now visited. Every subject's duty
is the King's, but every subject's soul is his own. There-

fore should every soldier in the wars do as every sick
man in his bed, wash every mote out of his conscience;
and dying so, death is to him advantage; or not dying,
the time was blessedly lost wherein such preparation
was gained; and in him that escapes, it were not sin to
think that, making God so free an offer, He let him
outlive that day to see His greatness, and to teach others
how they should prepare.   180

WILLIAMS 'Tis certain, every man that dies ill, the ill
upon his own head – the King is not to answer it.

BATES I do not desire he should answer for me, and yet I
determine to fight lustily for him.

KING HENRY I myself heard the King say he would not be
ransomed.

WILLIAMS Ay, he said so, to make us fight cheerfully:
but when our throats are cut he may be ransomed, and
we ne'er the wiser.

KING HENRY If I live to see it, I will never trust his word   190
after.

WILLIAMS You pay him then! That's a perilous shot out
of an elder-gun, that a poor and a private displeasure
can do against a monarch! You may as well go about to
turn the sun to ice, with fanning in his face with a pea-
cock's feather. You'll never trust his word after! Come,
'tis a foolish saying.

KING HENRY Your reproof is something too round. I
should be angry with you, if the time were convenient.

WILLIAMS Let it be a quarrel between us, if you live.   200

KING HENRY I embrace it.

WILLIAMS How shall I know thee again?

KING HENRY Give me any gage of thine, and I will wear
it in my bonnet: then, if ever thou dar'st acknowledge it,
I will make it my quarrel.

WILLIAMS Here's my glove: give me another of thine.

KING HENRY There.

WILLIAMS This will I also wear in my cap. If ever thou
come to me and say, after tomorrow, 'This is my glove,'
210   by this hand, I will take thee a box on the ear.

KING HENRY If ever I live to see it, I will challenge it.

WILLIAMS Thou dar'st as well be hanged.

KING HENRY Well, I will do it, though I take thee in the
King's company.

WILLIAMS Keep thy word. Fare thee well.

BATES Be friends, you English fools, be friends! We have
French quarrels enow, if you could tell how to reckon.

KING HENRY Indeed, the French may lay twenty French
crowns to one they will beat us, for they bear them on
220   their shoulders; but it is no English treason to cut
French crowns, and tomorrow the King himself will be
a clipper.   *Exeunt Soldiers*

Upon the King! Let us our lives, our souls,
Our debts, our careful wives,
Our children, and our sins, lay on the King!
We must bear all. O hard condition,
Twin-born with greatness, subject to the breath
Of every fool, whose sense no more can feel
But his own wringing! What infinite heart's ease
230   Must kings neglect that private men enjoy!
And what have kings that privates have not too,
Save ceremony, save general ceremony?
And what art thou, thou idol ceremony?
What kind of god art thou, that suffer'st more
Of mortal griefs than do thy worshippers?
What are thy rents? What are thy comings-in?
O ceremony, show me but thy worth!
What is thy soul of adoration?
Art thou aught else but place, degree, and form,
240   Creating awe and fear in other men?

Wherein thou art less happy, being feared,
Than they in fearing.
What drink'st thou oft, instead of homage sweet,
But poisoned flattery? O, be sick, great greatness,
And bid thy ceremony give thee cure!
Thinks thou the fiery fever will go out
With titles blown from adulation?
Will it give place to flexure and low bending?
Canst thou, when thou command'st the beggar's knee,
Command the health of it? No, thou proud dream,   250
That play'st so subtly with a king's repose.
I am a king that find thee, and I know
'Tis not the balm, the sceptre, and the ball,
The sword, the mace, the crown imperial,
The intertissued robe of gold and pearl,
The farcèd title running fore the king,
The throne he sits on, nor the tide of pomp
That beats upon the high shore of this world –
No, not all these, thrice-gorgeous ceremony,
Not all these, laid in bed majestical,   260
Can sleep so soundly as the wretched slave,
Who, with a body filled, and vacant mind,
Gets him to rest, crammed with distressful bread;
Never sees horrid night, the child of hell,
But, like a lackey, from the rise to set,
Sweats in the eye of Phoebus, and all night
Sleeps in Elysium; next day after dawn
Doth rise and help Hyperion to his horse;
And follows so the ever-running year
With profitable labour to his grave: 270
And but for ceremony, such a wretch,
Winding up days with toil, and nights with sleep,
Had the fore-hand and vantage of a king.
The slave, a member of the country's peace,

Enjoys it, but in gross brain little wots
What watch the king keeps to maintain the peace,
Whose hours the peasant best advantages.

    Enter Erpingham

ERPINGHAM

My lord, your nobles, jealous of your absence,
Seek through your camp to find you.

KING HENRY   Good old knight,

280   Collect them all together at my tent.
I'll be before thee.

ERPINGHAM   I shall do't, my lord.   *Exit*

KING HENRY

O God of battles, steel my soldiers' hearts;
Possess them not with fear; take from them now
The sense of reckoning, if th'opposèd numbers
Pluck their hearts from them. Not today, O Lord,
O not today, think not upon the fault
My father made in compassing the crown!
I Richard's body have interrèd new,
And on it have bestowed more contrite tears

290   Than from it issued forcèd drops of blood.
Five hundred poor I have in yearly pay,
Who twice a day their withered hands hold up
Toward heaven, to pardon blood: and I have built
Two chantries where the sad and solemn priests
Sing still for Richard's soul. More will I do,
Though all that I can do is nothing worth,
Since that my penitence comes after all,
Imploring pardon.

    Enter Gloucester

GLOUCESTER

My liege!

KING HENRY My brother Gloucester's voice? Ay,

300   I know thy errand, I will go with thee.

The day, my friends, and all things stay for me.

Exeunt

ORLEANS

The sun doth gild our armour: up, my lords!

DAUPHIN

Montez à cheval! My horse! *Varlet! Lacquais!*
Ha!

ORLEANS

O brave spirit!

DAUPHIN   *Via! Les eaux et la terre!*

ORLEANS

Rien puis? L'air et le feu?

DAUPHIN   *Ciel*, cousin Orleans!

Enter the Constable

Now, my Lord Constable!

CONSTABLE

Hark how our steeds for present service neigh!

DAUPHIN

Mount them and make incision in their hides,
That their hot blood may spin in English eyes
And dout them with superfluous courage, ha!

RAMBURES

What, will you have them weep our horses' blood?   10
How shall we then behold their natural tears?

Enter a Messenger

MESSENGER

The English are embattled, you French peers.

CONSTABLE

To horse, you gallant Princes, straight to horse!
Do but behold yon poor and starvèd band,
And your fair show shall suck away their souls,

Leaving them but the shales and husks of men.
There is not work enough for all our hands,
Scarce blood enough in all their sickly veins
To give each naked curtle-axe a stain
20   That our French gallants shall today draw out,
And sheathe for lack of sport. Let us but blow on them,
The vapour of our valour will o'erturn them.
'Tis positive 'gainst all exceptions, lords,
That our superfluous lackeys, and our peasants,
Who in unnecessary action swarm
About our squares of battle, were enow
To purge this field of such a hilding foe,
Though we upon this mountain's basis by
Took stand for idle speculation:
30   But that our honours must not. What's to say?
A very little little let us do,
And all is done. Then let the trumpets sound
The tucket sonance and the note to mount;
For our approach shall so much dare the field
That England shall couch down in fear and yield.

        Enter Grandpré

GRANDPRÉ
Why do you stay so long, my lords of France?
Yon island carrions, desperate of their bones,
Ill-favouredly become the morning field.
Their ragged curtains poorly are let loose,
40   And our air shakes them passing scornfully.
Big Mars seems bankrupt in their beggared host,
And faintly through a rusty beaver peeps.
The horsemen sit like fixèd candlesticks,
With torch-staves in their hand; and their poor jades
Lob down their heads, dropping the hides and hips,
The gum down-roping from their pale-dead eyes,
And in their pale dull mouths the gimmaled bit

Lies foul with chawed grass, still and motionless;
And their executors, the knavish crows,
Fly o'er them all, impatient for their hour.   50
Description cannot suit itself in words
To demonstrate the life of such a battle
In life so lifeless as it shows itself.

CONSTABLE
They have said their prayers, and they stay for death.

DAUPHIN
Shall we go send them dinners, and fresh suits,
And give their fasting horses provender,
And after fight with them?

CONSTABLE
I stay but for my guidon. To the field!
I will the banner from a trumpet take,
And use it for my haste. Come, come away!   60
The sun is high, and we outwear the day.   *Exeunt*

Enter Gloucester, Bedford, Exeter, Erpingham with   IV.3
all his host; Salisbury and Westmorland

GLOUCESTER
Where is the King?

BEDFORD
The King himself is rode to view their battle.

WESTMORLAND
Of fighting men they have full three-score thousand.

EXETER
There's five to one: besides, they all are fresh.

SALISBURY
God's arm strike with us! 'Tis a fearful odds.
God bye you, Princes all: I'll to my charge.
If we no more meet till we meet in heaven,
Then joyfully, my noble Lord of Bedford,

My dear Lord Gloucester, and my good Lord Exeter,
10   And my kind kinsman, warriors all, adieu!

BEDFORD

Farewell, good Salisbury, and good luck go with thee!

EXETER

Farewell, kind lord: fight valiantly today –
And yet I do thee wrong to mind thee of it,
For thou art framed of the firm truth of valour.

Exit Salisbury

BEDFORD

He is as full of valour as of kindness,
Princely in both.

Enter the King

WESTMORLAND   O that we now had here
But one ten thousand of those men in England
That do no work today!

KING HENRY   What's he that wishes so?
My cousin Westmorland? No, my fair cousin.
20   If we are marked to die, we are enow
To do our country loss: and if to live,
The fewer men, the greater share of honour.
God's will! I pray thee wish not one man more.
By Jove, I am not covetous for gold,
Nor care I who doth feed upon my cost;
It yearns me not if men my garments wear;
Such outward things dwell not in my desires.
But if it be a sin to covet honour,
I am the most offending soul alive.
30   No, faith, my coz, wish not a man from England:
God's peace! I would not lose so great an honour
As one man more methinks would share from me
For the best hope I have. O, do not wish one more!
Rather proclaim it, Westmorland, through my host,

That he which hath no stomach to this fight,
Let him depart: his passport shall be made,
And crowns for convoy put into his purse.
We would not die in that man's company
That fears his fellowship to die with us.
This day is called the Feast of Crispian: 40
He that outlives this day, and comes safe home,
Will stand a-tiptoe when this day is named,
And rouse him at the name of Crispian.
He that shall see this day, and live old age,
Will yearly on the vigil feast his neighbours,
And say, 'Tomorrow is Saint Crispian.'
Then will he strip his sleeve, and show his scars,
And say, 'These wounds I had on Crispin's day.'
Old men forget; yet all shall be forgot,
But he'll remember, with advantages,   50
What feats he did that day. Then shall our names,
Familiar in his mouth as household words,
Harry the King, Bedford and Exeter,
Warwick and Talbot, Salisbury and Gloucester,
Be in their flowing cups freshly remembered.
This story shall the good man teach his son;
And Crispin Crispian shall ne'er go by,
From this day to the ending of the world,
But we in it shall be rememberèd –
We few, we happy few, we band of brothers: 60
For he today that sheds his blood with me
Shall be my brother; be he ne'er so vile,
This day shall gentle his condition;
And gentlemen in England now abed
Shall think themselves accursed they were not here,
And hold their manhoods cheap, whiles any speaks
That fought with us upon Saint Crispin's day.

Enter Salisbury

SALISBURY
  My sovereign lord, bestow yourself with speed.
  The French are bravely in their battles set,
70   And will with all expedience charge on us.
KING HENRY
  All things are ready, if our minds be so.
WESTMORLAND
  Perish the man whose mind is backward now!
KING HENRY
  Thou dost not wish more help from England, coz?
WESTMORLAND
  God's will, my liege, would you and I alone,
  Without more help, could fight this royal battle!
KING HENRY
  Why, now thou hast unwished five thousand men,
  Which likes me better than to wish us one.
  You know your places. God be with you all!
    Tucket. Enter Montjoy
MONTJOY
  Once more I come to know of thee, King Harry,
80   If for thy ransom thou wilt now compound,
  Before thy most assurèd overthrow:
  For certainly thou art so near the gulf
  Thou needs must be englutted. Besides, in mercy,
  The Constable desires thee thou wilt mind
  Thy followers of repentance, that their souls
  May make a peaceful and a sweet retire
  From off these fields, where, wretches, their poor bodies
  Must lie and fester.
KING HENRY   Who hath sent thee now?
MONTJOY
  The Constable of France.

KING HENRY

I pray thee bear my former answer back: 90
Bid them achieve me, and then sell my bones.
Good God, why should they mock poor fellows thus?
The man that once did sell the lion's skin
While the beast lived, was killed with hunting him.
A many of our bodies shall no doubt
Find native graves; upon the which, I trust,
Shall witness live in brass of this day's work.
And those that leave their valiant bones in France,
Dying like men, though buried in your dunghills,
They shall be famed; for there the sun shall greet them,   100
And draw their honours reeking up to heaven,
Leaving their earthly parts to choke your clime,
The smell whereof shall breed a plague in France.
Mark then abounding valour in our English,
That being dead, like to the bullet's crasing,
Break out into a second course of mischief,
Killing in relapse of mortality.
Let me speak proudly: tell the Constable
We are but warriors for the working-day;
Our gayness and our gilt are all besmirched   110
With rainy marching in the painful field.
There's not a piece of feather in our host –
Good argument, I hope, we will not fly –
And time hath worn us into slovenry.
But, by the mass, our hearts are in the trim;
And my poor soldiers tell me, yet ere night
They'll be in fresher robes, or they will pluck
The gay new coats o'er the French soldiers' heads,
And turn them out of service. If they do this –
As, if God please, they shall – my ransom then   120
Will soon be levied. Herald, save thou thy labour;

Come thou no more for ransom, gentle Herald.
They shall have none, I swear, but these my joints,
Which if they have as I will leave 'em them
Shall yield them little, tell the Constable.

MONTJOY
I shall, King Harry. And so fare thee well:
Thou never shalt hear herald any more.   *Exit*

KING HENRY I fear thou wilt once more come again for
a ransom.

Enter York

YORK
130   My lord, most humbly on my knee I beg
The leading of the vaward.

KING HENRY
Take it, brave York. Now, soldiers, march away:
And how Thou pleasest, God, dispose the day! *Exeunt*

IV.4   *Alarum. Excursions. Enter Pistol, French Soldier, Boy*

PISTOL
Yield, cur!

FRENCH SOLDIER *Je pense que vous êtes le gentilhomme de
bonne qualité.*

PISTOL
Calitie! 'Calen o custure me!'
Art thou a gentleman? What is thy name? Discuss.

FRENCH SOLDIER *O Seigneur Dieu!*

PISTOL
O Signieur Dew should be a gentleman:
Perpend my words, O Signieur Dew, and mark.
O Signieur Dew, thou diest on point of fox,
10   Except, O Signieur, thou do give to me
Egregious ransom.

FRENCH SOLDIER *O, prenez miséricorde! Ayez pitié de
moy!*

PISTOL
    Moy shall not serve: I will have forty moys,
    Or I will fetch thy rim out at thy throat
    In drops of crimson blood!

FRENCH SOLDIER *Est-il impossible d'échapper la force de*
    ton bras?

PISTOL
    Brass, cur?
    Thou damnèd and luxurious mountain goat,   20
    Offer'st me brass?

FRENCH SOLDIER *O, pardonne-moy!*

PISTOL
    Say'st thou me so? Is that a ton of moys?
    Come hither, boy: ask me this slave in French
    What is his name.

BOY *Écoutez: comment êtes-vous appelé?*

FRENCH SOLDIER *Monsieur le Fer.*

BOY He says his name is Master Fer.

PISTOL Master Fer! I'll fer him, and firk him, and ferret
    him. Discuss the same in French unto him.   30

BOY I do not know the French for fer, and ferret, and firk.

PISTOL
    Bid him prepare, for I will cut his throat.

FRENCH SOLDIER *Que dit-il, monsieur?*

BOY *Il me commande à vous dire que vous faites vous prêt,*
    car ce soldat içi est disposé tout à cette heure de couper
    votre gorge.

PISTOL
    Owy, cuppele gorge, permafoy,
    Peasant, unless thou give me crowns, brave crowns;
    Or mangled shalt thou be by this my sword.

FRENCH SOLDIER *O, je vous supplie, pour l'amour de Dieu,*   40
    me pardonner! Je suis le gentilhomme de bonne maison.
    Gardez ma vie, et je vous donnerai deux cents écus.

PISTOL
    What are his words?

BOY He prays you to save his life. He is a gentleman of a
good house, and for his ransom he will give you two
hundred crowns.

PISTOL

Tell him my fury shall abate, and I
The crowns will take.

FRENCH SOLDIER *Petit monsieur, que dit-il?*

50 BOY *Encore qu'il est contre son jurement de pardonner aucun
prisonnier; néanmoins, pour les écus que vous l'avez
promis, il est content à vous donner la liberté, le franchisement.*

FRENCH SOLDIER *Sur mes genoux je vous donne mille
remercîments; et je m'estime heureux que je suis tombé
entre les mains d'un chevalier, je pense, le plus brave,
vaillant, et très distingué seigneur d'Angleterre.*

PISTOL

Expound unto me, boy.

BOY He gives you upon his knees a thousand thanks; and
60 he esteems himself happy that he hath fallen into the
hands of one – as he thinks – the most brave, valorous,
and thrice-worthy signieur of England.

PISTOL

As I suck blood, I will some mercy show.
Follow me!   *Exit*

BOY *Suivez-vous le grand capitaine.* (*Exit French Soldier*)
I did never know so full a voice issue from so empty a
heart; but the saying is true, 'The empty vessel makes
the greatest sound.' Bardolph and Nym had ten times
more valour than this roaring devil i'th'old play, that
70 everyone may pare his nails with a wooden dagger; and
they are both hanged – and so would this be, if he durst
steal anything adventurously. I must stay with the
lackeys, with the luggage of our camp. The French
might have a good prey of us, if he knew of it, for there
is none to guard it but boys.   *Exit*

Enter the Constable, Orleans, Bourbon, Dauphin,   IV.5
and Rambures

CONSTABLE *O diable!*

ORLEANS *O Seigneur! Le jour est perdu, tout est perdu!*

DAUPHIN

   Mort Dieu! Ma vie! All is confounded, all!

   Reproach and everlasting shame

   Sits mocking in our plumes. *O méchante fortune!*

    A short alarum

   Do not run away!

CONSTABLE   Why, all our ranks are broke.

DAUPHIN

   O perdurable shame! Let's stab ourselves.

   Be these the wretches that we played at dice for?

ORLEANS

   Is this the King we sent to for his ransom?

BOURBON

   Shame, and eternal shame, nothing but shame!   10

   Let's die in honour! Once more back again!

   And he that will not follow Bourbon now,

   Let him go hence, and with his cap in hand,

   Like a base pander, hold the chamber-door

   Whilst by a slave, no gentler than my dog,

   His fairest daughter is contaminated.

CONSTABLE

   Disorder that hath spoiled us, friend us now!

   Let us on heaps go offer up our lives.

ORLEANS

   We are enow yet living in the field

   To smother up the English in our throngs,   20

   If any order might be thought upon.

BOURBON

   The devil take order now! I'll to the throng.

   Let life be short, else shame will be too long. *Exeunt*

IV.6   *Alarum. Enter the King and his train, Exeter and*
            others, with prisoners

KING HENRY

Well have we done, thrice-valiant countrymen;
But all's not done – yet keep the French the field.

EXETER

The Duke of York commends him to your majesty.

KING HENRY

Lives he, good uncle? Thrice within this hour
I saw him down; thrice up again, and fighting.
From helmet to the spur all blood he was.

EXETER

In which array, brave soldier, doth he lie,
Larding the plain; and by his bloody side,
Yoke-fellow to his honour-owing wounds,
10   The noble Earl of Suffolk also lies.
Suffolk first died; and York, all haggled over,
Comes to him, where in gore he lay insteeped,
And takes him by the beard, kisses the gashes
That bloodily did yawn upon his face.
He cries aloud, 'Tarry, my cousin Suffolk!
My soul shall thine keep company to heaven.
Tarry, sweet soul, for mine, then fly abreast,
As in this glorious and well-foughten field
We kept together in our chivalry!'
20   Upon these words I came and cheered him up;
He smiled me in the face, raught me his hand,
And, with a feeble grip, says, 'Dear my lord,
Commend my service to my sovereign.'
So did he turn, and over Suffolk's neck
He threw his wounded arm, and kissed his lips,
And so espoused to death, with blood he sealed
A testament of noble-ending love.
The pretty and sweet manner of it forced

Those waters from me which I would have stopped;
But I had not so much of man in me,   30
And all my mother came into mine eyes
And gave me up to tears.

KING HENRY   I blame you not;
For, hearing this, I must perforce compound
With mistful eyes, or they will issue too.

    Alarum

But hark! what new alarum is this same?
The French have reinforced their scattered men.
Then every soldier kill his prisoners!
Give the word through.   *Exeunt*

    Enter Fluellen and Gower   **IV.7**

FLUELLEN Kill the poys and the luggage? 'Tis expressly
  against the law of arms; 'tis as arrant a piece of knavery,
  mark you now, as can be offert – in your conscience now,
  is it not?

GOWER 'Tis certain there's not a boy left alive, and the
  cowardly rascals that ran from the battle ha' done this
  slaughter. Besides, they have burnt and carried away
  all that was in the King's tent, wherefore the King most
  worthily hath caused every soldier to cut his prisoner's
  throat. O, 'tis a gallant King!   10

FLUELLEN Ay, he was porn at Monmouth, Captain
  Gower. What call you the town's name where Alexander
  the Pig was born?

GOWER Alexander the Great.

FLUELLEN Why, I pray you, is not 'pig' great? The pig,
  or the great, or the mighty, or the huge, or the magnanimous, are all one reckonings, save the phrase is a little
  variations.

GOWER I think Alexander the Great was born in Macedon;
20   his father was called Philip of Macedon, as I take it.

FLUELLEN I think it is in Macedon where Alexander is
      porn. I tell you, Captain, if you look in the maps of the
      'orld, I warrant you sall find, in the comparisons between
      Macedon and Monmouth, that the situations, look you,
      is both alike. There is a river in Macedon, and there is
      also moreover a river at Monmouth – it is called Wye
      at Monmouth, but it is out of my prains what is the
      name of the other river; but 'tis all one, 'tis alike as my
      fingers is to my fingers, and there is salmons in both.
30   If you mark Alexander's life well, Harry of Monmouth's
      life is come after it indifferent well; for there is figures in
      all things. Alexander, God knows and you know, in his
      rages, and his furies, and his wraths, and his cholers,
      and his moods, and his displeasures, and his indigna-
      tions, and also being a little intoxicates in his prains,
      did in his ales and his angers, look you, kill his best
      friend Cleitus.

GOWER Our King is not like him in that: he never killed
      any of his friends.

40 FLUELLEN It is not well done, mark you now, to take the
      tales out of my mouth, ere it is made and finished. I
      speak but in the figures and comparisons of it. As
      Alexander killed his friend Cleitus, being in his ales
      and his cups, so also Harry Monmouth, being in his
      right wits and his good judgements, turned away the
      fat knight with the great-belly doublet – he was full of
      jests, and gipes, and knaveries, and mocks: I have forgot
      his name.

GOWER Sir John Falstaff.

50 FLUELLEN That is he. I'll tell you, there is good men porn
      at Monmouth.

GOWER Here comes his majesty.

Alarum. Enter King Henry and Bourbon, with
prisoners; also Warwick, Gloucester, Exeter, and
others. Flourish

KING HENRY

I was not angry since I came to France
Until this instant. Take a trumpet, Herald;
Ride thou unto the horsemen on yon hill.
If they will fight with us, bid them come down,
Or void the field: they do offend our sight.
If they'll do neither, we will come to them,
And make them skirr away as swift as stones
Enforcèd from the old Assyrian slings.   60
Besides, we'll cut the throats of those we have,
And not a man of them that we shall take
Shall taste our mercy. Go and tell them so.
     Enter Montjoy

EXETER

Here comes the Herald of the French, my liege.

GLOUCESTER

His eyes are humbler than they used to be.

KING HENRY

How now, what means this, Herald? Know'st thou not
That I have fined these bones of mine for ransom?
Com'st thou again for ransom?

MONTJOY   No, great King;
I come to thee for charitable licence,
That we may wander o'er this bloody field   70
To book our dead, and then to bury them,
To sort our nobles from our common men.
For many of our princes – woe the while! –
Lie drowned and soaked in mercenary blood;
So do our vulgar drench their peasant limbs
In blood of princes, and their wounded steeds
Fret fetlock-deep in gore, and with wild rage

Yerk out their armèd heels at their dead masters,
Killing them twice. O, give us leave, great King,
To view the field in safety, and dispose
Of their dead bodies!

KING HENRY   I tell thee truly, Herald,
I know not if the day be ours or no;
For yet a many of your horsemen peer
And gallop o'er the field.

MONTJOY   The day is yours.

KING HENRY
Praisèd be God, and not our strength, for it!
What is this castle called that stands hard by?

MONTJOY
They call it Agincourt.

KING HENRY
Then call we this the field of Agincourt,
Fought on the day of Crispin Crispianus.

FLUELLEN Your grandfather of famous memory, an't
please your majesty, and your great-uncle Edward the
Plack Prince of Wales, as I have read in the chronicles,
fought a most prave pattle here in France.

KING HENRY They did, Fluellen.

FLUELLEN Your majesty says very true. If your majesties
is remembered of it, the Welshmen did good service in a
garden where leeks did grow, wearing leeks in their
Monmouth caps, which your majesty know to this hour
is an honourable badge of the service; and I do believe
your majesty takes no scorn to wear the leek upon Saint
Tavy's day.

KING HENRY
I wear it for a memorable honour;
For I am Welsh, you know, good countryman.

FLUELLEN All the water in Wye cannot wash your
majesty's Welsh plood out of your pody, I can tell you

that. God pless it and preserve it, as long as it pleases
His grace, and His majesty too!

KING HENRY Thanks, good my countryman.

FLUELLEN By Jeshu, I am your majesty's countryman, I
care not who know it; I will confess it to all the 'orld.   110
I need not to be ashamed of your majesty, praised be
God, so long as your majesty is an honest man.

KING HENRY

God keep me so!

Enter Williams

Our heralds go with him.
Bring me just notice of the numbers dead
On both our parts.   *Exeunt Heralds with Montjoy*

Call yonder fellow hither.

EXETER Soldier, you must come to the King.

KING HENRY Soldier, why wear'st thou that glove in thy
cap?

WILLIAMS An't please your majesty, 'tis the gage of one
that I should fight withal, if he be alive.   120

KING HENRY An Englishman?

WILLIAMS An't please your majesty, a rascal that
swaggered with me last night: who, if 'a live and ever
dare to challenge this glove, I have sworn to take him a
box o'th'ear: or if I can see my glove in his cap, which he
swore as he was a soldier he would wear if alive, I will
strike it out soundly.

KING HENRY What think you, Captain Fluellen, is it
fit this soldier keep his oath?

FLUELLEN He is a craven and a villain else, an't please   130
your majesty, in my conscience.

KING HENRY It may be his enemy is a gentleman of
great sort, quite from the answer of his degree.

FLUELLEN Though he be as good a gentleman as the
devil is, as Lucifer and Belzebub himself, it is necessary,

look your grace, that he keep his vow and his oath. If
he be perjured, see you now, his reputation is as arrant
a villain and a Jack-sauce as ever his black shoe trod
upon God's ground and His earth, in my conscience, la!

140 KING HENRY Then keep thy vow, sirrah, when thou
meet'st the fellow.

WILLIAMS So I will, my liege, as I live.

KING HENRY Who serv'st thou under?

WILLIAMS Under Captain Gower, my liege.

FLUELLEN Gower is a good captain, and is good knowledge
and literatured in the wars.

KING HENRY Call him hither to me, soldier.

WILLIAMS I will, my liege.   *Exit*

KING HENRY Here, Fluellen, wear thou this favour for
150 me, and stick it in thy cap. When Alençon and myself
were down together, I plucked this glove from his
helm. If any man challenge this, he is a friend to Alençon,
and an enemy to our person: if thou encounter any such,
apprehend him, an thou dost me love.

FLUELLEN Your grace doo's me as great honours as can
be desired in the hearts of his subjects. I would fain see
the man that has but two legs that shall find himself
aggriefed at this glove, that is all: but I would fain see it
once, and please God of His grace that I might see.

160 KING HENRY Know'st thou Gower?

FLUELLEN He is my dear friend, an please you.

KING HENRY Pray thee go seek him, and bring him to
my tent.

FLUELLEN I will fetch him.   *Exit*

KING HENRY
My Lord of Warwick, and my brother Gloucester,
Follow Fluellen closely at the heels.
The glove which I have given him for a favour
May haply purchase him a box o'th'ear.

It is the soldier's: I by bargain should
Wear it myself. Follow, good cousin Warwick.   170
If that the soldier strike him, as I judge
By his blunt bearing he will keep his word,
Some sudden mischief may arise of it;
For I do know Fluellen valiant,
And, touched with choler, hot as gunpowder,
And quickly will return an injury.
Follow, and see there be no harm between them.
Go you with me, uncle of Exeter.   *Exeunt*

    Enter Gower and Williams   IV.8
WILLIAMS I warrant it is to knight you, Captain.
    Enter Fluellen
FLUELLEN God's will and His pleasure, Captain, I
    beseech you now, come apace to the King. There is
    more good toward you, peradventure, than is in your
    knowledge to dream of.
WILLIAMS Sir, know you this glove?
FLUELLEN Know the glove? I know the glove is a glove.
WILLIAMS I know this; and thus I challenge it.
    He strikes him
FLUELLEN 'Sblood! an arrant traitor as any's in the
    universal world, or in France, or in England!   10
GOWER How now, sir? You villain!
WILLIAMS Do you think I'll be forsworn?
FLUELLEN Stand away, Captain Gower: I will give treason
    his payment into plows, I warrant you.
WILLIAMS I am no traitor.
FLUELLEN That's a lie in thy throat. I charge you in his
    majesty's name, apprehend him: he's a friend of the
    Duke Alençon's.
    Enter Warwick and Gloucester

WARWICK How now, how now, what's the matter?

20 FLUELLEN My Lord of Warwick, here is – praised be
God for it! – a most contagious treason come to light,
look you, as you shall desire in a summer's day. Here is
his majesty.

Enter the King and Exeter

KING HENRY How now, what's the matter?

FLUELLEN My liege, here is a villain and a traitor, that,
look your grace, has struck the glove which your majesty
is take out of the helmet of Alençon.

WILLIAMS My liege, this was my glove, here is the fellow
of it; and he that I gave it to in change promised to wear
30 it in his cap. I promised to strike him if he did. I met
this man with my glove in his cap, and I have been as
good as my word.

FLUELLEN Your majesty hear now, saving your majesty's
manhood, what an arrant, rascally, beggarly, lousy knave
it is. I hope your majesty is pear me testimony and
witness, and will avouchment, that this is the glove of
Alençon that your majesty is give me, in your conscience,
now.

KING HENRY Give me thy glove, soldier. Look, here is the
40 fellow of it.
'Twas I indeed thou promisèd'st to strike,
And thou hast given me most bitter terms.

FLUELLEN An please your majesty, let his neck answer for
it, if there is any martial law in the world.

KING HENRY How canst thou make me satisfaction?

WILLIAMS All offences, my lord, come from the heart:
never came any from mine that might offend your
majesty.

KING HENRY It was ourself thou didst abuse.

50 WILLIAMS Your majesty came not like yourself: you
appeared to me but as a common man – witness the

night, your garments, your lowliness; and what your
highness suffered under that shape, I beseech you take
it for your own fault, and not mine; for had you been
as I took you for, I made no offence: therefore, I beseech your highness, pardon me.

KING HENRY
Here, uncle Exeter, fill this glove with crowns,
And give it to this fellow. Keep it, fellow,
And wear it for an honour in thy cap
Till I do challenge it. Give him the crowns;   60
And, Captain, you must needs be friends with him.

FLUELLEN By this day and this light, the fellow has
mettle enough in his belly. Hold, there is twelve pence
for you, and I pray you to serve God, and keep you out
of prawls, and prabbles, and quarrels, and dissensions,
and I warrant you it is the better for you.

WILLIAMS I will none of your money.

FLUELLEN It is with a good will: I can tell you it will serve
you to mend your shoes. Come, wherefore should you
be so pashful? – your shoes is not so good; 'tis a good   70
silling, I warrant you, or I will change it.

   Enter an English Herald

KING HENRY Now, Herald, are the dead numbered?

HERALD
Here is the number of the slaughtered French.

   He gives him a paper

KING HENRY
What prisoners of good sort are taken, uncle?

EXETER
Charles Duke of Orleans, nephew to the King;
John Duke of Bourbon, and Lord Bouciqualt;
Of other lords and barons, knights and squires,
Full fifteen hundred, besides common men.

KING HENRY
 This note doth tell me of ten thousand French
80 That in the field lie slain. Of princes, in this number,
 And nobles bearing banners, there lie dead
 One hundred twenty-six: added to these,
 Of knights, esquires, and gallant gentlemen,
 Eight thousand and four hundred; of the which,
 Five hundred were but yesterday dubbed knights.
 So that, in these ten thousand they have lost,
 There are but sixteen hundred mercenaries;
 The rest are princes, barons, lords, knights, squires,
 And gentlemen of blood and quality.
90 The names of those their nobles that lie dead:
 Charles Delabreth, High Constable of France,
 Jaques of Chatillon, Admiral of France,
 The Master of the Cross-bows, Lord Rambures,
 Great Master of France, the brave Sir Guichard
   Dauphin,
 John Duke of Alençon, Antony Duke of Brabant,
 The brother to the Duke of Burgundy,
 And Edward Duke of Bar: of lusty earls,
 Grandpré and Roussi, Faulconbridge and Foix,
 Beaumont and Marle, Vaudemont and Lestrake.
100 Here was a royal fellowship of death!
 Where is the number of our English dead?
  The Herald gives him another paper
 Edward the Duke of York, the Earl of Suffolk,
 Sir Richard Kikely, Davy Gam, esquire;
 None else of name; and of all other men
 But five-and-twenty. O God, Thy arm was here!
 And not to us, but to Thy arm alone,
 Ascribe we all! When, without stratagem,
 But in plain shock and even play of battle,
 Was ever known so great and little loss

On one part and on th'other? Take it, God,   110
For it is none but Thine!

EXETER   'Tis wonderful!

KING HENRY

Come, go we in procession to the village:
And be it death proclaimèd through our host
To boast of this, or take that praise from God
Which is His only.

FLUELLEN Is it not lawful, an please your majesty, to tell
how many is killed?

KING HENRY

Yes, Captain, but with this acknowledgement,
That God fought for us.

FLUELLEN Yes, my conscience, He did us great good.   120

KING HENRY

Do we all holy rites:
Let there be sung *Non Nobis* and *Te Deum*,
The dead with charity enclosed in clay;
And then to Calais, and to England then,
Where ne'er from France arrived more happy men.

Exeunt

*

Flourish. Enter Chorus   V

CHORUS

Vouchsafe to those that have not read the story
That I may prompt them; and of such as have,
I humbly pray them to admit th'excuse
Of time, of numbers, and due course of things,
Which cannot in their huge and proper life
Be here presented. Now we bear the King
Toward Calais. Grant him there: there seen,

Heave him away upon your wingèd thoughts
Athwart the sea. Behold, the English beach
10   Pales in the flood with men, with wives, and boys,
Whose shouts and claps outvoice the deep-mouthed sea,
Which like a mighty whiffler fore the King
Seems to prepare his way. So let him land,
And solemnly see him set on to London.
So swift a pace hath thought that even now
You may imagine him upon Blackheath,
Where that his lords desire him to have borne
His bruisèd helmet and his bended sword
Before him through the city. He forbids it,
20   Being free from vainness and self-glorious pride,
Giving full trophy, signal, and ostent
Quite from himself to God. But now behold,
In the quick forge and working-house of thought,
How London doth pour out her citizens:
The Mayor and all his brethren in best sort,
Like to the senators of th'antique Rome,
With the plebeians swarming at their heels,
Go forth and fetch their conquering Caesar in:
As, by a lower but loving likelihood,
30   Were now the General of our gracious Empress –
As in good time he may – from Ireland coming,
Bringing rebellion broachèd on his sword,
How many would the peaceful city quit
To welcome him! Much more, and much more cause,
Did they this Harry. Now in London place him –
As yet the lamentation of the French
Invites the King of England's stay at home.
The Emperor's coming in behalf of France
To order peace between them; and omit
40   All the occurrences, whatever chanced,
Till Harry's back-return again to France.

There must we bring him; and myself have played
The interim, by remembering you 'tis past.
Then brook abridgement, and your eyes advance,
After your thoughts, straight back again to France.

Exit

Enter Fluellen and Gower   V. I

GOWER Nay, that's right; but why wear you your leek
today? Saint Davy's day is past.

FLUELLEN There is occasions and causes why and wherefore in all things. I will tell you ass my friend, Captain
Gower: the rascally, scauld, beggarly, lousy, pragging
knave Pistol – which you and yourself and all the world
know to be no petter than a fellow, look you now, of no
merits – he is come to me and prings me pread and salt
yesterday, look you, and bid me eat my leek. It was in a
place where I could not breed no contention with him;   10
but I will be so bold as to wear it in my cap till I see
him once again, and then I will tell him a little piece of
my desires.

Enter Pistol

GOWER Why, here he comes, swelling like a turkey-cock.

FLUELLEN 'Tis no matter for his swellings nor his turkey-
cocks. God pless you, Aunchient Pistol! you scurvy,
lousy knave, God pless you!

PISTOL

Ha, art thou bedlam? Dost thou thirst, base Troyan,
To have me fold up Parca's fatal web?
Hence! I am qualmish at the smell of leek.   20

FLUELLEN I peseech you heartily, scurvy, lousy knave,
at my desires, and my requests, and my petitions, to eat,
look you, this leek. Because, look you, you do not love
it, nor your affections, and your appetites, and your

digestions, doo's not agree with it, I would desire you to
eat it.

PISTOL

Not for Cadwallader and all his goats!

FLUELLEN There is one goat for you. (*He strikes him*)
Will you be so good, scauld knave, as eat it?

PISTOL

30 Base Troyan, thou shalt die!

FLUELLEN You say very true, scauld knave, when God's
will is. I will desire you to live in the meantime, and
eat your victuals – come, there is sauce for it. (*He strikes
him again*) You called me yesterday mountain-squire,
but I will make you today a squire of low degree. I pray
you fall to – if you can mock a leek, you can eat a leek.

GOWER Enough, Captain, you have astonished him.

FLUELLEN I say, I will make him eat some part of my leek,
or I will peat his pate four days. Bite, I pray you, it is

40 good for your green wound and your ploody coxcomb.

PISTOL Must I bite?

FLUELLEN Yes, certainly, and out of doubt, and out of
question too, and ambiguities.

PISTOL By this leek, I will most horribly revenge – I eat
and eat, I swear –

FLUELLEN Eat, I pray you; will you have some more
sauce to your leek? There is not enough leek to swear
by.

PISTOL Quiet thy cudgel, thou dost see I eat.

50 FLUELLEN Much good do you, scauld knave, heartily.
Nay, pray you throw none away, the skin is good for
your broken coxcomb. When you take occasions to see
leeks hereafter, I pray you mock at 'em, that is all.

PISTOL Good!

FLUELLEN Ay, leeks is good. Hold you, there is a groat to
heal your pate.

PISTOL Me a groat?

FLUELLEN Yes, verily and in truth you shall take it, or I
    have another leek in my pocket which you shall eat.

PISTOL I take thy groat in earnest of revenge.   60

FLUELLEN If I owe you anything, I will pay you in
    cudgels – you shall be a woodmonger, and buy nothing
    of me but cudgels. God bye you, and keep you, and heal
    your pate.   *Exit*

PISTOL
    All hell shall stir for this!

GOWER Go, go, you are a counterfeit cowardly knave.
    Will you mock at an ancient tradition, begun upon an
    honourable respect, and worn as a memorable trophy
    of predeceased valour, and dare not avouch in your
    deeds any of your words? I have seen you gleeking and   70
    galling at this gentleman twice or thrice. You thought,
    because he could not speak English in the native garb,
    he could not therefore handle an English cudgel. You
    find it otherwise, and henceforth let a Welsh correction
    teach you a good English condition. Fare ye well. *Exit*

PISTOL
    Doth Fortune play the housewife with me now?
    News have I that my Doll is dead i'th'spital
    Of malady of France,
    And there my rendezvous is quite cut off.
    Old I do wax, and from my weary limbs   80
    Honour is cudgellèd. Well, bawd I'll turn,
    And something lean to cutpurse of quick hand.
    To England will I steal, and there I'll – steal;
    And patches will I get unto these cudgelled scars,
    And swear I got them in the Gallia wars.   *Exit*

V.2   *Enter, at one door, King Henry, Exeter, Bedford,*
Gloucester, Clarence, Warwick, Westmorland,
Huntingdon, and other Lords; at another, the French
King, Queen Isabel, the Princess Katherine, Alice,
and other French; the Duke of Burgundy and his train

KING HENRY
Peace to this meeting, wherefor we are met!
Unto our brother France, and to our sister,
Health and fair time of day. Joy and good wishes
To our most fair and princely cousin Katherine;
And, as a branch and member of this royalty,
By whom this great assembly is contrived,
We do salute you, Duke of Burgundy;
And, Princes French, and peers, health to you all!

FRENCH KING
Right joyous are we to behold your face,
10   Most worthy brother England: fairly met!
So are you, Princes English, every one.

QUEEN ISABEL
So happy be the issue, brother England,
Of this good day, and of this gracious meeting,
As we are now glad to behold your eyes –
Your eyes which hitherto have borne in them,
Against the French that met them in their bent,
The fatal balls of murdering basilisks.
The venom of such looks, we fairly hope,
Have lost their quality, and that this day
20   Shall change all griefs and quarrels into love.

KING HENRY
To cry 'Amen' to that, thus we appear.

QUEEN ISABEL
You English Princes all, I do salute you.

BURGUNDY
My duty to you both, on equal love,

Great Kings of France and England! That I have
    laboured
With all my wits, my pains, and strong endeavours,
To bring your most imperial majesties
Unto this bar and royal interview,
Your mightiness on both parts best can witness.
Since, then, my office hath so far prevailed
That face to face, and royal eye to eye,   30
You have congreeted, let it not disgrace me
If I demand, before this royal view,
What rub or what impediment there is
Why that the naked, poor, and mangled peace,
Dear nurse of arts, plenties, and joyful births,
Should not in this best garden of the world,
Our fertile France, put up her lovely visage?
Alas, she hath from France too long been chased,
And all her husbandry doth lie on heaps,
Corrupting in it own fertility.   40
Her vine, the merry cheerer of the heart,
Unprunèd dies; her hedges even-pleached,
Like prisoners wildly overgrown with hair,
Put forth disordered twigs; her fallow leas
The darnel, hemlock, and rank fumitory
Doth root upon, while that the coulter rusts
That should deracinate such savagery.
The even mead, that erst brought sweetly forth
The freckled cowslip, burnet, and green clover,
Wanting the scythe, all uncorrected, rank,   50
Conceives by idleness, and nothing teems
But hateful docks, rough thistles, kecksies, burs,
Losing both beauty and utility;
And as our vineyards, fallows, meads, and hedges,
Defective in their natures, grow to wildness,
Even so our houses and ourselves and children

Have lost, or do not learn for want of time,
The sciences that should become our country,
But grow like savages – as soldiers will
60 That nothing do but meditate on blood –
To swearing and stern looks, diffused attire,
And everything that seems unnatural.
Which to reduce into our former favour
You are assembled; and my speech entreats
That I may know the let why gentle peace
Should not expel these inconveniences,
And bless us with her former qualities.

KING HENRY
If, Duke of Burgundy, you would the peace
Whose want gives growth to th'imperfections
70 Which you have cited, you must buy that peace
With full accord to all our just demands,
Whose tenors and particular effects
You have, enscheduled briefly, in your hands.

BURGUNDY
The King hath heard them, to the which as yet
There is no answer made.

KING HENRY   Well then, the peace
Which you before so urged lies in his answer.

FRENCH KING
I have but with a cursitory eye
O'erglanced the articles. Pleaseth your grace
To appoint some of your Council presently
80 To sit with us once more, with better heed
To re-survey them, we will suddenly
Pass our accept and peremptory answer.

KING HENRY
Brother, we shall. Go, uncle Exeter,
And brother Clarence, and you, brother Gloucester,
Warwick, and Huntingdon, go with the King;

And take with you free power to ratify,
Augment, or alter, as your wisdoms best
Shall see advantageable for our dignity,
Anything in or out of our demands,
And we'll consign thereto. Will you, fair sister,   90
Go with the Princes, or stay here with us?

QUEEN ISABEL
Our gracious brother, I will go with them.
Haply a woman's voice may do some good,
When articles too nicely urged be stood on.

KING HENRY
Yet leave our cousin Katherine here with us;
She is our capital demand, comprised
Within the fore-rank of our articles.

QUEEN ISABEL
She hath good leave.
                    Exeunt all but Henry, Katherine, and Alice
KING HENRY   Fair Katherine, and most fair,
Will you vouchsafe to teach a soldier terms
Such as will enter at a lady's ear   100
And plead his love-suit to her gentle heart?

KATHERINE Your majesty shall mock at me; I cannot
speak your England.

KING HENRY O fair Katherine, if you will love me soundly
with your French heart, I will be glad to hear you confess
it brokenly with your English tongue. Do you like me,
Kate?

KATHERINE *Pardonnez-moi*, I cannot tell wat is 'like me'.

KING HENRY An angel is like you, Kate, and you are like
an angel.   110

KATHERINE *Que dit-il? que je suis semblable à les anges?*

ALICE *Oui, vraiment, sauf votre grâce, ainsi dit-il.*

KING HENRY I said so, dear Katherine, and I must not
blush to affirm it.

KATHERINE *O bon Dieu! Les langues des hommes sont*
    pleines de tromperies.

KING HENRY What says she, fair one? that the tongues of
    men are full of deceits?

ALICE *Oui*, dat de tongues of de mans is be full of deceits —
    dat is de *Princesse*.

KING HENRY The Princess is the better Englishwoman.
    I'faith, Kate, my wooing is fit for thy understanding. I
    am glad thou canst speak no better English; for if thou
    couldst, thou wouldst find me such a plain king that
    thou wouldst think I had sold my farm to buy my crown.
    I know no ways to mince it in love, but directly to say,
    'I love you': then if you urge me farther than to say,
    'Do you, in faith?' I wear out my suit. Give me your
    answer, i'faith, do; and so clap hands, and a bargain.
    How say you, lady?

KATHERINE *Sauf votre honneur*, me understand well.

KING HENRY Marry, if you would put me to verses, or to
    dance for your sake, Kate, why, you undid me. For the
    one, I have neither words nor measure; and for the
    other, I have no strength in measure, yet a reasonable
    measure in strength. If I could win a lady at leapfrog,
    or by vaulting into my saddle with my armour on my
    back, under the correction of bragging be it spoken, I
    should quickly leap into a wife. Or if I might buffet for
    my love, or bound my horse for her favours, I could lay
    on like a butcher, and sit like a jackanapes, never off.
    But, before God, Kate, I cannot look greenly, nor gasp
    out my eloquence, nor I have no cunning in protestation:
    only downright oaths, which I never use till urged, nor
    never break for urging. If thou canst love a fellow of this
    temper, Kate, whose face is not worth sunburning, that
    never looks in his glass for love of anything he sees
    there, let thine eye be thy cook. I speak to thee plain

soldier. If thou canst love me for this, take me; if not,
to say to thee that I shall die is true – but for thy love,   150
by the Lord, no – yet I love thee too. And while thou
liv'st, dear Kate, take a fellow of plain and uncoined
constancy; for he perforce must do thee right, because
he hath not the gift to woo in other places. For these
fellows of infinite tongue, that can rhyme themselves
into ladies' favours, they do always reason themselves
out again. What! A speaker is but a prater, a rhyme is
but a ballad. A good leg will fall; a straight back will
stoop; a black beard will turn white; a curled pate will
grow bald; a fair face will wither; a full eye will wax   160
hollow: but a good heart, Kate, is the sun and the moon
– or rather, the sun, and not the moon; for it shines
bright and never changes, but keeps his course truly.
If thou would have such a one, take me; and take me,
take a soldier; take a soldier, take a king. And what
say'st thou then to my love? Speak, my fair, and fairly,
I pray thee.

KATHERINE Is it possible dat I sould love de *ennemi* of
France?

KING HENRY No, it is not possible you should love the   170
enemy of France, Kate; but in loving me you should
love the friend of France, for I love France so well that
I will not part with a village of it – I will have it all mine:
and Kate, when France is mine, and I am yours, then
yours is France, and you are mine.

KATHERINE I cannot tell wat is dat.

KING HENRY No, Kate? I will tell thee in French, which
I am sure will hang upon my tongue like a new-married
wife about her husband's neck, hardly to be shook off.
Je – quand sur le possession de France, et quand vous avez   180
le possession de moi, – let me see, what then? Saint Denis
be my speed! – *donc vôtre est France, et vous êtes mienne.*

It is as easy for me, Kate, to conquer the kingdom as to
speak so much more French. I shall never move thee in
French, unless it be to laugh at me.

KATHERINE *Sauf votre honneur, le français que vous
parlez, il est meilleur que l'anglais lequel je parle.*

KING HENRY No, faith, is't not, Kate; but thy speaking
of my tongue, and I thine, most truly-falsely, must
190 needs be granted to be much at one. But Kate, dost
thou understand thus much English – canst thou love
me?

KATHERINE I cannot tell.

KING HENRY Can any of your neighbours tell, Kate?
I'll ask them. Come, I know thou lovest me; and at
night, when you come into your closet, you'll question
this gentlewoman about me; and I know, Kate, you will
to her dispraise those parts in me that you love with
your heart. But, good Kate, mock me mercifully; the
200 rather, gentle Princess, because I love thee cruelly.
If ever thou beest mine, Kate, as I have a saving faith
within me tells me thou shalt, I get thee with scambling,
and thou must therefore needs prove a good soldier-
breeder. Shall not thou and I, between Saint Denis and
Saint George, compound a boy, half French, half
English, that shall go to Constantinople and take the
Turk by the beard? Shall we not? What say'st thou,
my fair flower-de-luce?

KATHERINE I do not know dat.

210 KING HENRY No, 'tis hereafter to know, but now to
promise. Do but now promise, Kate, you will endeavour
for your French part of such a boy, and for my English
moiety take the word of a king and a bachelor. How
answer you, *la plus belle Katherine du monde, mon
très cher et devin déesse?*

KATHERINE Your majestee 'ave *fausse* French enough to
deceive de most *sage demoiselle* dat is *en France*.

KING HENRY Now fie upon my false French! By mine
honour, in true English, I love thee, Kate: by which
honour I dare not swear thou lovest me, yet my blood   220
begins to flatter me that thou dost, notwithstanding the
poor and untempering effect of my visage. Now beshrew
my father's ambition! He was thinking of civil wars
when he got me; therefore was I created with a stubborn
outside, with an aspect of iron, that when I come to woo
ladies I fright them. But in faith, Kate, the elder I wax,
the better I shall appear. My comfort is, that old age,
that ill layer-up of beauty, can do no more spoil upon
my face. Thou hast me, if thou hast me, at the worst;
and thou shalt wear me, if thou wear me, better and   230
better; and therefore tell me, most fair Katherine, will
you have me? Put off your maiden blushes, avouch the
thoughts of your heart with the looks of an empress,
take me by the hand, and say, 'Harry of England, I am
thine': which word thou shalt no sooner bless mine ear
withal but I will tell thee aloud, 'England is thine,
Ireland is thine, France is thine, and Henry Plantagenet
is thine' – who, though I speak it before his face, if he
be not fellow with the best king, thou shalt find the best
king of good fellows. Come, your answer in broken   240
music – for thy voice is music, and thy English broken;
therefore, Queen of all, Katherine, break thy mind to
me in broken English – wilt thou have me?

KATHERINE Dat is as it shall please de *Roi mon père*.

KING HENRY Nay, it will please him well, Kate – it shall
please him, Kate.

KATHERINE Den it sall also content me.

KING HENRY Upon that I kiss your hand, and I call you
my Queen.

250 KATHERINE *Laissez, mon seigneur, laissez, laissez! Ma foi,*
je ne veux point que vous abaissiez votre grandeur en
baisant la main d'une – notre Seigneur – indigne serviteur.
Excusez-moi, je vous supplie, mon très puissant seigneur.

KING HENRY Then I will kiss your lips, Kate.

KATHERINE *Les dames et demoiselles pour être baisées*
devant leurs noces, il n'est pas la coutume de France.

KING HENRY Madam my interpreter, what says she?

ALICE Dat it is not be de fashion *pour les* ladies of *France* –
I cannot tell wat is *baiser en* Anglish.

260 KING HENRY To kiss.

ALICE Your majestee *entendre* bettre *que moi.*

KING HENRY It is not a fashion for the maids in France to
kiss before they are married, would she say?

ALICE *Oui, vraiment.*

KING HENRY O Kate, nice customs curtsy to great kings.
Dear Kate, you and I cannot be confined within the
weak list of a country's fashion. We are the makers of
manners, Kate, and the liberty that follows our places
stops the mouth of all find-faults – as I will do yours for
270 upholding the nice fashion of your country in denying
me a kiss; therefore, patiently, and yielding. (*He kisses
her*) You have witchcraft in your lips, Kate: there is
more eloquence in a sugar touch of them than in the
tongues of the French Council, and they should sooner
persuade Harry of England than a general petition of
monarchs. Here comes your father.

> *Enter the French King and Queen, Burgundy, and*
> *English and French Lords*

BURGUNDY God save your majesty! My royal cousin,
teach you our Princess English?

KING HENRY I would have her learn, my fair cousin, how
280 perfectly I love her, and that is good English.

BURGUNDY Is she not apt?

KING HENRY Our tongue is rough, coz, and my condition
is not smooth; so that, having neither the voice nor the
heart of flattery about me, I cannot so conjure up the
spirit of love in her that he will appear in his true
likeness.

BURGUNDY Pardon the frankness of my mirth, if I answer
you for that. If you would conjure in her, you must
make a circle; if conjure up love in her in his true likeness, he must appear naked and blind. Can you blame   290
her, then, being a maid yet rosed over with the virgin
crimson of modesty, if she deny the appearance of a
naked blind boy in her naked seeing self? It were, my
lord, a hard condition for a maid to consign to.

KING HENRY Yet they do wink and yield, as love is blind
and enforces.

BURGUNDY They are then excused, my lord, when they
see not what they do.

KING HENRY Then, good my lord, teach your cousin to
consent winking.   300

BURGUNDY I will wink on her to consent, my lord, if you
will teach her to know my meaning: for maids, well
summered and warm kept, are like flies at Bartholomew-
tide, blind, though they have their eyes, and then they
will endure handling, which before would not abide
looking on.

KING HENRY This moral ties me over to time and a hot
summer; and so I shall catch the fly, your cousin, in the
latter end, and she must be blind too.

BURGUNDY As love is, my lord, before it loves.   310

KING HENRY It is so; and you may, some of you, thank
love for my blindness, who cannot see many a fair
French city for one fair French maid that stands in my
way.

FRENCH KING Yes, my lord, you see them perspectively,

the cities turned into a maid; for they are all girdled
with maiden walls, that war hath never entered.

KING HENRY Shall Kate be my wife?

FRENCH KING So please you.

320 KING HENRY I am content, so the maiden cities you talk
of may wait on her: so the maid that stood in the way
for my wish shall show me the way to my will.

FRENCH KING
We have consented to all terms of reason.

KING HENRY
Is't so, my lords of England?

WESTMORLAND
The King hath granted every article:
His daughter first, and then, in sequel, all,
According to their firm proposèd natures.

EXETER
Only he hath not yet subscribèd this:
Where your majesty demands that the King of France,
330 having any occasion to write for matter of grant, shall
name your highness in this form, and with this addition,
in French, *Notre très cher fils Henri, Roi d'Angleterre,
Héritier de France*: and thus in Latin, *Praeclarissimus
filius noster Henricus, Rex Angliae et Haeres Franciae.*

FRENCH KING
Nor this I have not, brother, so denied
But your request shall make me let it pass.

KING HENRY
I pray you then, in love and dear alliance,
Let that one article rank with the rest,
And thereupon give me your daughter.

FRENCH KING
340 Take her, fair son, and from her blood raise up
Issue to me, that the contending kingdoms
Of France and England, whose very shores look pale

With envy of each other's happiness,
May cease their hatred, and this dear conjunction
Plant neighbourhood and Christian-like accord
In their sweet bosoms, that never war advance
His bleeding sword 'twixt England and fair France.

LORDS Amen!

KING HENRY
Now welcome, Kate; and bear me witness all
That here I kiss her as my sovereign Queen.   350
    Flourish

QUEEN ISABEL
God, the best maker of all marriages,
Combine your hearts in one, your realms in one!
As man and wife, being two, are one in love,
So be there 'twixt your kingdoms such a spousal
That never may ill office, or fell jealousy,
Which troubles oft the bed of blessèd marriage,
Thrust in between the paction of these kingdoms
To make divorce of their incorporate league;
That English may as French, French Englishmen,
Receive each other, God speak this 'Amen'!   360

ALL Amen!

KING HENRY
Prepare we for our marriage; on which day,
My Lord of Burgundy, we'll take your oath,
And all the peers', for surety of our leagues.
Then shall I swear to Kate, and you to me,
And may our oaths well kept and prosperous be!

                              Sennet. Exeunt

Epilogue

Enter Chorus

CHORUS

Thus far, with rough and all-unable pen,
  Our bending author hath pursued the story,
In little room confining mighty men,
  Mangling by starts the full course of their glory.
Small time, but in that small most greatly lived
  This star of England. Fortune made his sword,
By which the world's best garden he achieved,
  And of it left his son imperial lord.
Henry the Sixth, in infant bands crowned King
  Of France and England, did this King succeed,
Whose state so many had the managing
  That they lost France, and made his England bleed:
Which oft our stage hath shown; and, for their sake,
In your fair minds let this acceptance take.   *Exit*

An Account of the Text

The earliest text, that of 1600, is a 'bad' Quarto, that is, one derived from Shakespeare's manuscript only by an irregular process resulting in much corruption. Second and third Quartos followed in 1602 and 1619 (misdated 1608); each is a reprint of the first, with even less authority. The first Folio edition (1623) provides the text on which all later reprints have been based. It was set up from Shakespeare's manuscript, though clearer, better punctuated and freer from irregularities than several other texts so derived; Shakespeare may have worked with more care than usual.

The evidence for this authenticity is presented by John Dover Wilson in his 1947 New Cambridge edition. It consists of apparent Shakespearian spellings transmitted into the text (such as 'vp-peer'd' for 'up'ard' (II.3.24), 'Deules' and 'Deule' for 'devils' and 'devil' (II.3.30, 33), 'Moth' for 'mote' (IV.1.174) and 'vawting' for 'vaulting' (V.2.137)), misprints resulting from Shakespeare's kind of script (for instance, 'name' for 'mare' (II.1.22), 'Straying' for 'Straining' (III.1.32), 'Leuitie' for 'lenitie' (III.6.109) and 'nam'd' for 'name' (IV.Chorus.16)). There are variations in the designating of characters, to be expected from an author in the process of composition; the Hostess, for instance, appears as '*Quickly*', '*Hostesse*' and '*Woman*'; Fluellen is sometimes '*Welch*'; '*King*' stands for Henry and for Charles of France – in V.2 there is a mixture of '*King*', '*France*', '*England*' and '*French King*', which needs editorial regularization. Characters may be introduced in stage directions and then given nothing to do in the scene; conversely, others may play a part without having been introduced. There are also stage directions which sound like authorial notes rather than exact instructions (for example, '*Enter two Bishops*' (I.2.6); '*Enter the King and all his Traine before the Gates*' (III.3.0); '*Drum and Colours. Enter the King and his poore Souldiers*' (III.6.84); '*Enter the French Power, and the English Lords*' (V.2.276)). The Folio text, then, is the indisputable authority.

The Quarto text is much shorter, some 1,620 lines as against some 3,380. It omits many passages, three complete scenes (I.1, III.1 and IV.2), and the Prologue, choruses and Epilogue. The surviving verse approximates roughly to that of the Folio, though the sense is often garbled and the metre irregular; at times it is no more than paraphrase. The prose scenes fare still worse; printed in irregular lines capitalized as if verse, they give a scrappy rendering of the corresponding parts of the original, sometimes conveying no more than the gist of the Folio version. The Quarto does, however, furnish some apparently authentic readings lost in the Folio, including two whole lines (II.1.101 and IV.3.48), and it preserves the verse form of Pistol's speeches, nearly all of which the Folio gives as prose (see Collations, below). It also includes several oaths, over and above those which appear in the Folio (see Collations, below). Since the 'copy' for several plays was to varying extents expurgated before the Folio was printed, some of these oaths may have been cut from the authentic text. Nine of them, out of the total of fifteen, come from Fluellen, and this may be significant of a cutting down of his exuberance. Unfortunately, so corrupt is the Quarto text that it is impossible to tell whether Shakespeare or the unauthorized compiler put them into Fluellen's mouth. Some, at least, are probably genuine expressions of his Welsh fieriness, but which cannot be ascertained. (Any expurgation to which *Henry V* may have been subjected was clearly incomplete; many oaths remain, particularly – though not solely – those that are serious and reverent.)

The brevity of the Quarto doubtless owes something to the forgetfulness of those compiling it. The text seems to be a reported one, written down from recitation probably by disloyal actors (the proper course was for the performing company to sell an authentic text to a publisher of its choice, when it judged such a sale advisable). Scholars have tried to assess the degrees of accuracy in various parts of the Quarto so as to ascertain which actors may have been involved, but the discussion has proved inconclusive.

The Quarto's deficiencies probably result also from heavy cutting of the original text to produce a shortened version for a provincial tour – in any case, the full text would need some pruning before it could be staged, though not nearly as much as it gets in the Quarto. This condensation saves eleven acting parts and much acting time. The phrasal changes are botchings to compensate for imperfect memory, and auditory errors resulting from a reporter's mishearings (for example, 'the function' for 'defunction' (I.2.58), 'Inger' for 'Lingare' (I.2.74), 'Foraging' for 'Forage in' (I.2.110), 'England' for 'inland' (I.2.142), 'a thing' for 'a sin' (II.4.74), 'shout' for 'suit' (III.6.76), 'partition' for 'perdition' (III.6.95) and 'de la Brute' for 'Delabreth' (IV.8.91)).

When a reading in the Quarto agrees with that in the Folio this agreement is strong evidence for correctness, since it has survived the hazards of abbreviation, recollection and reporting. Now and then the Quarto offers a better reading than the Folio, but its authority is of the slightest, and the Folio reading must prevail unless clearly erroneous.

COLLATIONS

The following lists are selective, not comprehensive. They include the more noteworthy variants but omit many minor changes which are insignificant in the determination of the true reading, changes such as obvious misprints, trifling omissions, small variations in word order and grammatical details not affecting the sense. Only the more interesting of editorial regularizations of the French passages have been recorded; to collate in full would have meant citing nearly every word. Variants between the first Quarto and first Folio texts, which are very numerous indeed since the Quarto is so irregular, have been noted only when the Quarto variant has been accepted, either in the present or in several earlier editions, or when it is unusually interesting; the interest may lie in its offering a possibly correct alternative to the accepted reading, or in its revealing compositorial vagaries or other operations in textual transmission (auditory errors, verbal alternatives and the like).

When a reading in the text exceeds a word or two, only its opening and closing words are quoted for identification, but the

whole passage is to be taken as representing the variant version.
Q1, Q2 and Q3 mean the first, second and third Quarto editions
(1600, 1602, 1619); F1, F2, F3 and F4 mean the first, second, third
and fourth Folio editions (1623, 1632, 1663–4, 1685). 'J. Dover
Wilson' and 'J. H. Walter' mean the New Cambridge (1947) and
Arden 2 (1954) editions respectively, by those editors.

1 Accepted Q1 Readings

(a) Variants

The following readings in the present text derive from Q1, not
from F1. Each represents the Q1 form in modernized spelling; if,
though derived from Q1, it differs interestingly, the actual Q1
form follows, in brackets. Each Q1 reading is followed by the F1
variant, unmodernized and unbracketed. Later interesting variants, if any, come last, in brackets.

I.2

    183 True:] *not in* F1
    209 several] *not in* F1
    213 End] And

II.1

    22 mare] name
    26 NYM] *not in* F1
        How now, mine host Pistol?] (*Nim.* How do you my
        Hoste? Q1) *In* F1 *this is a continuation of Bardolph's
        speech at 25.*
    69 thee defy] defie thee
    101 NYM I shall have . . . betting?] *not in* F1
    112 came] come

II.2

    147 Henry] *Thomas*
    176 you have] you (you three F2)

II.3

    15 fingers' ends] fingers end

III.6

    30 her] his
    109 lenity] Leuitie

IV.1

> 35 *Qui va là?*] (Ke ve la? Q1) *Che vous la?*
>
> 301 friends] friend

IV.3

> 13–14 And yet . . . valour.] Q1 *locates this correctly, though making Clarence the speaker of lines 12–14 and garbling the text.* F1 *makes this a continuation of Bedford's speech at 11.*
>
> 48 And say, 'These wounds . . . day.'] *not in* F1

IV.5

> 11 Let's die in honour] (Lets dye with honour Q1) Let vs dye in (Let us die instant) (Let's die in harness) (Let's die in arms)
>
> 15 Whilst by a] (Why least by a Q1) Whilst a base

V.1

> 85 swear] swore

(b) Metrical Speeches

The following metrical speeches (from Pistol) appear in Q1 as verse (though sometimes so erratically that the verse form may be accidental) and in F1 as prose. Editors follow Q1 in presenting them as verse, though basing the text on F1. It is not clear in Q1 and F1 whether several one-line speeches are meant as verse or prose. They are given as verse in this edition if they sound histrionic. Metrical speeches which are not in Q1 and which F1 gives as prose are listed on p. 123.

II.1

> 27–9 Base tike, . . . lodgers.
>
> 43–50 'Solus', egregious dog? . . . follow.
>
> 68–76 'Couple a gorge!' . . . enough.
>
> 102–8 A noble . . . hand.

II.3

> 44–53 Come, let's away . . . blood to suck!

III.6

> 20–21 Captain, . . . well.
>
> 24–8 Bardolph, . . . stone –
>
> 38–48 Fortune is . . . requite.

IV.1

    37–8 Discuss unto me, . . . popular?
    44–8 The King's . . . name?

IV.4

    47–8 Tell him . . . take.
    63–4 As I suck blood, . . . me!

V.1

    18–20 Ha, art thou bedlam? . . . leek.
    76–83 Doth Fortune . . . steal;

2 *Accepted Readings Later Than F1*

(a) *Variants*

The following readings in the present text (given first) originate
in editions later than F1; if proposed by a modern editor, they are
identified in brackets. The F1 variant comes next, unmodernized
and unbracketed. Other interesting variants, whether earlier than
F1 or later, come last, in brackets; the sources are given of such
of them as originate in the quartos or the later folios, or in modern
scholarly editions.

I.2

        94 imbare] imbarre (imbace Q1, embrace Q3, imbar F3)
       163 her] their (your Q1)
      208–9 Come to . . . town,] *one line in* F1, 'several' *omitted*

II.1

        34 drawn] hewne (here)
       76–7 enough. | Go to!] enough to go to.
        79 you, Hostess] your Hostesse

II.2

        87 him] *not in* F1
       114 All] And
       139 mark the] make thee
       159 I] *not in* F1

II.3

        16 'a babbled] a Table

II.4

       107 privèd (J. H. Walter)] priuy (pining Q1)

III.Chorus

    4 Hampton] Douer
    6 fanning] fayning

III.1

    7 conjure (J. H. Walter)] commune (summon)
    17 noblest] Noblish (noble)
    24 men] me
    32 Straining] Straying

III.2

    114 hear] heard

III.3

    32 heady] headly (deadly)
    35 Defile] Desire
    54 all. For us, dear uncle,] all for vs, deare Vnckle.

III.4

    7–13 KATHERINE De hand. Et les doigts? . . . les ongles?] F1
        gives to Alice 'Et les doigts?' (*7*), *to Katherine* 'Les
        doigts? Ma foi, j'oublie . . . oui, de fingres' (*8–10*), *to
        Alice* 'La main, de hand . . . le bon écolier' (*11–12*), *and
        to Katherine the remainder.*
    38 N'avez-vous pas déjà] *N'aue vos y desia*

III.5

    11 *Mort Dieu! Ma vie!*] *Mort du ma vie* (Mordeu ma via
        (*at 5*) Q1, mor du (*at 11*) Q1)
    26 Lest poor we (this edition)] Poore we (Poore we may F2)
    46 Knights] Kings

III.7

    12 pasterns] postures
    63 *et la truie*] *est la leuye*

IV.Chorus

    16 name] nam'd
    27 Presenteth] Presented

IV.1

    92 Thomas] *John*
    174 mote] Moth
    226–30 We must . . . enjoy!] *six lines in* F1, *ending* 'beare all. |
        . . . Greatnesse, | . . . sence | . . . wringing. | . . .
        neglect, | . . . enioy?'

238 What is thy soul of adoration?] What? is thy Soule of
   Odoration?

284 if] of (lest); or (J. Dover Wilson)

284–5 numbers | Pluck] numbers: | Pluck

293–5 Toward heaven, . . . do,] *four lines in* F1, *ending* 'blood:
   | . . . Chauntries, | . . . still | . . . doe:'

IV.2

9 dout] doubt

58 guidon. To the field! | I will] Guard: on | To the field,
   I will

IV.4

4 *Calitie* (this edition)] Qualtitie (Quality F4)
   Calen o] calmie

15 Or] for

35 *à cette heure*] asture

51–2 *l'avez promis*] layt a promets

55 *remercîments*] remercious
   suis tombé] intombe

65 *Suivez*] Saaue

IV.6

34 mistful] mixtfull

IV.7

76 their] with (the)

123 'a live] aliue

V.Chorus

10 with wives] Wiues

V.2

12 England] Ireland

50 all] withall

54–5 as . . . wildness,] all . . . wildnesse.

77 cursitory (J. Dover Wilson)] curselarie (cursenary Q1,
   cursorary Q3)

93 Haply] Happily

186–7 *que vous parlez, il est meilleur*] ques vous parleis, il &
   melieus

317 never] *not in* F1

326 then] *not in* F1

(b) Metrical Speeches

The following speeches (mostly from Pistol) have been arranged as verse by editors, though they are given as prose in F1. There is either nothing or very little in Q1 to correspond to them. Metrical speeches given as verse in Q1 but as prose in F1 are listed on p. 119–20.

II.1

  64–5 Give me thy fist, ... tall.

 118–19 Nym, ... corroborate.

II.3

  3–6 No, for my manly heart ... therefor.

III.2

  6–10 The plainsong ... fame.

  14–19 If wishes ... bough.

  22–5 Be merciful, ... chuck!

IV.1

  54–5 Tell him ... day.

IV.4

  4–5 *Calitie!* ... Discuss.

  7–11 O Signieur Dew ... ransom.

  14–16 Moy shall not ... blood!

  19–21 Brass, cur? ... brass?

  23–5 Say'st thou ... name.

  37–9 *Owy,* ... sword.

(c) Act and Scene Divisions

Q1 has no act and scene divisions at all. F1 has '*Actus Primus. Scæna Prima*' before I.1 but marks no later scenes. It puts '*Actus Secundus*' before III.Chorus, '*Actus Tertius*' before IV.Chorus, '*Actus Quartus*' before IV.7 and '*Actus Quintus*' before V.Chorus. Editors have amended the act divisions and inserted scene numbers as in the present text.

(d) Stage Directions

The wording of the stage directions in this text follows as closely as practicable that in F1. Amendments and additions have been made only when necessary to clarify the action or to assimilate the entry and exit directions to it. The following stage directions, introduced by editors, differ sufficiently from those of F1 to qualify

for recording; added *Exits* and *Exeunts*, when self-evident, are
not listed, nor are characters' names when these merely regularize
entry and exit directions. The reading in the present text is given
first, that of F1 second.

I.2

   6 *Enter the Archbishop . . . Ely*] *Enter two Bishops.*
  222 *Exeunt some attendants*] *not in* F1

II.1

   33 *Nym draws his sword*] *not in* F1
   42 *He sheathes his sword*] *not in* F1
   59 *They both draw*] *not in* F1
   62 *He draws*] *not in* F1
   63 *Pistol and Nym sheathe their swords*] *not in* F1
   97 *He sheathes his sword*] *not in* F1
  108 *Nym sheathes his sword*] *not in* F1

II.2

  181 *Exeunt Cambridge, Scroop, and Grey, guarded*] *Exit.*

II.3

   56 *He kisses her*] *not in* F1

II.4

   67 *Exeunt Messenger and certain lords*] *not in* F1

III.2

   21 *He drives them forward*] *not in* F1
   27 *Exeunt all but the Boy*] *Exit.*
   53 *Enter Fluellen, Gower following*] *Enter Gower.*

III.3

   0 *Some citizens . . . walls.*] *not in* F1.

IV.1

  222 *Exeunt Soldiers*] *Exit Souldiers.* (*after 217*)

IV.8

   73 *He gives him a paper*] *not in* F1
  101 *The Herald gives him another paper*] *not in* F1

V.1

 33–4 (*He strikes him again*)] *not in* F1

V.2

 271–2 (*He kisses her*)] *not in* F1
  276 *Enter the French King . . . Lords*] *Enter the French Power,*
     and the English Lords.

3 Rejected Variants

The following list contains some of the more interesting and important variants (whether earlier or later than F1) and proposed emendations not accepted in the present text. The reading of this edition is (unless otherwise identified) that of F1, modernized; it is followed by the rejected variants, unmodernized. The sources are given of such variants as originate in the quartos or later folios or in modern scholarly editions. When no source is given, the reading is one proposed by an earlier editor which has not gained general acceptance. Only a small selection of the very numerous Q1 variants is offered.

I.1

    49 wonder] wand'rer

I.2

    72 find] fine Q1

    99 man] sonne Q1

    112 pride] power Q1

    142 Our inland] your *England* Q1

    165 sumless] shiplesse Q1

    166 ELY] *Lord* Q1, WESTMORLAND

    173 'tame] spoyle Q1, tear, taint

    175 crushed] curst Q1, crude

    199 kneading] lading Q1

    208 Come] flye Q1

    234 waxen] paper Q1

    244 is] are Q1

    255 spirit] study Q1

II.Chorus

    20–21 But see, thy fault France hath in thee found out, | A nest] But see thy fault! France hath in thee found out | A nest

    31 we'll] well

    32 distance, force] distance while we force

II.1

    49 take] talke Q1

    49–50 Pistol's cock is up, | And flashing fire will follow] *Pistolls* flashing firy cock is vp Q1

II.1

    80 face] nose Q1
   111 that's] (that F1) theres Q1

II.2

   118 tempered] tempted

II.3

    14 play with] talk of Q1
    24 knees,] knees, and they were as cold as any stone Q1
    39 hell] hell fire Q1
    50 *Caveto*] cophetua Q1
    59 Adieu!] adieu. | *Pist.* Keepe fast thy buggle boe. Q1

II.4

    57 his mountain] his mounting, his mighty

III.5

    15 Where] whence Q1
    54 captive chariot] chariot, captive (J. Dover Wilson)

III.6

    59 FLUELLEN Very good.] *Flew.* That is very well. | *Pist.*
        I say the fig within thy bowels and thy durty maw. |
        Exit Pistoll. | *Fle.* Captain *Gour*, cannot you hear it
        lighten & thunder? Q1
    76 suit] shout Q1

III.7

    14 *chez*] *qui a, avec*

IV.1

    65 fewer] lewer Q1, lower Q3

IV.3

    44 shall see] outliues ⎫ *These* Q1 *variants occur in the*
        and live] and sees ⎭ *corresponding line (41).*
   105 crasing] grazing
 128–9 thou wilt once more come again for a ransom] thou'lt
        once more come again for ransom

IV.4

    64 Follow me] Follow me cur Q1

IV.5

    14 base pander] bace leno Q1
    16 contaminated] contamuracke Q1
    18 our lives] our liues | Vnto these English, or else die
        with fame Q1

IV.6

    15 He cries] And cryde Q1
        my] deare Q1

  37–8 kill his prisoners! | Give the word through.] kill his
        prisoner. | *Pist.* Couple gorge. Q1

IV.8

  79–111 KING HENRY This note . . . Thine!] Q1 *gives this passage*
        as a continuation of Exeter's speech but prefixes 'Exe.'
        also to ''Tis wonderful' (111). Q3 *continues lines 79–99*
        to Exeter ('This note . . . Lestrake') *and then gives lines*
        100–101 to the King ('Here was . . . dead?'), *lines 102–*
        5 to Exeter ('Edward the Duke of York . . . five and
        twenty') *and lines 105–11 to the King* ('O God, . . .
        Thine!').

   123 enclosed] enterred Q1

V.1

    77 Doll] Nell (*see Commentary*)

V.2

  180–82 *Je – quand sur le possession . . . mienne.*] Let me see,
        Saint *Dennis* be my speed. | Quan *France* et mon. |
        Kate. Dat is, when *France* is yours. | *Harry.* Et vous
        ettes amoy. | *Kate.* And I am to you. | *Harry.* Douck
        France ettes a vous: | *Kate.* Den *France* sall be mine. |
        Harry. Et Ie suyues a vous. | *Kate.* And you will be to
        me. Q1

   222 untempering] untempting

   252 *d'une – notre Seigneur – indigne*] (*d'une nostre Seigneur*
        indignie F1) d'une vostre indigne d'une de votre
        seigneurie indigne

4 Oaths

The following list shows the oaths that occur in Q1 but not in F1;
the F1 reading, which is that also of the present text, is given first,
modernized. On this difference between the two texts, see p. 116.
A few more oaths occur in parts of Q1 to which nothing in F1
corresponds.

II.1

    28 Now by this hand] Now by gads lugges

II.3

> 7 Would I were with him] God be with him
> 40 Well] Well, God be with him

III.2

> 3 Pray thee] Before God
> 20 Up to the breach] Godes plud vp to the breaches

III.6

> 3 I assure you, there is] By Iesus thers
> 13 in my very conscience] by Iesus
> 62 I'll assure you] By Iesus
> 102 but his nose] But god be praised, now his nose

IV.1

> 76 If the enemy] Godes sollud [*sic*], if the enemy
> 88–9 I think we shall never see] God knowes whether we shall see
> 192 You pay him then] Mas youle pay him then

IV.7

> 1 Kill the poys] Godes plud kil the boyes
> 66 How now, what means] Gods will what meanes

IV.8

> 62 By this day and this light] By Iesus

V.1

> 38 I say] by *I*esu

V.2

> 272 You have witchcraft] Before God *Kate*, you have witchcraft

5 Stage Directions in Q1 and F1

The following are the more interesting of the stage-direction variants between Q1 and F1. The Q1 directions are given before the square bracket, F1 after.

I.2

> 0 *Enter King* Henry, Exeter, 2. *Bishops*, Clarence, *and other Attendants.*] *Enter the King, Humfrey, Bedford, Clarence, Warwick, Westmerland, and Exeter. (after 6˙) Enter two Bishops.*

II.1

23 *Enter* Pistoll *and Hostes Quickly, his wife.*] *Enter Pistoll,
    & Quickly.*

II.2

0   *Enter Exeter and Gloster.*] *Enter Exeter, Bedford, &
    Westmerland.*

11 *Enter the King and three Lords.*] *Sound Trumpets. Enter
    the King, Scroope, Cambridge, and Gray.*

II.4

0   *Enter King of* France, Bourbon, Dolphin, *and others.*]
    *Flourish. Enter the French King, the Dolphin, the Dukes
    of Berry and Britaine.*

III.2

21 *Enter* Flewellen *aud* [sic] *beates them in.*] *Enter Fluellen.*

27 (*after 53*) *Exit* Nim, Bardolfe, Pistoll, *and the Boy.*]
    (*after 27*) *Exit.*

III.3

0   *Enter the King and his Lords alarum.*] *Enter the King and
    all his Traine before the Gates.*

III.4

0   *Enter* Katherine, Allice.] *Enter Katherine and an old
    Gentlewoman.*

III.5

0   *Enter King of* France *Lord Constable, the Dolphin, and*
    Burbon.] *Enter the King of France, the Dolphin, the
    Constable of France, and others.*

III.6

0   *Enter* Gower.] *Enter Captaines, English and Welch,
    Gower and Fluellen.*

84 *Fnter* [sic] *King*, Clarence, Gloster *and others.*] *Drum
    and Colours. Enter the King and his poore Souldiers.*

III.7

0   *Enter* Burbon, Constable, Orleance, Gebon.] *Enter the
    Constable of France, the Lord Ramburs, Orleance,
    Dolphin, with others.*

IV.1

34 *Enter the King disguised, to him* Pistoll.] (*at 1*) *Enter the
    King, Bedford, and Gloucester.* (*at 34*) *Enter Pistoll.*

IV.1

83 *Enter three Souldiers.*] *Enter three Souldiers, Iohn Bates,*
    Alexander Court, and Michael Williams.

IV.3

0 *Enter* Clarence, Gloster, Exeter, *and* Salisburie.] *Enter*
   Gloucester, Bedford, Exeter, Erpingham with all his
   Hoast: Salisbury, and Westmerland.

78 *Enter the Herald from the French.*] *Tucket. Enter Montioy.*

IV.4

0 *Enter Pistoll, the French man, and the Boy.*] *Alarum.*
   Excursions. Enter Pistoll, French Souldier, Boy.

IV.5

0 *Enter the foure French Lords.*] *Enter Constable, Orleance,*
   Burbon, Dolphin, and Ramburs.

IV.6

0 *Enter the King and his Nobles,* Pistoll.] *Alarum. Enter*
   the King and his trayne, with Prisoners.

IV.7

52 *Enter King and the Lords.*] *Alarum. Enter King Harry*
    and Burbon with prisoners. Flourish.

V.2

0 *Enter at one doore, the King of* England *and his Lords.*
   And at the other doore, the King of France, *Queene*
   Katherine, *the Duke of* Burbon, *and others.*] *Enter at one*
   doore, King Henry, Exeter, Bedford, Warwicke, and other
   Lords. At another, Queene Isabel, the King, the Duke of
   Bourgongne, and other French.

98 *Exit King and the Lords. Manet,* Hrry [*sic*], Katherine,
    and the Gentlewoman.] *Exeunt omnes. Manet King and*
    Katherine.

276 *Enter the King of France, and the Lordes.*] *Enter the French*
     Power, and the English Lords.

Genealogical Tables

Table 1: Henry V and the Throne of France

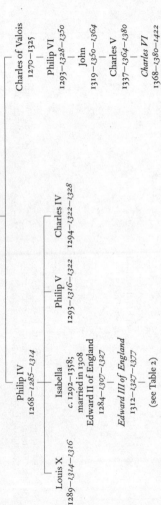

Philip III
1245–1270–1285

Philip IV
1268–1285–1314

Charles of Valois
1270–1325

Louis X
1289–1314–1316

Philip V
1293–1316–1322

Charles IV
1294–1322–1328

Isabella
c. 1292–1358;
married in 1308
Edward II of England
1284–1307–1327

Edward III of England
1312–1327–1377

(see Table 2)

Philip VI
1293–1328–1350

John
1319–1350–1364

Charles V
1337–1364–1380

Charles VI
1368–1380–1422

Louis the Dauphin
1396–1415

Katherine
1401–38;
married in 1420
Henry V of England
1387–1413–1422;
married c. 1428
Owain Tudwr

Charles VII
1403–1422–1461

NOTE: Names in italics are those of persons in or closely relevant to the play. Italicized dates are those of reigns; other dates are those of births and deaths. Collateral kindred irrelevant to Henry's claim to the French crown have been omitted; nor has any attempt been made to illustrate the Archbishop's Salic Law speech. The 'Lewis the Tenth' of that speech (1.2.77) was in fact Louis IX, not the Louis X shown above. The point at issue between the kings of France and those of England was whether the latter, descending from Philip IV through Isabella (the senior line), had a stronger claim than the descendants of Charles of Valois (the junior line). When Louis X died in 1316, Isabella was debarred by law from succeeding and from transmitting the right to succeed, whereupon her younger brothers succeeded and then her cousin, Philip VI.

Table 2: Claimants to the Throne of England

Edward III 1312–*1327*–1377

1	2	3	4	5	6	7
Edward, the Black Prince 1330–76	William of Hatfield d. infancy	Lionel, Duke of Clarence 1338–68	John of Gaunt, Duke of Lancaster 1340–99	Edmund Langley, 1st Duke of York 1341–1402	Thomas of Woodstock, Duke of Gloucester 1355–97 (murdered, probably on Richard II's order)	William of Windsor d. infancy
Richard II 1367–*1377*–1400		Philippa 1355–c. 1380; married in 1368 Edmund Mortimer, 3rd Earl of March 1351–81	*Henry IV* 1367–*1399*–1413	*Richard, Earl of Cambridge* d. 1415; executed for conspiracy		
		Roger Mortimer, 4th Earl of March 1374–98	*Henry V* 1387–*1413*–1422	Richard Plantagenet, 3rd Duke of York 1411–60		
	Edmund Mortimer, 5th Earl of March 1391–1425; declared heir presumptive to Richard II in 1398	Anne 1388–c. 1413	*Henry VI* 1421–*1422*–*1461*–1471 deposed 1461, restored 1470, again deposed 1471 and murdered	Edward IV 1442–*1461*–1483	George, Duke of Clarence 1449–78	Richard III 1452–*1483*–1485

NOTE: Names in italics are those of persons in or closely relevant to the play. Italicized dates are those of reigns; other dates are those of births and deaths. Collateral kindred irrelevant to claims under lines 3, 4 and 5 have been omitted. The contest arose from the fact that Richard II should have been succeeded not by the Lancastrian Henry IV but by Edmund Mortimer. The Yorkist Richard, Earl of Cambridge, married Mortimer's sister Anne and conspired against Henry V to seat the childless Mortimer on the throne and thereafter have his own descendants succeed – this is the motive very obliquely hinted at in II.2.155–7.

Commentary

The chief sources of the play are the chronicles of Raphael Holinshed and, to a lesser extent, Edward Hall. References here are to the following editions: Holinshed's *Chronicles of England, Scotland, and Ireland* (2nd edn, 1587), vol. III; Hall's *Union of the Two Noble and Illustre Families of Lancaster and York* (1548). Biblical quotations are from the Bishops' Bible (1568, etc.), the official English translation of Elizabeth's reign.

The Characters in the Play: No list of these is provided in the first Quarto (Q) or the first Folio (F). Many editions omit the Duke of Clarence and the Earl of Huntingdon, since, though they are passingly addressed in the final scene (V.2.84–5), neither is given anything at all to say. They are included here as having at least an action to perform, whereas Talbot, mentioned at IV.3.54, says and does nothing whatever, and so is omitted from this list.

The action takes place in England and France.

Prologue

The speeches of the Chorus are not in Q.

0 *Flourish*: Fanfare. F has flourishes before Acts II and III only; they are inserted here before each act for uniformity.

1 *a Muse of fire*: Inspiration as brilliant and aspiring as the brightest and highest of the four 'elements' (earth, water, air and fire). Cf. III.7.20–21. Drayton described Marlowe's poetic 'raptures' as 'All air, and fire' (*Epistle to Henry Reynolds, Esquire, Of Poets and Poesie*).

2 *invention*: (1) Imagination *or* (2) the discovery or

thinking up of material and arguments (known as 'topics') with which to persuade, the first and principal of the five parts of classical rhetoric. The terminal -*ion* is pronounced as two syllables.

3–4 *A kingdom ... swelling scene*: The Chorus wishes that it could re-enact historical events on their former scale and with a cast on a social par with the originals for an audience composed exclusively of monarchs so that the performance could match the epic grandeur of its subject.

4 *swelling*: Magnificent, stately, majestic.

5 *warlike*: Martial, courageous.

like himself: In his own manner, i.e., in a heroic manner in keeping with Henry's greatness.

6 *port*: Bearing.

7 *Leashed in*: A 'leash' was a trio of dogs on a lead.

famine, sword, and fire: In Holinshed, the archbishop urges Henry to wage war with blood, sword and fire, and replying to the French ambassador Henry threatens to do so. The presentation of the king here perhaps echoes Henry's declaration, when besieging Rouen, 'that the goddess of battle, called Bellona, had three handmaidens, ever of necessity attending upon her, as blood, fire, and famine' (Holinshed, p. 567); similarly *Henry VI, Part I*, IV.2.11: 'lean famine, quartering steel, and climbing fire'.

8 *gentles*: Gentlewomen and gentlemen (a complimentary form of address, as many playgoers would have been socially ranked below the gentry).

9 *flat*: Dull, lifeless.

unraisèd: Unanimated, uninspired (a denigrating reference to the actors); with wordplay on the raising of supernatural *spirits* through magical incantations.

hath: Plural nouns with singular verbs, and vice versa, are frequent in Elizabethan English.

10 *scaffold*: Stage.

11 *cockpit*: Round theatre (the *wooden O* of 13). Shakespeare may refer to the existing Curtain Theatre or to the Globe, which was under construction while he was writing the play.

12 *vasty*: Spacious.

15–16 *a crookèd figure . . . a million*: Like the additional nought or zero which turns 100,000 into 1,000,000.

15 *crookèd*: Curved (*figure* refers apologetically to the stage actor).

17 *ciphers*: Figures of no value.
    account: (1) Sum total *or* (2) narrative.

18 *imaginary forces*: (1) Powers of imagination *or* (2) imaginary armies.

19 *girdle*: Confines.

22 *perilous*: Pronounced as 'parlous' (two syllables).
    narrow ocean: I.e., the English Channel.

23 *Piece out . . . thoughts*: I.e., make our imperfect theatrical re-enactment go further by supplementing what you see on stage with your thoughts.

25 *imaginary puissance*: (1) Fictional armed force *or* (2) power of imagination.

28 *deck our kings*: Adorn our supposed kings like real ones.

30 *many years*: The play covers events between 1414 and 1420.

31 *for the which supply*: To assist you and reinforce your efforts (of imagination).

32 *Chorus*: Commentator.

33 *Prologue-like*: In the obsequious manner of a prologue-speaker. The second prologue in Heywood's *Four Prentices of London* (1615) asks, 'Do you not know that I am the Prologue? Do you not see this long black velvet cloak upon my back?', suggesting that prologue-speakers may have worn such a cloak as one of the conventional signs of their role.

I.1

The scene is omitted in Q, which begins with Exeter's line at I.2.2.

1 *That self bill*: The self-same, the very same bill in Parliament.

3 *like*: Likely.

4 *scambling*: Turbulent. Because of civil disorders, a bill proposed by Lollard lords to dispossess the clergy was withdrawn from Parliament in 1413.

5   *question*: Consideration.

8   *our possession*: What we possess.

9   *temporal*: Secular.

10   *By testament*: In their wills.

14   *esquires*: Candidates for knighthood, attending on a
     knight.

15   *to relief*: For the relief.
     lazars: Lepers.

16   *indigent*: Poor, needy.
     corporal toil: Physical labour.

22   *grace*: (1) God's grace, in two related senses: the favour
     of God as manifest in the salvation of sinners, and the
     divine influence which inspires virtuous impulses *or* (2)
     social grace. 'Favour' and 'charm' are less likely here,
     but the prelates' ensuing discussion of Henry's 'refor-
     mation' and its relation to his rhetorical skill brings all
     three senses into play.
     fair regard: Good, just intentions.

26   *mortified*: Accepted word for the old sinning self
     (*th'offending Adam*, 29) dying before the onset of grace.
     The Archbishop uses many biblical and theological
     phrases.

28   *Consideration*: (1) Spiritual self-examination *or* (2) atten-
     tive thought. The former sense is primary at this point,
     but by 63–9 the bishops are agreed that Henry delib-
     erately *obscured his contemplation* | *Under the veil of wild-
     ness*. In *Henry IV, Part I*, I.2.192–214, Henry announces
     that he will reject his Eastcheap companions and sets
     out the political considerations that guide his actions.

28–31 *like an angel ... spirits*: Like the angel sent by God to
     drive the sinning Adam – and Eve – out of Eden or
     Paradise, which thereafter was left to blessed spirits
     only (see Genesis 3:23–4).

34   *heady currance*: Impetuous, violent current.

35   *Hydra-headed*: Manifold and proliferating. The Hydra
     was a many-headed monster encountered by Hercules;
     two heads grew to replace each head that was cut off,
     unless a burning brand was thrust into the stump.

36   *seat*: Throne, power.

38 *reason in divinity*: Henry, according to Holinshed, was an able theological disputant; he argued matters of faith with the Lollard Sir John Oldcastle, imprisoned for heresy (p. 544).

43 *List*: Listen to (imperative).

44 *fearful*: Frightful.

45 *cause of policy*: Political question.

46 *Gordian knot*: Seemingly insoluble problem. The peasant Gordius devised so intricate a knot that, tradition held, whoever undid it would rule over Asia. Alexander cut it with his sword. By implication, Henry outdoes Alexander by untying it easily.

47 *Familiar as his garter*: As if it were as commonplace to untie as his garter (a band tied around the leg to keep the stocking from falling down).

48 *chartered*: Licensed.
   libertine: One free to roam, unrestricted; associated with licentiousness.

50 *sentences*: Pithy sayings, maxims.

51–2 *the art . . . this theoric*: Practical skill and experience must govern his theoretical knowledge.

55 *companies*: Companions.
   unlettered: Illiterate, uneducated.
   rude: Synonymous with unlettered.

56 *riots*: Unruly revels.
   sports: Entertainments, amusements.

58–9 *sequestration . . . popularity*: Keeping aloof from places of common resort and from mixing with the people.

60–62 *The strawberry . . . quality*: The Bishops of Ely had a celebrated strawberry garden in Holborn, referred to in *Richard III* (III.4.32–3). T. Hill's *Profitable Arte of Gardeninge* (1572) observes that '[s]trawberry . . . aptly groweth in shadowy places, and rather joyeth under the shadow of other herbs, than by growing alone'; and Montaigne describes refined plants as growing best near coarse ones, since the latter absorb the 'ill savours' of the ground (*Essays*, III.9).

66 *crescive in his faculty*: Growing in accordance with its natural capacity.

70 *mitigation*: Moderating (the severity).

72 *indifferent*: Impartial.

74 *exhibiters*: Proposers of the bill.

76 *Upon*: On behalf of.

77 *causes*: Matters of concern.

85 *fain*: Gladly.

86 *severals*: Details.

   unhidden passages: Clear lines of descent.

88 *generally*: With no exceptions.

89 *Edward*: I.e., Edward III.

95 *embassy*: Message committed to an ambassador.

I.2

2 *presence*: Present. (See also II.4.111.)

4 *cousin*: The word is often used loosely for 'kinsman', but in fact Westmorland was Henry's cousin by marriage.

   would be resolved: Desire to be freed from uncertainty.

8 *become*: (1) Grace, adorn *or* (2) occupy with fitting grace, honour.

10 *justly*: Accurately.

   religiously: Faithfully, scrupulously.

   unfold: Reveal, explain.

11 *the law Salic*: The supposed law by which the crown of France could descend only through males. *Edward III* (I.1.11–41) also has a discourse on the Salic law in relation to Edward's claim to France.

12 *our claim*: Henry laid claim to the French throne through his descent from Isabella, daughter of Philip IV of France and mother of Henry's great-grandfather, Edward III.

13 *faithful*: Religious.

14 *fashion, wrest, or bow*: Shape, pervert the meaning, distort.

   reading: Interpretation.

15 *nicely . . . soul*: Sophistically burden your soul with guilt by knowingly misrepresenting the case.

16 *With opening titles miscreate*: By setting out falsely invented titles.

17 *native*: Natural.

19 *drop their blood*: I.e., be injured or die.

approbation: Putting to the proof.

20 *incite*: Induce, encourage. (This is an example of the ambiguous diction that marks this diplomacy.)

21 *impawn*: Pledge, commit (by offering a guarantee of moral justification).

26–8 *sore complaint ... brief mortality*: Grave accusation against him who wrongfully wages war, so destroying the brief lives of men. The question of who bears moral responsibility in a war is debated by the disguised Henry and his soldiers on the night before Agincourt, IV.1.84–222.

29 *conjuration*: Solemn appeal.

33–95 *Then hear me ... progenitors*: This address follows Holinshed (pp. 545–6) very closely. It is notable that all three of the historical examples the archbishop cites of monarchs who laid claim to the French crown through the female line were either usurpers or, like Henry V, the heir to a usurper (see 65, 69, 72–3, 78).

37 *Pharamond*: Legendary king of the Salian Franks.

40 *gloze*: Gloss.

42 *female bar*: Bar against inheritance through the female line (the basis of Henry's claim).

45 *floods*: Rivers.

46 *Charles the Great*: Charlemagne, king of the Franks and Holy Roman Emperor (AD 742?–814).

49 *dishonest*: Unchaste.

57 *four hundred one-and-twenty years*: Shakespeare retains Holinshed's faulty arithmetic unaltered (see 61–4). The actual date was AD 379.

58 *defunction*: The death.

62 *seat*: Settle, establish.

66 *heir general*: Legal heir whether through male or female line.

72 *find*: Provide.
    shows: Specious appearances.

74 *Conveyed himself*: Passed himself off.

75 *Charlemain*: Hall and Holinshed, followed by Shakespeare, give this name in error for Charles II, also known as Charles the Bald.

77 *Lewis the Tenth*: An error, in Holinshed and Shakespeare, for Lewis the Ninth. Hall records the correct thirteenth-century king of France.

82 *lineal*: A direct descendant.

86 *as clear as is the summer's sun*: Proverbial. (The line often provokes audience laughter.)

88 *satisfaction*: I.e., of the lineage of his grandmother, Queen Isabel.

    appear: Are plainly seen.

93 *hide them in a net*: I.e., try to conceal what is plain to see.

94 *amply to imbare*: (1) Fully lay bare *or* (2) openly invalidate.

95 *progenitors*: Ancestors.

99–100 *When the man ... daughter*: Numbers 27:8 reads: 'If a man die and have no son, ye shall turn his inheritance unto his daughter.' Shakespeare omits 'and have no son'.

103 *great-grandsire*: Edward III, whose son the Black Prince won a famous victory at Crécy in 1346.

108 *on a hill*: Holinshed tells how Edward III watched from 'a windmill hill' (p. 372) as the Black Prince waged the battle of Crécy; the play of *Edward III* treats the incident (III.5.1–2).

114 *for action*: For the want of action.

119 *thrice-puissant*: Triply powerful for the reasons outlined at 117–19.

120 *the very May-morn of his youth*: Henry was 27; the prime of youth (the Roman '*juventus*') was held to be between 20 and 35.

123–4 *rouse yourself ... former lions*: To 'rouse' was a hunting term for disturbing a large animal from its lair, as in *Henry IV, Part I*, 'rouse a lion' (I.3.196); *Titus Andronicus*, 'rouse the proudest panther' (II.2.21); Marlowe, *Tamburlaine the Great, Part One*, 'As princely lions when they rouse themselves' (I.2.52).

126 *So hath your highness*: So indeed you *have* (with emphasis on *hath*).

129 *pavilioned*: Tented.

136–9 *We must not ... all advantages*: Henry turns from the moral and legal justifications for war to the pragmatic

matter of ensuring the safety of his kingdom. In
Holinshed it is Westmorland, Warden of the Northern
Marches, who first raises the threat posed by the Scots.

140 *marches*: The border territories.

145 *still*: Constantly.

151 *gleanèd*: Stripped (of defenders).
    assays: Assaults.

155 *feared*: Frightened.

156 *hear her ... herself*: Listen to the examples she (i.e.,
    England) can provide from her own history.

160 *taken and impounded as a stray*: Taken to the pound like
    a stray animal.

161–2 *The King of Scots ... prisoner kings*: King David II of
    Scotland was captured at Neville's Cross in 1346 while
    the main English army was in France. A story circu-
    lated, not in fact true, that he was sent to Edward III's
    camp at Calais, and the supposed episode occurs in the
    play of *Edward III* (V.1.63).

166–73 *But ... eat*: In Q this is spoken by '*Lord*', in F by the
    Bishop of Ely. The corresponding speech in Holinshed
    is by Westmorland, and in *The Famous Victories* both
    the archbishop and the Earl of Oxford have versions
    of it. In view of this uncertainty it seems best to follow
    F, though many editors change to Westmorland.

169 *in prey*: In search of prey.

173 *'tame*: Attame, broach, break into.

175 *Yet ... necessity*: Yet the conclusion that that is neces-
    sary is a forced one.

177 *pretty*: Cunning.

180–83 *For government ... like music*: Sir Thomas Elyot uses this
    commonplace analogy between music and government
    in *The Boke named The Governour* (1531): 'In everything
    is order, and without order may be nothing stable or
    permanent: and it may not be called order, except it do
    contain in it degrees, high and base, according to the
    merit or estimation of the thing that is ordered' (Bk 1,
    ch. 1), and 'music, ... how necessary it is for the better
    attaining the knowledge of a public weal: which ... is
    made of an order of estates and degrees, and by reason

thereof containeth in it a perfect harmony' (Bk 1, ch. 7).

181–2 *parts ... consent ... close*: These are musical terms for the separate melodies combining in a concluding cadence; *consent* unites the senses of 'agreement' and 'concent' (singing together). There may be an echo of Lyly's *Euphues* (1580; see also note to 187 below), for, telling how bees delight in 'sweet and sound Music', Lyly says they are called the Muses' birds, 'because they follow not the sound so much as the consent' (*Works* (1902), ed. Bond, II.44).

182 *Congreeing*: Coming together, agreeing.

186 *butt*: Archery target.

187 *honey-bees*: Elyot, in *The Governour* (Bk 1, ch. 2), uses the bee to illustrate the need for a just ruler and obedient subjects and describes the ordered hive in a way which anticipates Shakespeare. The political analogy of the beehive in Lyly's *Euphues* is more detailed; he tells how the commonwealth of bees 'live under a law' and 'choose a King'. 'They call a parliament, wherein they consult for laws, statutes, penalties, choosing officers, and creating their king', and 'every one hath his office, some trimming the honey, some working the wax, one framing hives, another the combs'. They 'keep watch and ward, as living in a camp to others', and their King 'goes up and down, entreating, threatening, commanding' (*Works*, ed. Bond, II.44–5). Shakespeare's bees are still more anthropomorphic, performing all the functions of citizens. The analogy can be traced back to Virgil's *Georgics* (Bk 4) and Pliny's *Natural History* (Bk 11).

188–9 *Creatures ... kingdom*: Elyot describes the bee as 'left to man by nature, as it seemeth, a perpetual figure of a just governance or rule' (*The Governour*, Bk 1, ch. 2).

190 *king*: Aristotle's assumption that the hive was ruled by a male bee stood uncorrected until 1586; however, the discovery that the hive was ruled by a 'queen' bee appears to have reached England only in 1609 with the printing of Charles Butler's *The Feminine Monarchy*.
sorts: Different ranks.

194 *Make boot*: Take booty, plunder.

200 *mechanic*: Engaged in manual labour, an artisan.

203 *executors*: Executioners.

207 *loosèd several ways*: Shot from several directions.

211 *dial's*: Sundial's.

215 *happy*: Fortunate.

217 *withal*: With that.

  Gallia: Gaul, i.e., France.

220 *worried*: Shaken, savaged (as by a dog; see also II.2.83).

221 *hardiness and policy*: Courage and statesmanship.

222 *Dauphin*: Title given to the eldest son of the King of France.

225 *bend it to our awe*: Force it to fear and respect our authority.

234 *Not ... epitaph*: Not honoured with even the most perishable memorial.

243 *grace*: (1) Majesty *or* (2) spiritual virtue (as being a *Christian* king).

253 *galliard*: Dance (in lively triple time).

255 *meeter*: More fitting.

256 *tun*: A large cask, barrel or chest.

262 *rackets*: (1) Tennis rackets *or* (2) noises (of gunfire).

264 *crown*: (1) Coin *or* (2) royal crown.

  hazard: (1) An opening in the wall of a tennis court into which if the ball was struck it was unplayable *or* (2) jeopardy.

265 *wrangler*: (1) Opponent *or* (2) quarrelsome disputant.

266 *courts*: (1) Tennis courts *or* (2) royal courts.

267 *chases*: (1) Tennis balls that the opponent fails to return before the second bounce (in 'real' tennis the nearness of the second impact to the end wall of the court determines the score) *or* (2) hunts *or* (3) pursuits of enemy forces.

271 *hence*: I.e., away from the court.

274 *keep my state*: (1) Retain my throne *or* (2) maintain the ceremonies of royalty.

275 *show my sail of greatness*: Unfurl the sail of my greatness, fully display my power.

278 *like a man for working-days*: I.e., like a common labourer.

279 *I will rise ... glory*: The metaphor is the frequent sun

image of royalty.

282 *pleasant*: Humorous.

283 *gun-stones*: Cannon balls (originally made of stone).

284 *chargèd*: Burdened.

288 *ungotten*: Not yet conceived.

294 *well-hallowed*: Sanctified, much blessed.

305 *proportions*: Monies and troops appointed.

308 *God before*: With God leading us.

II.*Chorus*

2 *silken dalliance*: (1) Luxurious clothing *or* (2) effeminate idleness.

6 *the mirror of all Christian kings*: The epithet conflates *A Mirror for Magistrates* (1559) and Erasmus's *Institutio Principis Christiani* (*Education of a Christian Prince*, 1516). Hall calls Henry the 'mirror of Christendom' (p. lxxxiᵛ), Holinshed 'a lode-star in honour' (p. 583; cf. Epilogue.6: *This star of England*) and 'mirror of magnificence' (p. 583).

   mirror: An exemplar or model.

7 *wingèd heels, as English Mercuries*: I.e., swiftly. Mercury (Hermes, in Greek), the messenger of Jove, herald of the gods and patron of traders and thieves, was represented with winged sandals, a winged hat and a purse.

9 *hilts*: Crosspiece at the base of the blade that guards the hand. Since the hilt was made of several parts it was often spoken of in the plural, as also at II.1.61.

10 *coronets*: Lesser crowns worn by the nobility (cf. *Henry VI, Part I*, V.4.134 and *Julius Caesar*, 1.2.236).

12 *intelligence*: Information obtained by spying.

13 *preparation*: Pronounced as five syllables.

14 *pale policy*: Cowardly and ineffectual intrigue prompted by fear (see 20–30).

16 *model*: Image in miniature.

19 *kind*: The senses of 'filial' and 'loving' are combined.

26 *gilt*: Gold, with wordplay on 'guilt'.

27 *fearful*: Frightened.

28 *this grace of kings*: This king who most honours the title (an echo, perhaps, of Chapman, *Seaven Bookes of the Iliades of Homere* (1598): 'with her [Chryseis] the grace

of kings | wise Ithacus ascended too' (Bk I, sig. C2ʳ)).

31–2 *digest . . . distance*: (1) Stomach the flouting of unity of place (as the action moves to Southampton) *or* (2) swallow the insult caused by the Chorus's abuse of proper social distance.

32 *force a play*: Produce a play by cramming its events into a small compass. (The metre is defective, suggesting corruption.)

41–2 *But till . . . our scene*: This couplet looks like an afterthought as it contradicts 35; possibly the chorus ended with the rhymed couplet at 39–40 and was followed by scene 2, scene 1 being inserted later and the extra couplet being added to explain the delay in reaching Southampton. The inclusion of the Eastcheap scene enables Shakespeare to dispose of Falstaff before the king embarks for France and establishes another group that, like the bishops, has a monetary motive for supporting Henry's war (see II.1.106–7), contradicting the Chorus's claim at 3–4.

II.1

0 *Corporal Nym*: Notable for his small stature and hairiness, Nym is not in the *Henry IV* plays. His first appearance is as one of Falstaff's followers in *The Merry Wives of Windsor*, I.1. 'To nim' is an archaic slang term meaning 'to steal', 'to take'; cf. the pun at 105.

Lieutenant Bardolph: Bardolph first appears in *Henry IV, Part I*, II.2; he is a corporal in *Henry IV, Part II* and becomes one again at III.2.3. As a lieutenant he is ranked above his confederates, Corporal Nym and 'Ancient' (Ensign) Pistol (see 3 below).

3 *Ancient*: Ensign, standard-bearer. Thomas Digges in *Stratioticos* (1579) defines the qualifications of an ensign, and Pistol should be measured against these:

above all other [he ought] to have honourable respect of his charge, and to be no less careful and jealous thereof, than every honest and honourable gentleman should be of his wife . . . Let the Ensign be a man of good account, honest and virtuous (pp. 93–4).

3 *Pistol*: Pronounced 'pizzle', with wordplay on 'penis'.

5–6 *that shall be as it may*: Proverbial. Nym's comic speech is marked by the tedious repetition of banal proverbs.

6 *wink*: Close my eyes.

7 *iron*: Sword, with phallic wordplay.
   what though: What of that.

8 *endure cold*: When not hot (toasting cheese) it stays cold (with inactivity).

9 *there's an end*: I.e., that's that, with wordplay on 'penis'.

11 *sworn brothers*: Faithful comrades (in thieving; strictly, companions-in-arms sworn to the laws of chivalry).

15 *rest*: I.e., resolve (a card-playing term meaning the final stake in the game).
   rendezvous: Refuge, retreat; Nym misuses the term to mean last resort.

18 *troth-plight*: Engaged to marry. (A mutual pledge to marry was contractually more binding than the modern engagement.)

22–3 *though patience . . . plod*: Horses were proverbially tired; Nym may be making a veiled threat of eventual revenge on Pistol.

26 *How now, mine host Pistol*: In F this forms the end of Bardolph's speech, but Q allots the corresponding words to Nym, and he rather than the inoffensive Bardolph seems the proper target of Pistol's wrath.
   host: (1) Innkeeper *or* (2) pimp (Pistol picks up on the latter sense).

27–9 *Base tike . . . lodgers*: F gives most of Pistol's verses as prose (see Collations, pp. 119–20, 123).

27 *tike*: (1) A mongrel *or* (2) a variant spelling of the modern 'tick' (parasite).

29 *keep lodgers*: (1) Rent out rooms *or* (2) run a brothel.

30 *troth*: Faith.

32 *honestly*: (1) Respectably, lawfully *or* (2) chastely. The Hostess intends the former but her comic idiom is the unwitting obscenity. In this play, as in *Henry IV, Part II*, she is given to self-contradictory remarks.
   by the prick . . . needles: The unconscious sexual innuendo begun by *honestly* and *board* culminates in an

unwitting pun on *prick* ('penis') and on *needles*
('vaginas').

33 *bawdy-house*: Brothel.

   straight: Straightaway.

34 *Lady*: I.e., by Our Lady (the Virgin Mary).

   drawn: Refers to Nym's sword being out, with wordplay on his penis being erect.

36 *Lieutenant*: As an ensign, Pistol was in effect a sub-
lieutenant; at III.6.12 he is *aunchient lieutenant*.

39 *Iceland dog*: Nym is evidently shaggy: 'Iceland dogs,
curled and rough all over, . . . by reason of the length
of their hair, make show neither of face nor of body'
(A. Fleming, *Of English Dogges* (1576)). They were
kept as lap-dogs, so a sexual slur compounds the insult.

   prick-eared: (1) Pointy-eared *or* (2) bearing a cuckold's
horns (popularly the sign of a man whose wife had
committed adultery).

40–41 *put up your sword*: The repeated drawing and sheathing
of swords comically underscores the sexual rivalry of
Pistol and Nym.

42 *shog off*: Go away.

   solus: Alone (theatre Latin). Pistol, a shaky linguist,
takes it as an insult; or he may take Nym to mean 'I'd
prefer you unmarried' (cf. 70).

43 *egregious*: Outrageous.

44 *mervailous*: F's form is worth retaining as more fitting
to the metre than 'marvellous'. The spelling may be
Shakespeare's normal one (similar spellings occur in
other of his plays) or it may represent Pistol's idio-
syncratic diction.

46 *perdy*: I.e., by God (French, '*par dieu*').

49 *take*: (1) Take offence, or take fire *or* (2) strike *or* (3)
perform sexually.

   cock is up: (1) Trigger is cocked *or* (2) penis is erect.

51 *Barbason*: This also occurs in *The Merry Wives of
Windsor* (II.2.283) among 'the names of fiends'; it is of
uncertain origin. Reginald Scot's *Discoverie of
Witchcraft* (1584) names among principal devils one
'Marbas, *alias* Barbas', who 'appeareth in the form of

a mighty lion; but at the commandment of a conjuror cometh up in the form of a man and answereth fully as touching anything which is hidden or secret' (p. 378). Shakespeare may have half-recalled this.

conjure: Exorcize. (Pistol's threats at 43–8 sound like the rigmaroles used for conjuring or exorcizing devils.)

53 *foul*: (1) Abusive *or* (2) dirty (the pistol barrel after firing) *or* (3) syphilitic (syphilis was known as 'the foul disease').

scour: (1) Thrash *or* (2) clean out (Nym will run his sword through Pistol as if it were a scouring rod) *or* (3) with connotations of vigorous sex.

rapier: Sword with a light, sharply tipped blade used for thrusting.

54 *in fair terms*: (1) Not in foul terms, like Pistol *or* (2) thoroughly.

55 *prick*: Stab, with sexual wordplay on phallic penetration.

57 *wight*: Person.

59 *exhale*: Draw (a Pistolian extravagance; used normally of the sun drawing phosphorescent vapours from the earth).

61 *run him up to the hilts*: I.e., run him straight through with my sword.

63 *mickle*: Much.

64 *fist . . . forefoot*: Hand, paw.

65 *tall*: Valiant.

68 *Couple a gorge*: Pistol intends '*couper la gorge*' or '*coupez la gorge*' ('Cut the throat!'), a French catchphrase he uses again at IV.4.37. The cutting of French throats features prominently at Agincourt.

70 *hound of Crete*: (1) Another shaggy dog insult, like *Iceland dog* (II.1.39) *or* (2) a reference to the ancient proverb 'all Cretans are liars'.

71 *spital*: Charitable hospital for treating the poor, especially lepers.

72 *powdering tub*: (1) Vat for salting meat *or* (2) sweating tub used in treating venereal disease (colloquial).

73 *lazar kite of Cressid's kind*: Leprous scavenging whore.

Leprosy was thought of as a venereal disease. In Henryson's *Testament of Cresseid* (written in the late fifteenth century; printed 1532), the God of Love strikes the faithless Cressida with leprosy; 'kites of Cressid's kind' was a proverbial phrase, kites being birds of prey. In *Henry IV, Part II*, Doll is hauled off to prison for brothel violence with Pistol.

74 *Doll Tearsheet*: She first appears in *Henry IV, Part II*, II.4. Doll was a name commonly used for a prostitute and Tearsheet is suggestive of vigorous sex.

   espouse: Marry.

75 *quondam*: Former (Latin).

76 *pauca*: 'Few', from the Latin tag *'pauca verba'* ('in few words').

77 *Enter the Boy*: The Boy is Falstaff's page, given him by Prince Hal in *Henry IV, Part II* (I.2.13).

78 *my master*: I.e., Falstaff (Henry's dissolute companion in *Henry IV, Parts I* and *II*).

81 *warming-pan*: Mocking reference to Bardolph's red nose and face, inflamed from drinking.

83 *yield the crow a pudding*: Die (proverbial phrase originally applied to a dead animal whose flesh the crows would peck; *pudding* = stuffed guts, as in 'black pudding').

84 *King has killed his heart*: On becoming king, Henry publicly rejected Falstaff (see *Henry IV, Part II*, V.5.50).

85 *presently*: At once.

92 *Base is the slave that pays*: Proverbial. *Base* = poor, low (lacking in spirit, money).

94 *As manhood shall compound*: In the way a brave man settles such differences.

97 *Sword*: Punning on ''s word' (by God's word), a common oath.

98 *an*: If.

101 *I shall have ... betting*: Not in F, but editors supply it from Q as necessary to Pistol's reply.

102 *noble*: Coin worth one-third of a pound sterling or six shillings and eight pence (less than Pistol owes, but with the advantage of *present pay*).

106 *sutler*: Provision-seller. Pistol does not in fact figure in this lucrative role.

107 *camp*: Military camp.

114 *quotidian tertian*: A quotidian fever recurred daily, a tertian every other day. The Hostess may be in a characteristic verbal muddle; alternatively, Taylor cites John Jones, *A Dial for all Agues* (1586), ch. 16, to show her diagnosis may be correct as it was thought different fevers could mix together to form 'compound agues', the worst and most fatal of these being when the tertian and quotidian fevers 'be joined in one'.

116 *run bad humours on*: Upset by his displeasure. Lines 116–21, in which the king is blamed for Falstaff's illness, are absent from Q.

117 *even*: Plain truth.

119 *fracted and corroborate*: Broken and healed (strictly strengthened). Pistol's fondness for Latinate terms results in nonsense.

121 *passes some humours and careers*: Lets himself go when he feels like it. To 'pass the career' in horsemanship was to do a short gallop at full stretch.

122 *condole*: Express condolences to.
   we will live: Despite Pistol's assurance and high hopes, Bardolph, Nym and the Boy are all dead by the end of Act IV.

II.2

3 *smooth and even*: Unperturbedly and calmly.

8 *bedfellow*: Close friend. It was not remarkable for friends to share a bed. Iago claims to have done so with Cassio in *Othello*, III.3.410. In *The Life of Sir John Oldcastle, Part I* (1599) Scroop is identified as Henry's bedfellow and proposes to assassinate him while he is in bed (l. 2095).

9 *dulled*: Blunted his appetite.
   cloyed: Satiated with sweetness.

10 *for a foreign purse*: I.e., a French bribe. Holinshed records the French bribe but also notes that Cambridge supported Mortimer's lineal right to the English crown. No explicit mention is made of this political motive in

the scene. See note to 155–7.

14 *gentle*: Noble (of gentle birth).

17 *execution*: Act of destruction, killing.

18 *in head*: As an armed force.

20–24 *I doubt ... on us*: Henry shows considerable compo-
sure and skill as an actor and a rhetorician as he lays a
trap for the traitors, who are lulled into a false sense
of security by his seemingly benign pronouncements.

22 *grows not in a fair consent*: Is not in total agreement.

25 *feared*: Held in awe, revered.

30 *galls*: Literally 'gall bladders', but here used to mean
bitterness of spirit (thought to have its source in the
gall bladder).

33 *the office*: I.e., how to use.

34 *quittance*: Due recompense.

40 *Enlarge*: Release.

43 *more advice*: Thinking better of it.

44 *security*: Over-confidence, complacency.

46 *sufferance*: Pardoning.

53 *orisons*: Prayers.

54 *on distemper*: From a disordered condition (in this case,
drunkenness).

55 *winked at*: Proverbially, small faults are or should be
winked at.
stretch: Open wide. If small faults are not allowed to
pass unregarded, then calculated treason must provoke
more than wide-eyed horror.

61 *late commissioners*: Those lately appointed regents to
rule England during the king's absence. This ploy of
handing out sealed papers of 'commission' is not in the
sources.

74 *paper*: I.e., paper-white.

79 *quick*: Alive.

83 *As dogs upon their masters*: Proverbial. The phrase recalls
the tale of Actaeon: transformed into a stag by Diana
after he glimpsed her bathing, the unfortunate hunter
was then chased and killed by his own hunting hounds.
worrying: Biting.

85 *English monsters*: The conspirators' treachery is the

more 'monstrous' because they are *English*; *monsters* were commonly shown as exotic marvels.

87 *appertinents*: Things appertaining, things appropriate.

90 *practices*: Plots.

92 *bounty*: (Kingly) generosity.

98 *coined me into gold*: I.e., used me to make as much money as you wished.

99 *practised on*: Plotted against.

103 *off as gross*: Out as plainly.

107 *grossly*: Openly, blatantly.

a natural cause: I.e., natural for *devils* but monstrous for humans.

108 *That admiration . . . them*: That wonder was beyond the power to exclaim.

109 *proportion*: Natural order.

112 *preposterously*: Unnaturally. The rhetorical figure of *hysteron proteron* or 'the preposterous' involves a (verbal) reversal or exchange of place and was associated by English Renaissance rhetoricians with a trespass against 'natural' order and hierarchy (see Patricia Parker, *Literary Fat Ladies: Rhetoric, Gender, Property* (1987), pp. 67–9).

113 *voice*: Vote.

114 *suggest*: Tempt.

115 *botch and bungle up damnation*: Clumsily disguise the damnable deeds they incite to.

116 *patches*: (1) Pieces of cloth (used to cover a hole) *or* (2) fools, rogues.

colours: (1) Outward appearances *or* (2) excuses, pretexts.

forms: Likenesses, outward appearances.

118 *he that tempered thee*: I.e., the tempting devil that moulded you to his will.

stand up: Rebel, make a stand.

119 *instance*: Motive.

120 *dub thee . . . traitor*: Knight you with the title 'traitor', parodying the act of a king knighting a subject by touching (dubbing) him on the shoulder.

121 *gulled*: Fooled.

122 *his lion gait*: His devil's stride (an echo of 1 Peter 5:8: 'Be sober, and watch, for your adversary the devil, as a roaring lion walketh about seeking whom he may devour').

123 *vasty*: Wide and waste (the two senses are combined). *Tartar*: Tartarus (the hell of classical mythology).

126 *jealousy*: Suspicion.

127 *affiance*: Trust.

133 *blood*: One of the four 'humours' of Renaissance medical theory. The source of the 'vital spirits', the hot and moist humour of the 'blood' was thought to provoke passionate and lustful behaviour.

134 *complement*: (1) Outward attributes of the 'complete' gentleman *or* (2) courtesy.

136 *purgèd*: Purified.

137 *bolted*: Sifted, refined.

139 *full-fraught*: Fully laden, packed (with virtues). *endued*: Endowed.

151 *discovered*: Revealed.

155–7 *For me ... intended*: Holinshed records that the plotters received bribes from the French king but notes that Cambridge was motivated by a desire to make the legitimate Yorkist claimant, Edmund Mortimer, Earl of March (the Mortimer of *Henry VI* and *Henry IV*), king. Cambridge's heirs would then have been next in line in the succession. The political motive is explained in *Henry VI, Part III*, I.1, especially 25–7.

155–60 *For me ... pardon me*: These lines, in which Cambridge hints at a political motive, are absent from Q.

159 *sufferance*: Suffering the penalty.

166 *quit*: Acquit.

169 *earnest*: Part-payment in advance.

175 *tender*: Hold dear.

181 *dear*: Dire.

183 *like*: Equally.

184 *fair*: Just, favourable. *lucky*: Fortunate.

188 *rub*: Obstacle (a bowling term).

190 *puissance*: Power.

191 *expedition*: Speedy motion (pronounced as five syllables).

192 *signs*: Ensigns, banners.

   advance: (1) Raise *or* (2) move forward.

II.3

2 *Staines*: Town with a bridge over the Thames, about
  seventeen miles from London on the road to
  Southampton.

3 *earn*: Yearn, grieve.

4 *blithe*: Merry, joyous.

   rouse thy vaunting veins: Raise your lively (*vaunting* =
   boasting) spirits, i.e., take heart.

6 *earn*: (1) Grieve *or* (2) make money.

9 *Arthur's*: Abraham's (cf. Luke 16:22: 'the beggar died,
  and was carried by the angels into Abraham's bosom').
  The Hostess merges the biblical heaven with the
  Arthurian Isle of Avalon, whither her knightly patron
  has gone to join the company of the Round Table.

10 *'A*: He.

11 *a finer end*: As fine an end as can be imagined (and
   certainly finer than going to hell).

   an: As if.

   christom: Newly christened (and so in perfect inno-
   cence). The Hostess amalgamates 'christen' and
   'chrisom', a chrisom child being one dying within a
   month of birth, during which time it wore the white
   chrisom cloth put on it at its christening. Bunyan's Mr
   Badman is reported to have 'died like a lamb, or, as
   they call it, like a chrisom child' (*The Life and Death
   of Mr Badman* (1680), p. 346).

12 *between twelve and one*: Between midnight and one in
   the morning.

13 *turning o'th'tide*: There is an ancient and widespread
   belief that a man at the point of death will die as the
   flood tide turns to the ebb.

13–17 *fumble ... fields*: Similar details are listed as symptoms
   of approaching death from the *Prognostics* of
   Hippocrates onwards. Dover Wilson cites Thomas
   Lupton, *A Thousand Notable Things* (1578): 'If the

forehead of the sick wax red, and his nose wax sharp,
if he pull straws or the clothes of his bed, these are
most certain tokens of death' (Bk IX). Taylor cites
a similar passage (A4ᵛ) in Peter Lowe's *The Whole
Course of Surgery, whereunto is annexed the Presages of
Hippocrates* (1597).

16–17 *'a babbled of green fields*: This reading, originated by
Theobald (1733), for F's *a Table of greene fields* is
perhaps the most famous of Shakespeare emendations.
Q reads *talk of floures*.

22–3 *I put . . . stone*: Emrys Jones, *The Origins of Shakespeare*
(p. 20), suggests the passage parodies Plato's account
of the death of Socrates in the *Phaedo*: 'And the man
who gave the poison . . . pressed his foot hard, and asked
him if he could feel; and he said "No"; and then his
leg, and so upwards and upwards, and showed us that
he was cold and stiff' (*The Four Socratic Dialogues of
Plato*, trans. B. Jowett (1903), p. 273). However, no
English translation of the *Phaedo* was available at the
time and this nineteenth-century translation may have
been influenced by the account of Falstaff's death.

25 *all . . . stone*: Inadvertently suggesting 'penis' ('awl')
and 'testicle' ('stone'), another example of the Hostess's
unwittingly sexual turn of phrase.
   as cold as any stone: Proverbial.

26 *of*: Against. Falstaff is making his *finer end* by repenting
his excesses.
   sack: White wine from Spain and the Canary Islands.

30 *incarnate*: In human form.

34 *handle*: Discuss (with an inadvertently sexual sense).

35 *rheumatic*: Literally, suffering from catarrh, but in this
instance a malapropism for lunatic, delirious; in *Henry
IV, Part II* she calls Falstaff and Doll 'as rheumatic as
two dry toasts' (II.4.54–5), though the 'rheumatic
humour' was in fact cold and damp. There is also a pun
on 'Rome-atic' (see note to 35–6 below).

35–6 *the Whore of Babylon*: Roman Catholic Church (in the
Protestant interpretation of Revelation 17:3–9: 'great
Babylon, the mother of whoredom and abominations

of the earth', a scarlet woman drunk with the blood of
the martyrs and riding a seven-headed beast symbol-
izing seven mountains on which she sits). This no doubt
put *rheumatic* into the Hostess's mind ('Rome' being
pronounced 'room').

40 *fuel*: I.e., alcohol provided by Falstaff.

41 *riches*: There is play on the normal sense and on 'rich'
as red(-faced, -nosed). Cf. *Henry IV, Part I*: 'Look
upon his face. What call you rich? Let them coin his
nose' (III.3.76–7); and Thomas Lodge, *A Looking
Glasse for London* (1594): 'You and I have been tossing
many a good cup of ale, your nose is grown very rich'
(ll. 1870–72).

42 *shog*: Be off.

45 *chattels . . . movables*: Personal possessions other than
real estate.

46 *Let senses rule*: Keep your wits about you, but may also
mean 'let your sensual desires govern your actions'.
Pitch and pay: Pay as you go, cash down, no credit
(proverbial).

48 *straws*: Proverbially worthless.
wafer-cakes: (Flimsy as) thin pastry.

49 *Holdfast is the only dog*: This echoes the punning
proverb: 'Brag is a good dog, but Holdfast is a better.'
(A 'brag' = a large nail; a 'holdfast' = a clamp or bolt;
and a 'dog' = a vice or clamp.)
duck: Term of endearment.

50 *Caveto*: 'Beware' (Latin imperative).

51 *clear thy crystals*: Wipe your eyes.
Yoke-fellows: Companions.

54 *And that's but unwholesome food*: Cf. Andrew Boorde,
Dyetary of Helth (1542): 'The blood of all beasts and
fowls is not praised, for it is hard of digestion' (ch.
xvii).

58 *housewifery*: Thifty housekeeping (pronounced
'hussif'ry').
Keep close: (1) Stay indoors *or* (2) be chaste.

59 *Farewell! Adieu*: This is the last we see of the Eastcheap
company in its familiar haunts.

II.4

0 *Berri*: Never speaks and need not be present on the two occasions he is referred to (II.4.4, III.5.41); however, an attendant lord is required. Taylor notes that Orleans, who features later in the play, is often substituted for Berri in performance.

Britaine: Brittany, Bretagne. Shakespeare's spelling indicates the required pronunciation.

Constable: The Lord Constable was the head of the royal household and commander-in-chief of the army in the absence of the king.

1 *Thus comes . . . us*: Following immediately upon the exit of Pistol and his crew these words can produce a comic-satiric effect.

7 *line*: Strengthen.

10 *gulf*: Whirlpool (cf. IV.3.82).

11 *provident*: Forward-thinking.

12 *late examples*: I.e., recent French defeats, notably at Crécy (1346) and at Poitiers (1356).

13 *fatal and neglected*: Fatally underrated.

14 *redoubted*: Respected.

25 *Whitsun*: Whit Sunday, the seventh Sunday after Easter and the beginning of the festal week of Whitsuntide.

Whitsun morris-dance: Folk dances known as morris dances were held at Whitsuntide or on May Day (1 May) as spring festivities; the performers commonly blackened their faces to make them look like Moors and wore bell-hung costumes. The name refers to their supposed Moorish origin.

28 *humorous*: Capricious.

31 *late*: Recent.

34 *modest in exception*: Reasonable in raising objections.

36 *vanities forespent*: Former frivolities (previously used up).

37 *Brutus*: Lucius Junius Brutus feigned stupidity ('*brutus*' = 'stupid' in Latin) to dupe his enemies while plotting to expel the tyrannous Tarquinius Superbus, last king of Rome; he became one of the first consuls, in 509 BC.

38 *coat of folly*: Coat of motley worn by the fool or jesters.

39 *ordure*: Manure.

40 _delicate_: Fine (in quality) and sensitive.

45 _So ... filled_: Thus the necessary defensive forces are fully provided.

46 _Which of_: Which (defence) if on.

projection: Scale.

47 _scanting_: Economizing on.

50 _fleshed_: Given their first taste of blood. Hounds and hawks used in hunting were given a taste of their prey to excite their interest in the chase.

52 _haunted_: Pursued (a hunting term).

54 _Crécy battle_: Edward, the Black Prince, won the battle of Crécy (1346) under the watchful gaze of his father, Edward III (see note to 57 below). Cf. Holinshed, p. 551.

56 _black name ... Black Prince_: Compares Edward, the Black Prince, to the devil. Cf. _All's Well That Ends Well_: 'The black prince, sir, alias the prince of darkness, alias the devil' (IV.5.40–41).

57 _mountain sire_: _mountain_ may be an error for 'mountant' by attraction from _mountain standing_. Edward III (Henry's great-grandfather) was in the ascendant at Crécy and watched the battle from a nearby hill (cf. note to I.2.108). _mountain_ suggests a man 'of more than human stature' who is 'as immovable as a mountain'.

64 _fate_: Destiny, with the suggestion that Henry may be destined to be fatal to the French.

68 _chase is hotly followed_: Hunt is eagerly pursued.

69 _Turn head_: Stand at bay (a hunting term), i.e., turn and face your pursuers.

69–71 _coward dogs ... them_: Proverbial.

70 _spend their mouths_: Bark energetically, as in _Venus and Adonis_:

> The hot scent-snuffing hounds are driven to doubt,
> Ceasing their clamorous cry till they have singled,
> With much ado, the cold fault cleanly out;
> Then do they spend their mouths. (ll. 692–5)

72 _short_: Abruptly, on a short lead.

83 _ordinance of times_: Time-honoured law, tradition.

85 *sinister*: (1) Illegitimate (in heraldry the bar or bend sinister indicated bastardy) *or* (2) deceitful (literally, 'left-handed').

awkward: Oblique, perverse.

88–90 *this most . . . pedigree*: Exeter presents a document setting out the king's lineage.

89 *demonstrative*: Making evident, illustrative.

90 *overlook*: Look over, scrutinize.

91 *evenly derived*: Directly descended.

94 *indirectly*: Crookedly, wrongfully.

95 *native*: Natural and rightful ('by right of birth').

challenger: Claimant.

99 *fierce*: Two syllables.

100 *Jove*: The Greek Zeus, Roman Jupiter or Jove, was lord of the heavens, ruler of gods and men. His weapon was the thunderbolt.

101 *requiring*: Demanding.

102 *in the bowels of the Lord*: For the love of Christ. The phrase originates in Philippians 1:8 ('in the bowels of Jesus Christ'), but here is carried over from Holinshed: '[Henry] exhorted the French king in the bowels of Jesus Christ, to render him that which was his own, whereby effusion of Christian blood might be avoided' (p. 548).

107 *privèd*: Deprived, bereaved; Q has *pining*.

121 *at large*: (1) In full *or* (2) as yet unsettled.

124 *womby vaultages*: Hollow recesses.

126 *second accent*: Echo.

ordinance: (1) Artillery *or* (2) lawful decree.

129 *odds*: (1) A quarrel *or* (2) a bet.

131 *Paris balls*: Tennis balls (so called because the game came to England from Paris).

132 *Louvre*: Palace in Paris.

133 *mistress court*: Principal royal and tennis court. Exeter makes plain that Henry will forcibly remind the *mistress court* who is the *master* if Henry's claim to the French crown is not duly acknowledged.

136 *greener*: Less mature.

140 *Flourish*: To mark the French king's rising.

143 *is footed . . . already*: Has already set foot. Historically,
   Henry did not invade France until 14 August 1415, some
   six months after Exeter's embassy.

III.*Chorus*

1 *imagined wing*: Wing of imagination.

2–3 *no less . . . thought*: 'As swift as thought' (proverbial).

4 *well-appointed*: Well-equipped.
   Hampton: Southampton. F's *Dover* is at odds with the
   sources and with Act II but is consistent with the later
   references to Dover and the unlikelihood of the
   compositor mistaking *Hampton* for *Dover*. However,
   this edition adopts Theobald's correction on the
   grounds that the army has been placed in Southampton
   in II.Chorus.30, II.2.91 and II.3.42–3; and in
   Holinshed the army lands near Harfleur. There
   appears to have been some geographical confusion on
   Shakespeare's part, as the Boy will later report that
   Nym and Bardolph have been in Calais (III.2.45) and
   at III.3.56 Henry proposes to retire from Harfleur to
   Calais. Dover is a more sensible embarkation port for
   a crossing to Calais.

5 *brave*: Splendid, finely decked (in the *silken streamers*
   of the next line).

6 *the young Phoebus fanning*: Fluttering against the early
   morning sun. Phoebus was the Roman sun god, *young
   Phoebus* suggests the rising sun.

7 *fancies*: Imaginations.

9 *whistle*: I.e., of the ship's master or boatswain.

10 *threaden*: Made of linen thread.

12 *bottoms*: I.e., ships (literally hulls).

13 *Breasting*: First known use of this verb to describe ships
   at sea.

14 *rivage*: Shore.

15 *inconstant billows*: Shifting waves.

17 *Harfleur*: French port at the mouth of the Seine
   (accented on the first syllable; F's *Harflew(e)* may indicate the pronunciation).

18 *Grapple*: Seize hold, fasten (with grappling irons).
   sternage: The sterns.

19 *as dead midnight still*: As quiet as the stillness at midnight
when nothing stirs (proverbial).

21 *pith and puissance*: Strength and power.

24 *culled and choice-drawn*: Selected and chosen with special
care (the two are virtually synonymous).
cavaliers: Gentlemen trained to arms.

26 *ordnance*: See note to II.4.126.

27 *girded*: (1) Encircled *or* (2) defensively prepared.

29–31 *Tells Harry ... dukedoms*: Henry subsequently accepts
this offer in V.2, with the critical addition that he be
acknowledged the heir to France (*Héritier de France*;
331–9).

32 *likes*: Pleases.

33 *linstock*: Staff with a forked end used to hold the gunner's
lighted match.
Alarum: Military signal, made with drums (for infantry)
or trumpets (for cavalry).
chambers: Small cannon (for giving salutes, or for theatre
use).

35 *eke out*: Supplement.

III.1

This scene does not appear in Q.

1 *breach*: Gap in the walls. The need for scaling ladders
suggests an upper section of the wall has been
destroyed; however, previous attempts to take advantage of this weak point have evidently failed, as will
this renewed attempt.

7 *conjure*: Walter's emendation, accepted in most recent
editions, supposes a minim misreading in F (*commune*
for 'coniure'). Contemporary Galenist medical theory
held that the blood contained 'vital spirits', and wordplay associating attempts to control the motion of these
physiological 'spirits' with conjuration was commonplace, as when Henry discounts his ability to *conjure up
the spirit of love* in Katherine (V.2.284–5).

8 *nature*: Both natural feeling and natural appearance.
hard-favoured: Hard-featured.

9 *aspect*: Appearance (accent on the second syllable).

10 *portage*: Porthole(s).

11 *o'erwhelm*: Overhang.

12 *gallèd*: Worn (by the sea).

13 *jutty*: Project beyond (synonymous with 'overhang').
   confounded: Ruined.

14 *Swilled*: Vigorously washed.
   wasteful: Destructive.

16 *bend up*: Tense, as in bending (drawing) a bow to add
   tension to the string before releasing the arrow.

17 *his*: Its.
   On, on, you noblest English: Henry addresses the English
   nobility first, turning his attention to the yeomen at 25.
   Although no nobles are listed in the stage direction
   accompanying his entry, the use of the conjunction *And
   you, good yeomen* at 25 disproves the suggestion that
   the speech is addressed to the common soldiers from
   the outset.

18 *fet*: Fetched, derived.
   of war-proof: Tested in war.

19 *Alexanders*: Alexander the Great famously regretted that
   there were no more worlds for him to conquer. Henry
   is twice compared to Alexander, but where the archbishop praises his singular skill as an orator (see note
   to I.1.46), Fluellen unwittingly draws attention to
   Henry's relatively modest achievements as a conqueror
   (IV.7.12–48).

21 *argument*: Further opposition.

24 *copy*: (An) example.
   grosser: Thicker, less fine (because lacking valiant
   fathers).

25 *yeomen*: Rural men of property under the rank of
   gentlemen, but used more generally of respectable
   commoners, especially those who served as foot
   soldiers.

27 *mettle of your pasture*: Quality of your breeding and
   nurture.

29 *mean and base*: Of low social rank, but also suggesting
   morally inferior.

31 *greyhounds in the slips*: Hunting hounds kept on a slip-
   leash for easy release.

32 *upon the start*: While waiting for the quarry to be flushed from cover.

The game's afoot: The quarry is on the run.

34 *St George*: Patron saint of England.

III.2

3 *Corporal*: Nym addresses Bardolph as a lieutenant at II.1.2.

knocks: Blows, fights.

4 *case*: Set or pair.

5 *humour*: Temper.

plainsong: I.e., plain truth (literally, a simple unadorned melody).

6 *humours*: Pistol uses the term loosely; several senses are appropriate here, among them (1) mists, vapours (caused by the smoke of gunpowder); (2) emotions; (3) temperaments, especially *hot* or angry ones.

7 *vassals*: Humble servants, i.e. men.

16 *hie*: Hurry, speed.

18 *truly*: I.e., melodiously.

19 *Fluellen*: Anglicized spelling of the Welsh name Lluellen.

20 *Avaunt*: Advance.

21 *cullions*: (1) Despicable fellows, rascals *or* (2) testicles'

22 *Duke*: Military leader (from the Latin '*dux*' = 'leader').

men of mould: Men made of earth, i.e., mortal men.

25 *bawcock*: Fine fellow (French '*beau coq*').

lenity: Mildness, mercifulness.

chuck: Chick (a term of endearment).

26–7 *wins bad humours*: Makes everyone angry.

29 *swashers*: Blustering braggarts, swaggerers.

boy: Servant, male youth.

30 *man to me*: (1) Manservant to me *or* (2) more manly than I am.

31 *antics*: Clowns.

32 *white-livered*: Cowardly ('lily livered').

red-faced: From drinking or shouting bombastically or both, causing him to look as though he is choleric (hot-tempered).

33 *faces it out*: Brazens it out, with a pun on 'face'.

35 *breaks words*: (1) Exchanges (hostile) words (not sword blows) *or* (2) breaks his word.

35–6 *keeps whole weapons*: Preserves weapons undamaged (because unused).

36–7 *men of few words are the best men*: Proverbial (*best* here means bravest).

42 *purchase*: Booty.

43 *twelve leagues*: Thirty-six miles (a league was approximately three miles).

44 *filching*: Stealing.

45 *Calais*: An English port (1347–1558) on the coast of northern France. Like *Dover* in F at III.Chorus.4, this appears to be another geographical error on Shakespeare's part.

46 *carry coals*: (1) Do any dirty work *or* (2) put up with insults (proverbial).

47 *familiar with men's pockets*: I.e., be a pick-pocket.

50 *pocketing up of wrongs*: (1) Putting up with insults (proverbial) *or* (2) stealing.

53 *cast it up*: (1) Abandon it *or* (2) vomit it up.

55 *mines*: Tunnels dug under enemy fortifications and packed with explosives.

58 *disciplines of the war*: Military science.

58–9 *concavities*: Concave sides or cavities, i.e., depth.

60 *discuss*: Declare.
    is digt: I.e., has dug.

60–61 *is digt . . . countermines*: Fluellen presumably means to say 'has dug himself countermines four yards under (our mines)'.

62 *plow*: Blow. F is inconsistent in its indications of dialect.

65 *gentleman*: The captains are addressed as gentlemen, a social rank between yeomen and nobles.

69 *in his beard*: I.e., to his face.

70–71 *the true disciplines . . . Roman disciplines*: Fluellen's antiquarian pedantry about the Roman disciplines parodies the manual advice offered in *An Arithmeticall Militare Treatise, named Stratioticos* (1579), a work on military tactics by Leonard and Thomas Digges (see Introduction, p. xxviii).

71 *Enter Captain Macmorris and Captain Jamy*: Macmorris
and Jamy are not in Q and much of the scene is omitted.
The inclusion of a Scottish captain and a captain from
Ireland in F to complement the Welsh and English
captains, Fluellen and Gower, symbolizes the presence
of soldiers from all four 'nations' in Henry's army. Each
captain was likely to command soldiers from his respec-
tive 'nation'. On Macmorris's national identity, see
Introduction, pp. lxii–lxiv.

75 *expedition*: Quickness of action or wit.

81 *Good-e'en*: Good evening (but used any time after
noon).

84 *pioneers*: Soldiers employed in digging trenches and
laying mines.

92 *voutsafe*: Vouchsafe, i.e., grant.

100 *quit*: Requite, repay.

107 *sa'*: Save.

110 *mess*: Mass (a common Catholic oath).

111 *lig*: Lie.

114 *full fain*: Very gladly.

118 *Of my nation*: See Introduction, pp. lxii–lxiii.

122 *peradventure*: Perhaps.

130 *parley*: Trumpet call inviting the enemy to talk (from
French '*parler*' = 'to talk').

III.3

0 *Some citizens . . . walls*: Capell's addition. Neither Q nor
F provides an entry for the inhabitants of Harfleur until
the close of Henry's threatening speech, at which point
both include the stage direction *Enter Governour*.
gates: Gates of the town.

1–43 *How yet resolves . . . destroyed*: Nothing corresponding
to Henry's speech to the citizens of Harfleur is found
in Holinshed and Q includes only lines 1–10 and 42–3.

2 *latest parle*: Last negotiation, before Henry's army
resumes its attack on Harfleur. (Presumably the
renewed assault on the breach failed.)

3 *best*: Fullest.

4 *proud of destruction*: Glorying in self-destruction
(*destruction* is pronounced as four syllables).

5 *to our worst*: I.e., to do our worst (proverbial).

7 *battery*: Bombardment.

10 *The gates of mercy*: The phrase 'gate of mercy' is used
in *Henry VI, Part III*, I.4.177. Taylor compares Robert
Parson's *Christian Directory* (1598): 'that most dreadful
shutting up of the gate, whereof Our Saviour spake in
such doleful manner when he said, "*Clausa est ianua*",
the gate is shut up and made fast forever. That is to
say, in hell the gate of all mercy . . . is shut up forever'
(Bk 1, Pt 1, ch. ix, p. 382; alluding to Matthew 25:10).

11 *fleshed*: See note to II.4.50.

12 *In . . . hand*: Licensed to spill blood freely.

14 *flowering*: Flourishing.

15 *impious*: Wicked.

16 *Arrayed*: Clothed.
   the prince of fiends: The devil, Lucifer.

17 *smirched*: Blackened (with gunpowder and the grime of
battle).
   fell feats: Ruthless and exceptional acts.

18 *Enlinked*: (1) Joined (like links in a chain) *or* (2) a link
was a torch used in lighting people along dark streets.

21 *hot and forcing violation*: Lustful and violent rape.

22–3 *hold . . . holds*: Restrain . . . maintains.

23 *fierce career*: Furious gallop.

24 *bootless*: Uselessly.
   spend: Expend, waste.
   vain: Futile.

25 *in their spoil*: In the act of plundering.

26 *precepts*: Writs of summons (accented on the second
syllable).
   leviathan: Huge biblical sea monster, i.e., whale.

31 *O'erblows*: Blows away.
   contagious clouds: Infectious and infecting clouds.
   (Pestilence was thought to be carried along by moist
   air.) The *clouds* are the smoke of battle.

32 *heady*: Impetuous, violent.

34 *blind*: (1) Morally blind, immoral *or* (2) undiscrimi-
nating, reckless.

35 *Defile the locks . . . daughters*: (1) Dirty the hair of your

daughters, i.e, by dragging them along the ground by the hair *or* (2) violate the chastity of your daughters by raping them.

38 *spitted*: Impaled (thrust through with a spit as if for roasting).

pikes: Weapons with long wooden shafts and pointed metal heads.

40 *break*: Tear, split.

Jewry: Judaea.

40–41 *as . . . Herod's bloody-hunting slaughtermen*: Herod ordered his soldiers to kill all male infants aged two years old and under in and around Bethlehem in the hope of killing the infant Jesus, prophesied to be the future king of the Jews: 'Then Herod . . . sent forth, and slew all the children that were in Bethlehem . . . In Rama was there a voice heard, lamentation, weeping, and great mourning' (Matthew 2:16–18).

43 *guilty in defence*: Guilty because defending yourselves in a wrongful cause.

45 *succours*: Relief.

46 *Returns*: Informs.

54 *Use . . . all*: Shakespeare diverges markedly from Holinshed, who relates that even after the surrender 'the town [was] sacked, to the great gain of the Englishmen' (p. 550).

55 *sickness growing*: Dysentery and other fevers. Holinshed records: 'The number of his people was much minished by the flix [flux] and other fevers' (p. 550).

56 *Calais*: See notes to III.Chorus.4 and III.2.45.

58 *addressed*: Prepared.

III.4

0 *Katherine*: Princess Katherine is not identified by name in the scene, but Alice addresses her as a social superior. Were Katherine to wear a coronet playgoers would be more likely to recognize that she is the daughter of the French king named by the Chorus (III.Chorus. 29–30). Historically, she was not quite fifteen at the time of Agincourt.

old gentlewoman: Alice's English proves somewhat

uneven, suggesting her visit to England may have been
in her youth. When Henry addresses Alice as *fair one*
at V.2.117 he may be flattering (or gently mocking)
Katherine's lady-in-waiting; alternatively, Shakespeare
may have been ambivalent about her age.

1–58 The French text in this edition has been regularized,
but not fully corrected, in many details. F is, however,
sufficiently comprehensible to suggest that the original
script was tolerably accurate. The French is translated
as nearly as possible in the notes below.

1–6 *Alice . . . hand*: 'Alice, you have been in England, and
you speak the language well.' 'A little, madam.' 'I pray
you, teach me – I must learn to speak [it]. How do you
say hand in English?' 'The hand? It is called *de hand*.'

6 *de*: Both speakers mispronounce English 'th' as 'd'.

7–14 *De hand . . . nailès*: 'De hand. And the fingers?' 'The
fingers? My faith, I forget the fingers, but I shall
remember. The fingers? I think that they are called *de
fingres*; yes, *de fingres*.' 'The hand, *de hand*; the fingers,
de fingres. I think that I am a good student; I have
acquired two words of English quickly. What do you
call the nails?' 'The nails? We call them *de nailès*.'

10 *fingres*: Possibly with inadvertent wordplay on 'penis'
(slang). Given the unconscious sexual innuendo that
follows, Taylor suggests that the mispronunciation of
'fingers' as '*fingres* might (appropriately) suggest *ingress*,
elsewhere used of sexual penetration' (see also 11 and
16). Either way, the mispronunciation further establishes Alice's uneven recollection of the language.

15–27 *De nailès . . . madame*: '*De nailès*. Listen: tell me if I
speak well – *de hand*, *de fingres*, and *de nailès*.' 'That's
well said, madam. It is very good English.' 'Tell me
the English for the arm.' '*De arm*, madam.' 'And the
elbow?' '*D'elbow*.' '*D'elbow*. I am going to repeat all
the words that you have taught me up to now.' 'It is
too difficult, madam, I think.' 'Excuse me, Alice; listen
– *d'hand, de fingre, de nailès, d'arma, de bilbow*.' '*D'elbow*,
madam.'

26 *bilbow*: Mispronunciation produces a pun on the English

word 'bilbo', meaning (1) a type of sword, originally
made in Bilbao, Spain, that was known for its well-
tempered blade *or* (2) an iron bar furnished with sliding
shackles used to fetter a prisoner's ankles.

28–33 *O Seigneur Dieu ... de sin*: 'O Lord God, I am forgetting them! *D'elbow*. What do you call the neck?' '*De
nick*, madam.' '*De nick*. And the chin?' '*De chin*.' '*De
sin*. The neck, *de nick*; the chin, *de sin*.'

   30 *nick*: Possible wordplay on a contemporary English
term for the anal cleft (slang). The first use of 'nick'
as a slang term for the female external genitals recorded
in the *OED* is 1625; however, Gordon Williams notes
that Fletcher appears to use 'nick' as a slang term for
'vagina' in *Wife for a Month* (1624) and states that it
was 'perhaps familiar enough in the 1590s to allow play
in *H5* III.iv.55', where wordplay on *con, foutre* and 'sin'
may prompt the audience to 'recognize undetected
bawdry amongst these last four words' (*A Glossary of
Shakespeare's Language* pp. 215–16).

34–46 *Oui ... la robe*: 'Yes. Saving your honour, in truth, you
pronounce the words as correctly as the natives of
England.' 'I have no doubt at all that I shall learn
[English], by the grace of God, and in little time.'
'Have you not already forgotten what I have taught
you?' 'No, I will recite it to you promptly: *d'hand, de
fingre, de mailès –*' '*De nailès*, madam.' '*De nailès, de
arm, de ilbow –*' 'Saving your honour, *d'elbow*.' 'That's
what I said: *d'elbow, de nick*, and *de sin*. What do you
call the foot and the gown?'

   41 *mailès*: Possible English pun on 'males'.

   43 *de ilbow*: Possible wordplay on 'bow', contemporary
English slang for 'vagina'. E. A. M. Colman comments
that *Love's Labour's Lost*, IV.i.110, and Thomas
Middleton's *Michaelmas Term*, II.1.27, 'raise the suspicion that *bow* could, in suggestive contexts, carry the
sense *vulva*' (*The Dramatic Use of Bawdy in Shakespeare*
(1974), p. 185).

47–58 *Le foot ... à dîner*: 'The *foot*, madam, and the *count*.'
'The *foot*, and the *count*? O Lord God! They are words

of evil sound, corrupting, coarse, and immodest, and
not for ladies of honour to use. I would not pronounce
these words before the lords of France for all the world.
Fie! The *foot* and the *count*! Nonetheless, I will repeat
my whole lesson one more time: *d'hand, de fingre, de
nailès, d'arm, d'elbow, de nick, de sin, de foot*, the *count*.'
'Excellent, madam!' 'That is enough for one time. Let
us go to dinner.'

47 *foot*: Sounds to Katherine like the French '*foutre*' ('to fuck').
   count: Alice's mispronunciation of 'gown' sounds like
   the French '*con*' ('cunt'). Taylor notes that 'the terminal
   t could easily be a misreading of *e*' by the compositor;
   however, the F spelling reflects Elizabethan pronunciation. Katherine reacts with distaste to the sound of the
   word (*de son mauvais*) and its similarity to French sexual
   slang.

III.5

1 *River Somme*: Just over halfway between Harfleur and
  Calais. The French do not regard Henry's march to
  Calais as a retreat (see III.3.56).

2 *withal*: With.

5 *O Dieu vivant*: 'O living God'.
  sprays: (Bastard) offshoots (as a consequence of the
  Norman conquest of 1066).

6 *emptying*: Ejaculate.
  luxury: Lust.

7 *scions*: Shoots used for grafting.
  put in: Grafted on to.
  wild and savage stock: I.e., the English.

8 *Spirt*: Sprout.

9 *overlook*: Rise above.
  grafters: (1) Those who did the grafting *or* (2) the stock
  from which the cultivated shoots were taken for
  grafting, i.e., the (Norman French) people from whom
  they are descended.

11 *Mort Dieu! Ma vie*: Q reads *Mordeu ma via* and F *Mort
   du ma vie*, which many editors render as '*Mort de ma vie*'.
   At IV.5.3 Q has *Mor du ma vie* and F *Mor Dieu ma vie*.
   vie here is a disyllable.

13 *slobbery*: Slimy, muddy or dirty.

14 *nook-shotten*: Having many corners, angles, or projections; i.e., misshapen.

Albion: Old name for the island comprising England, Scotland and Wales.

15 *Dieu de batailles*: 'God of battles' (*batailles* is three syllables).

mettle: Spirited temperament, courage.

17 *as in despite*: As if despising them.

18 *sodden*: Boiled.

19 *drench*: Medicinal dose or drink, especially for horses.

sur-reined: Over-ridden. (For an *Edward III* echo, see the note to III.7.148 (*out of beef*), below.)

jades: Horses (contemptuous), of inferior breed, worn-out, ill-tempered.

barley broth: Strong ale.

20 *Decoct*: Boil up.

21 *quick*: Lively.

23 *roping*: Hanging like ropes.

26 *Lest poor we*: F reads *Poore we*, which is defective; F2 reads *Poore we may*, which mends the metre and makes sense if *Poore* is stressed: 'Rather we should call them poor because they have bred such poor-spirited masters' (Walter). The proposed reading maintains the train of thought ('Let us not hang ... Lest ...').

28 *madams*: Ladies, wives.

29 *bred out*: Exhausted by breeding.

33 *lavoltas*: The *lavolta* was a lively dance comprising a whirl of the body followed by a high leap (Italian '*la volta*' = 'the turn').

corantos: The *coranto* was a French dance with a running step (from the French '*courante*' = 'running').

34–5 *our grace ... runaways*: Quibbles abound; the sense is: 'The only thing that distinguishes us is our agility (in dancing, or in fleeing), and we are lofty (high-born, or high-leaping) performers in running (*corantos*, or away from danger).'

36 *Mountjoy*: Like 'Garter' in Britain, this is the title of the chief herald of France, not a personal name.

37 *England*: The King of England.

40–45 *Charles Delabreth, High Constable ... Charolois*: These names occur in Holinshed's list of the French lords captured or slain at Agincourt, except for Berri and Charolois, who take part in the council of war but not in the battle. Holinshed spells *Burgundy* 'Burgognie' (F *Burgonie*), *Faulconbridge* 'Fauconberge' (earlier 'Fauconbridge') and *Foix* 'Fois' (F *Loys*); Holinshed's 'Lestrake' becomes *Lestrale* in F, which most editors follow.

47 *For your great seats*: For the sake of your great estates (and ranks).

   quit you: Absolve, rid yourselves.

48 *Bar*: (1) Stop, obstruct *or* (2) prevent Henry from enforcing his claim.

49 *pennons*: Pennants, long, narrow, triangular-shaped banners attached to the heads of lances (or the top of helmets).

50 *host*: Army.

51 *vassal*: Abject, base. A vassal was a tenant who owed homage and allegiance to his feudal overlord.

52 *The Alps ... upon*: I.e., in avalanches. The image has been compared to a burlesque by Horace (*Satires* 2.5.41) of a line of verse by the Latin poet Furius Bibaculus: '*Iuppiter hibernas cana nive conspuit Alpes*' ('Jupiter spits upon the wintry Alps with white snow').

   voids his rheum: Discharges his phlegm, spits (here, the runoff from melting snow).

54 *Rouen*: Capital of Normandy, a coastal region in northern France.

59 *sink*: Cesspit.

60 *for achievement*: As his sole accomplishment, instead of victory.

64 *Prince Dauphin ... Rouen*: Shakespeare here follows Holinshed, who reports that the French king forbade the Dauphin to fight. In III.7, IV.2 and IV.5, however, the Dauphin is taking part, as he evidently was also in the *Henry V* play mentioned by Nashe (see Introduction, p. xl) and in the episode Shakespeare had referred to

when Henry 'made the Dauphin and the French to stoop'
(*Henry VI, Part III*, I.1.108). The idea may have
originated in a later remark of Holinshed's, that the
French mob who pillaged the English camp would have
been punished 'if the Dauphin had longer lived' (p. 554).

68 *England's fall*: King Henry's defeat.

III.6

1–2 *the bridge*: The keeping of the bridge over the River
Ternoise at Blangy was essential for the English march
to Calais. Holinshed records that Henry,

> doubting [fearing] lest if the same bridge should be broken it
> would be greatly to his hindrance, appointed certain captains,
> with their bands, to go thither with all speed before him, and
> to take possession thereof, and to keep it, till his coming thither.
> Those that were sent, finding the Frenchmen busy to break
> down the bridge, assailed them so vigorously that they discom-
> fited them, and took and slew them; and so the bridge was
> preserved (p. 552).

3–4 *services committed*: Military feats performed.

6 *magnanimous*: Great-souled (the literal sense).

7 *Agamemnon*: Leader of the Greeks at Troy.

9 *is not*: Has not.

12 *aunchient*: Ancient, i.e., ensign (historically, a soldier
marked out for his courage who carried the regimental
flag into battle). See notes to II.1.3, 36.

14 *Mark Antony*: Famous Roman general (the first reference to him in Shakespeare's plays).
estimation: Esteem, repute.

25 *buxom*: Lively.

26–8 *giddy Fortune's . . . stone*: Pistol mixes up two traditional
emblems of Fortune, as the power turning the wheel
on which men rise and fall, and as the blindfold figure
balancing upon the rolling stone of change and chance.

30 *muffler*: Blindfold.

34 *fixed*: Standing securely (a physical impossibility given
that the sphere is perpetually rolling).

37 *moral*: Allegorical figure.

38 *Fortune . . . him*: Echoes the familiar tag, 'Fortune's my foe', and the ballad line, 'Fortune, my foe! Why dost thou frown on me?'

39 *pax*: Peace (Latin); the 'kiss of peace' in Christian ritual. Holinshed records that Henry executed a soldier for stealing a 'pix' from a church. Hall states that the soldier ate the communion wafers, though this detail is absent from Holinshed. Shakespeare substitutes Bardolph for the anonymous soldier and a *pax of little price* (44) for the more precious and more sacred 'pix'. A pix was a box of consecrated communion wafers; a pax was a small metal tablet depicting the crucifixion which was kissed by the priest celebrating the Mass and then by the communicants. Both objects were often made of silver or gold.

41 *Let gallows gape for dog*: Animals were sometimes hanged for misdemeanours; cf. the phrase 'hangdog look' and Thomas Dekker's *Honest Whore*, Part One (1604): 'Now you look like an old he-cat, going to the gallows' (II.1.131–2).

42 *let not . . . suffocate*: In Holinshed (p. 552), Henry orders that the pix be restored and the unnamed soldier strangled; in Shakespeare it is Exeter who orders Bardolph's execution, but Bardolph is still alive when Henry learns that his former companion *is like to be executed* (97–8), news to which he responds impassively at 104–5.
   hemp: I.e., rope made of hemp.

46 *vital thread*: Thread of life, which, according to myth, is spun, measured and cut by the three Fates; here it is synonymous with the windpipe.

48 *requite*: Repay (hints at a bribe).

56 *figo*: Fig (Spanish '*figo*'). A contemptuous exclamation often accompanied by an obscene gesture known as the 'fig of Spain', which consisted in thrusting the thumb between two closed fingers or into the mouth, and is comparable in tone to modern 'fuck off' or 'up yours'. Cf. 58.

60 *arrant*: Notorious.

61 *cutpurse*: Pickpocket, thief.

63 *as you shall . . . day*: I.e., a long day (proverbial).

65 *time is serve*: There is opportunity.

66 *gull*: Fool.

69 *perfect*: Word perfect.

71 *sconce*: Small fort or earthwork.

72 *came off*: Acquitted himself.

73 *what terms the enemy stood on*: I.e., what conditions the enemy insisted on.

   con: Memorize.

74 *trick up*: Dress up.

75 *new-tuned*: Newly invented, fashionable.

75–6 *beard of the general's cut*: Beard trimmed in the same style as the general's. On returning to popular acclaim from his Cadiz expedition of 1596, the Earl of Essex set a fashion for wearing long, square-cut beards. The passage suggests that Pistol may have worn just such a 'Cadiz beard' when the play was originally performed.

76 *suit of the camp*: Military uniform.

82 *find a hole in his coat*: Find a weak spot in him (proverbial).

84 *from*: I.e., about.

   colours: Military flags or banners.

   poor: Shabby, sick, tired.

90 *passages*: Passages of arms, i.e., hand-to-hand combats.

95 *perdition*: Losses, destruction.

99–100 *his face . . . o'fire*: Shakespeare may be recalling Chaucer's Summoner, with his 'fyr-reed' face blotched with 'whelkes white' and 'knobbes sittynge on his chekes' (*Canterbury Tales*, General Prologue, ll. 624–33).

99 *bubukles*: Inflamed sores, tumours. Fluellen conflates '*bubo*' (Latin = 'abscess') and 'carbuncle' (an inflamed skin tumour).

100 *whelks*: Pimples.

   blows: I.e., like a bellows blowing on a fire.

108 *upbraided*: Reproached.

110 *Tucket*: Preliminary trumpet signal.

111 *You know me by my habit*: A terse, discourteous opening, which Henry answers in the same vein.

   habit: Clothing, i.e., herald's tabard, a coat with short or no sleeves, emblazoned with the coat of arms of his king.

118 *Advantage*: The restraint which awaits a favourable opportunity.

120 *bruise an injury*: (1) Squeeze out an abscess *or* (2) hit back at the cause of our harm.

123 *admire our sufferance*: Marvel at our forbearance (realizing our inaction was due to patience not weakness).

126–7 *pettiness*: Weakness, small military force.

138–45 *tell thy King ... French*: In Holinshed (p. 552), Henry replies: 'Mine intent is to do as it pleaseth God. I will not seek your master at this time; but if he or his seek me, I will meet with them, God willing. ... And yet wish I not any of you so unadvised as to be the occasion that I dye your tawny ground with your red blood' (cf. 158–60). He does not, however, admit his army's plight, as he so frankly does here.

140 *impeachment*: Impediment (French, '*empêchement*').
    sooth: Truth.

III.7

0 *Dauphin*: For the Dauphin's presence at Agincourt, contrary to the chronicles, see note to III.5.64. The Dauphin does not appear at Agincourt in Q; instead Bourbon is substituted for the Dauphin both in this scene and in IV.5, and IV.2 is omitted.

12 *pasterns*: Hooves (strictly, the part of a horse's leg between the fetlock and the hoof).

13 *as if ... hairs*: I.e., as if he was virtually weightless, like a tennis ball stuffed with hair (as they were at the time).

14 *le cheval volant*: 'The flying horse'.
    Pegasus: Winged horse of classical mythology.
    chez les narines de feu: 'With the fiery nostrils'. Some editors emend F's *ches* to '*qui a*' ('who has').

17 *pipe of Hermes*: The Greek god Hermes (Roman Mercury) invented the reed pipe and with it charmed asleep the hundred-eyed giant Argus (see Golding's *Ovid*, ll. 843–56).

18 *nutmeg*: Dull brown. Horses' colours were thought to reflect their temperaments: 'A good horse cannot be of a bad colour' (proverbial).

20 *Perseus*: Son of Zeus in classical mythology; his winged

sandals and cap (which he later gave to Hermes) bore
him through the air to slay the Gorgon Medusa. The
winged horse Pegasus sprang from the blood of her
severed head.

air and fire: Considered the 'higher', more noble elements
because they rise upwards whereas the 'baser' elements
of earth and water fall downwards. Cf. Prologue.1
(note); also *Antony and Cleopatra*, V.2.288–9: 'I am fire
and air; my other elements | I give to baser life.'

23 *all other . . . beasts*: All other horses are poor specimens,
merely animals.

26 *palfreys*: Saddle-horses for ordinary riding (especially
by women), as distinguished from war-horses; also
associated with tales of wandering knights.
neigh: With a pun on 'nay'.

30–31 *from . . . lamb*: I.e., all day long. 'To go to bed with the
lark and rise with the lamb' was proverbial.

31 *vary*: Express variations on a theme, a standard rhetorical exercise.

34 *argument*: Theme, subject matter.

35 *sovereign's sovereign*: Sovereign reason, the faculty that
ought to rule all others.

38–40 *I once . . . mistress*: The idea may come from *Edward
III*, where Edward orders a poem of surpassing praise,
and, when the poet asks about the intended recipient,
replies: 'Thinkest thou I did bid thee praise a horse?'
(I.2.98).

42 *courser*: Swift horse, charger.

43 *Your mistress bears well*: (1) Your horse carries her rider
well *or* (2) punningly, your mistress carries your weight
during sex well. The sexual pun is taken up by the
Constable at 46–7.

44 *prescript*: Prescribed.

45 *particular*: Private, personal.

47 *shrewdly*: Sharply, with a pun on 'shrewishly', bad-
temperedly.
shook your back: I.e., jolted you in the saddle, but also
develops the sexual innuendo.

49 *bridled*: I.e., not a horse or a shrew but a woman. Women

punished as shrews were sometimes forced to wear a 'scold's bridle', a gag that prevented them from speaking.

51 *rode*: (1) Rode his horse *or* (2) had sex with his mistress.

kern: A lightly armed Irish footsoldier or skirmisher drawn from the poorer classes; more generally, a peasant, a rascal.

French hose: Wide breeches.

52 *strait strossers*: Tight trousers (worn by the Irish), i.e., bare legs.

53 *horsemanship*: Possibly with a pun on 'whores' (see note to 57).

55 *foul bogs*: (1) Filthy wet spongy ground (associated with Ireland) *or* (2) vaginas (more generally, women) infected with venereal disease.

57 *jade*: (1) Strictly, a worn-out horse *or* (2) punningly, a prostitute.

59 *own hair*: Implying the Constable's mistress wears a wig because she has gone bald through syphilis. Taylor cites *A Comedy of Errors*, II.2.82–93, and *Timon of Athens*, IV.3.161, as other examples of Shakespeare associating venereal disease with baldness.

62–3 *Le chien ... bourbier*: 'The dog is turned to his own vomit again, and the sow that was washed is turned again to her wallowing in the mire' (2 Peter 2:22). The sentence was proverbial, and Shakespeare had already made powerful use of it in *Henry IV, Part II* (I.3.97–9) when the Archbishop calls the populace 'thou common dog', and continues: '[thou] didst ... disgorge | Thy glutton bosom of the royal Richard; | And now thou wouldn't eat thy dead vomit up.'

63 *use*: With wordplay on use sexually.

71 *a many*: A lot.

79–80 *faced out of my way*: (1) Put out of countenance *or* (2) outfaced, intimidated, driven away.

82 *go to hazard*: Place a bet (*hazard* = a dice game).

84 *go yourself to hazard*: Place yourself at risk.

89 *he will eat all he kills*: I.e., he will not kill anyone, a proverbial joke.

92 *foot*: Perhaps with wordplay on French '*foutre*' ('fuck'),
   as in Katherine's language lesson at III.4.48–50, or on
   English slang for 'vulva'.

   tread out: Rub out with her foot, perhaps with wordplay
   on 'have sex', although this requires the copulative sense
   of 'treading', a term for 'the action of the male bird in
   coition' (*OED sb.* 9a), to be applied to a female.

94 *active*: (1) Energetic *or* (2) sexually virile.

96 *Doing is . . . doing*: (1) Busy to no effect *or* (2) having sex.

108 *lackey*: Footman, implying the servant has been beaten
   by the Dauphin.

   hooded: Concealed, referring to the practice in falconry
   of keeping the falcon hooded until it is released to fly
   at game.

109 *bate*: A satirical pun. (1) Flutter its wings for action *or*
   (2) abate, lessen.

119 *bolt*: (1) A short, blunted arrow *or* (2) penis.

   soon shot: With wordplay on 'ejaculates prematurely'.

120 *shot over*: Overshot the target (with his proverb).

121 *overshot*: (1) Outshot in archery *or* (2) mistaken.

130 *mope*: Wander about aimlessly.

   fat-brained: Thick-witted, stupid.

131 *knowledge*: Familiar bearings.

138 *mastiffs*: Large, powerful dogs known for their courage
   and violence. Harrison's 'Description of England' (in
   Holinshed, vol. I, pp. 230–31) reports that English
   mastiffs were employed as watchdogs, being 'terrible
   and fearful to behold', and for bull- and bear-baitings
   where they were sent out 'without any collar to defend
   their throats'.

139 *winking*: With their eyes closed.

143 *sympathize with*: Resemble.

148 *shrewdly*: Severely.

   out of beef: Short of beef; this seems to echo *Edward
   III* (III.3.159–62) when the King of France says of the
   English soldiers, 'but scant them of their chines of
   beef, | . . . And presently they are as resty stiff | As
   'twere a many over-ridden jades' (cf. *sur-reined jades*,
   III.5.19, above).

IV.*Chorus*

1   *entertain conjecture of*: Imagine.

2   *poring*: Eye-straining (transferred epithet: the darkness makes the observer strain to see).

5   *stilly*: Quietly.

8   *paly*: Pale.

9   *battle*: Army.
    umbered: Shadowed or umber-coloured (lit by the camp-fires).

12 *accomplishing*: Finish equipping.

14 *note*: Sound.
    preparation: Pronounced as five syllables.

17 *secure*: Over-confident.

18 *over-lusty*: (1) Overly cheerful *or* (2) arrogant, self-confident.

19 *play*: Gamble for.

20 *tardy-gaited*: Slow-paced.

23 *Like sacrifices*: Like animals awaiting sacrificial slaughter. Cf. *Henry IV, Part I*, IV.1.113–15: 'They come like sacrifices in their trim, | And to the fire-eyed maid of smoky war | All hot and bleeding will we offer them.'
    watchful fires: Watch-fires, but also awake by their fires (transferred epithet).

24 *inly*: Inwardly.
    ruminate: Turn over and over in the mind, meditate.

25 *gesture sad*: Sorrowful bearing.

26 *Investing*: Enveloping.

28 *who will behold*: Whoever wishes to see.

30 *watch*: Sentinel or group of soldiers on guard.

35 *note*: Sign.

36 *dread an army*: An army greatly to be feared.
    enrounded: Encircled. Hall records that Henry's tactics stemmed from his fear that the French would 'compass and beset him about' (p. xlviiiᵛ). In truth, the French had simply blocked the route to Calais, but the statement conveys the numerical superiority of the French forces.

37 *dedicate*: Sacrifice.
    jot: Least bit.

38 *all-watchèd*: All passed in wakefulness.

39 *overbears attaint*: Overcomes exhaustion.

40 *semblance*: Appearance.

43–4 *largess universal . . . one*: Quintilian, *Institutio*, 1.2.14, 'ut
sol universes idem lucis caloris largitur' ('as the sun abun-
dantly gives the same light and warmth to all men'),
has been suggested as a possible source for
Shakespeare's phrasing of the familiar proverb 'the sun
shines on everyone'. Jorgensen quotes *A Mirror for
English Soldiers* (1595): 'Let every general know himself
to be the sun in the heaven of his host, from whose
beams every soldier borroweth his shine' (p. C1).

44 *liberal*: Generous.

45 *that*: So that.
mean and gentle: I.e., low- and high-born. Henry draws
a similar social distinction between *noblest English* and
yeomen at III.1.17 and 25.

46 *as may unworthiness define*: The Chorus contrasts
Henry's worth with the unworthiness of (1) the
Chorus's own capacity to describe *or* (2) the theatre's
(or actor's) capacity to present.

47 *touch*: Trace or impression.

49–53 *we shall . . . mockeries be*: Stage battles were often sati-
rized; cf. Sidney's *The Defence of Poesy* (1595): 'Two
armies fly in, represented with four swords and buck-
lers; and then what hard heart will not receive it for a
pitched field?' (ll. 1279–80). Jonson is equally derisive
in the prologue to *Every Man in His Humour* (1598)
about 'three rusty swords' set to fight the Wars of the
Roses (l. 9).

51 *Right ill-disposed*: Very unskilfully handled.

53 *Minding*: Calling to mind.
mockeries: Ridiculous imitations.

IV.1

4 *soul*: Element, trace.

5 *observingly*: Observantly.

6 *bad neighbour . . . stirrers*: Proverbial ('he that has an ill
neighbour has often times an ill morning').

7 *husbandry*: Management.

10 *dress us*: Prepare ourselves. Holinshed reports that
    though the English were 'hungry, weary, sore travelled,
    and vexed with many cold diseases' they took holy
    communion and made confession (p. 552); cf. 172–80
    below.

11 *gather honey from the weed*: Proverbial.

12 *make a moral of*: Draw a moral from.

15 *churlish*: Unyielding.

20 *quickened*: Revived.

22 *newly*: (1) Anew, afresh *or* (2) immediately.

23 *With casted slough . . . legerity*: I.e., with the new nimble-
    ness (*fresh legerity*) of a snake that has shed its old skin
    (*casted slough*).

26 *anon*: Shortly.

31 *bosom*: I.e., heart.

34 *God-a-mercy*: I thank thee (strictly, 'God have mercy',
    but confused with 'gramercy' ('graunt mercy', i.e.,
    'great thanks')).

35 *Qui va là*: 'Who goes there?'

38 *base, common, and popular*: I.e., a common soldier.

39 *gentleman of a company*: Gentleman volunteer who
    chose the captain or general under whom he served and
    whose military rank, between that of an officer and a
    common soldier, was deemed more honourable than
    that of a sergeant. Cf. *Henry IV, Part I*, IV.2.24.

40 *Trail'st thou the puissant pike*: I.e., are you an
    infantryman? The pike, which consisted of a long
    wooden handle with a pointed metal head, was a
    favourite weapon of the English infantry. When not
    on the march or in use, the pike was commonly held
    near the head allowing the base of its long handle to
    trail along the ground.

42 *As good . . . Emperor*: Proverbial.
    Emperor: Holy Roman Emperor.

44 *bawcock*: Fine fellow (French, '*beau coq*'); cf. III.2.25.

45 *imp*: Scion, son. Pistol calls the King 'most royal imp
    of fame' in *Henry IV, Part II*, V.5.43.

48 *lovely bully*: Fine fellow, a term of endearment and
    familiarity.

49 *Harry le Roy*: Harry the King (French '*le roi*' = 'the king').

55 *Saint Davy's day*: Feast day of David, patron saint of Wales, celebrated on 1 March, when the Welsh wear their national emblem, the leek, to mark the supposed anniversary of their victory over the Saxons on that date in AD 540.

60 *figo*: Cf. III.6.56 and note.

63 *sorts*: Fits.

65 *fewer*: Speak less. F reads *fewer*, Q *lewer* (*lower* in Q3). Since Gower has spoken only two words, and later promises to *speak lower* (80), many editors read 'lower' here. But Fluellen's reproof is against *tiddle-taddle* and *pibble-pabble*, and the comedy is in his long-winded warning to the taciturn Gower not to talk so much.

66 *admiration*: Wonder (here derogatory).

67 *prerogatifes*: Prerogatives, due rights.

70 *tiddle-taddle*: Tittle-tattle, trifling talk about trivial matters.

72–3 *ceremonies . . . cares . . . forms*: Formalities . . . duties . . . correct procedures, codes of conduct.

73 *modesty*: Constraint, discipline.

78–9 *coxcomb*: Fool.

82–3 *Though . . . Welshman*: These lines are printed as verse in F; Henry again speaks to himself in verse in his soliloquy after the common soldiers leave, at 223.

82 *out of fashion*: (1) Out of the expected order of things *or* (2) unconventional in manner.

94 *estate*: Condition.

95 *sand*: Sandbank.

101 *element shows*: Sky appears.

102 *conditions*: (1) Limitations *or* (2) characteristics, qualities.
   ceremonies: External symbols of state and kingly pomp.

104 *affections . . . higher mounted*: Feelings more lofty, more sophisticated.

105 *stoop*: Swoop (a falconry term for the descent of a bird of prey on its quarry).
   with the like wing: I.e., like ours do.

106 *of fears*: To fear.

107 *relish*: Taste.

107–8 *in reason . . . fear*: It is reasonable that no one should show any sign of his own fear.

112 *Thames*: The River Thames, which flows through London.

113 *at all adventures*: At all events, whatever the consequences.

123–4 *his cause . . . just*: The moral bearing of this discussion and the validity of the king's argument depend on the justice of his cause.

131 *reckoning*: (Spiritual) account.

133 *the latter day*: The last day, the Day of Judgement (Job 19:25).

136 *rawly left*: Left too young, unprovided for.

137 *die well*: I.e., die a Christian death.

138 *charitably*: In Christian charity.

141–2 *proportion of subjection*: The proper relation of subject to ruler.

144 *sinfully miscarry*: Die in a state of sin.

148–9 *irreconciled*: Unreconciled to God, unabsolved.

149 *iniquities*: Sins.

155–6 *arbitrement of*: Settlement by.

159 *broken seals of perjury*: Violation of a solemn oath.

160 *bulwark*: (1) Military fortification *or* (2) refuge (from punishment for crimes).

164 *beadle*: Parish officer who whipped petty offenders.

167 *the death*: The death penalty.
borne life away: I.e., escaped with their lives.

169 *unprovided*: Spiritually unprepared (for death).

171 *visited*: Punished (by God).

174 *mote*: Spot, blemish.

175 *death is to him advantage*: This echoes Philippians 1:21: 'Christ is to me life, and death is to me advantage.'

181 *ill*: Ill-prepared, in sin.

182 *to answer it*: Responsible, accountable for it.

192 *pay*: Punish.

193 *elder-gun*: Pop-gun (made from a hollow elder stick).
a poor and a private displeasure: I.e., the displeasure of a commoner.

198 *round*: Blunt.

203 *gage*: Pledge.

210 *take thee a box*: Give you a blow.

217 *could tell how to reckon*: Knew how to count.

218 *lay*: Bet.

218–19 *French crowns*: (1) French *écus* (gold coins) *or* (2) French heads.

220–21 *but it is . . . crowns*: For an Englishman to clip bits of silver or gold off English coins was a capital offence under the law of treason, but it is not treasonable (1) to clip French coins *or* (2) to cut the hair from Frenchmen's heads (i.e., to cut off French heads).

222 *clipper*: (1) Clipper of coins *or* (2) barber (i.e., the king will be cutting off French heads).

224 *careful*: (1) Full of cares, anxious *or* (2) grieving.

227 *Twin-born*: Born a twin; born at the same birth.
    subject: Subjected.
    breath: I.e., opinion.

229 *wringing*: Pain.

231 *privates*: Those who do not hold public office.

232 *ceremony*: Royal pomp, forms of deference or ceremonious respect.
    general: Public.

234 *thou, that suffer'st*: *thou* means ceremony in this instance, but sometimes it means greatness, and at other times (i.e. at 239) the king.

236 *comings-in*: Income.

238 *soul of adoration*: It is unclear whether the line is exclamatory or interrogative: made of insubstantial adoration (if exclamatory), or composed of the virtue or essence that inspires adoration (if interrogative). (*adoration* is pronounced as five syllables.)

239 *place, degree, and form*: Social rank, eminence.

246 *go out*: Be extinguished.

247 *blown*: (1) Breathed out *or* (2) inflated, puffed up *or* (3) corrupted.
    from adulation: By flattery. (*adulation* is pronounced as five syllables.)

248 *flexure and low bending*: Knee-bending (kneeling) and bowing low, i.e., displays of deference.

252 *find thee*: (1) Has found you out *or* (2) suffers from you.

253 *balm*: Consecrated oil used to anoint the monarch in
     the coronation ceremony.

     ball: Orb of sovereignty given to the monarch at coro-
     nation.

255 *intertissued*: Interwoven.

256 *farcèd*: Stuffed, bombastic.

265 *lackey*: Footman, especially one who runs alongside his
     master's carriage (here, the chariot of the sun god).

     the rise to set: Sunrise to sunset.

266 *Phoebus*: Greek and Roman sun god.

267 *Elysium*: I.e., perfect contentment (in Greek mythology,
     the dwelling place of the blessed after death).

268 *Hyperion*: Father of Helios (the charioteer of the sun),
     often taken for the sun god himself.

270 *profitable*: Useful.

273 *fore-hand and vantage of*: Upper hand and advantage
     over.

274 *member*: Sharer.

275 *gross*: Dull.

     wots: Knows.

277 *advantages*: Benefits from.

278 *jealous of*: Anxious about.

284 *reckoning*: Counting (pronounced as two syllables).

     th'opposèd numbers: The numbers of enemy soldiers.

287 *My father . . . crown*: Henry's father, Henry Bolingbroke
     (Henry IV), deposed Richard II, who was later
     murdered in prison.

     compassing: Attaining, achieving.

288 *I Richard's body . . . new*: The body of Richard II had
     been moved from Westminster Abbey to King's Langley
     by Henry IV. Henry V exhumed Richard's coffin and
     reinterred it with much ceremony in Westminster
     alongside Queen Anne, Richard's first wife.

293 *blood*: I.e., the murder of Richard II.

294 *chantries*: A chantry was an endowment for the main-
     tenance of one or more priests to sing daily mass for
     the souls of the founders or others specified by them
     (Richard II, in this instance). Henry founded two

religious houses, Bethlehem at Sheen and Sion at
Twickenham.

sad: Grave.

295 *still*: To this day, perpetually.

IV.2

There is no corresponding scene in Q.

2 *Montez à cheval*: 'Mount up'.

Varlet: (1) Groom *or* (2) rascal.

Lacquais: 'Lackey' (pejorative), 'footman'.

3–4 *Via . . . Orleans*: In F these speeches read: '*Via les ewes
& terre.*' '*Rien puis le air & feu.*' '*Cien, Cousin Orleance.*'
The meaning of *Via* is uncertain. Used as an interjec-
tion its most likely sense here is 'go', 'be off'. (The first
instance cited in the *OED* of '*via*' as a preposition
meaning 'by way of' or 'through' is dated 1779.) Either
the Dauphin is urging his horse to go through the waters
and over the earth, or he is banishing the baser elements
from his own constitution, having declared his horse
is made of air and fire at III.7.20. Two alternative translations of the dialogue would be: (1) 'Be off! [Through]
waters and [over] earth!' 'Nothing else? [Not] air and
fire?' '[Yes,] the sky [heavens], cousin Orleans!' *or* (2)
'Be off! Water and earth [from our constitutions]!'
'Nothing left [in our constitutions]? [Only] air and fire
[i.e., 'hot air']?' 'The sky [heavens], cousin Orleans!'
Others editors substitute '*Cieux*' ('the heavens') or
'*Rien*' ('nothing') for F's *Cien*. If the latter is adopted,
the final line would be 'Nothing, cousin Orleans!'

4 *Ciel*: 'Sky' (*Cien* in F).

7 *make incision*: I.e., with spurs.

8 *spin*: Spurt.

9 *dout*: Extinguish.

superfluous courage: An excess of blood (identified with
courage).

12 *embattled*: In battle formation.

16 *shales*: Shells, outer cases.

19 *curtle-axe*: Cutlass.

20 *gallants*: Fine, brave young men.

23 *positive*: Certain.

23 *exceptions*: Objections.

26 *squares of battle*: Square-shaped battle formations.

27 *hilding*: Worthless, contemptible.

28–9 *Though we . . . speculation*: Cf. the French king's account of Edward III at Crécy at II.4.53–62.

28 *mountain's basis by*: Nearby mountain's base or foot.

29 *speculation*: Onlooking.

33 *tucket sonance*: Resounding trumpet-call to march. Jorgensen (*Shakespeare's Military World*, p. 22) notes that the signals to march and to mount are named in reverse order. *sonance* is from the Italian '*sonanza*', defined in John Florio's dictionary, *World of Words* (1598), as 'a sound, a resounding, a noise, a ringing' (p. 375).

34 *dare the field*: (1) Defy the foe *or* (2) daze the prey (a fowling term, 'to dare' being to dazzle or fascinate birds so that they can be captured).

37 *island*: I.e., English.
    carrions: Corpses for birds to scavenge. A parallel notion to that here and at 49–50 occurs in *Edward III* (IV.5.49–51): 'these ravens for the carcasses | Of those poor English that are marked to die | Hover about.' (Cf. *If we are marked to die . . .*, IV.3.20, below.)
    desperate: Reckless.

38 *Ill-favouredly become*: Ill-suit, disgrace.

39 *curtains*: Banners.

40 *passing*: Very.

41 *Big Mars*: Mighty Mars, Roman god of war.

42 *faintly*: Faint-heartedly.
    beaver: Helmet's visor.

43–4 *candlesticks . . . hand*: Candlesticks were sometimes made in the form of horsemen, the candle being the lance held upright; Webster wrote: 'he showed like a pewter candlestick, fashioned like a man in armour, holding a tilting-staff in his hand' (*The White Devil* (1612), III.1.69–70).

45 *Lob*: Droop.

46 *gum*: Gummy secretion, rheum.
    down-roping: Cf. III.5.23 and note.

47 *gimmaled*: Jointed (of twin parts). F reads *Iymold*.
'Gymould mayle' occurs in *Edward III* (I.2.29).

49 *their executors*: Disposers of their remains.
knavish: Rascally, mischievous.

50 *hour*: I.e., of death. See 37 and note (*carrions*).

52–3 *demonstrate ... itself*: Depict in a manner true to life
what such an army is like that appears so lifeless.

56 *provender*: Fodder.

58 *guidon*: Standard or pennant, i.e., the commander's sign.
Many editions, following F, read 'Guard: on', but the
detail clearly derives from Holinshed, who writes: 'The
Duke of Brabant, when his standard was not come,
caused a banner to be taken from a trumpet [cf. 59]
and fastened to a spear, the which he commanded to
be borne before him instead of his standard' (p. 554).

59 *trumpet*: Trumpeter.

IV.3

1 *Where is the King*: King Henry exited with Gloucester
at the end of IV.1 – *I know thy errand, I will go with
thee* (300) – though theatre audiences are unlikely to
notice the inconsistency.

3 *three-score thousand*: Sixty thousand.

4 *five to one*: This would make Henry's army 12,000
strong, though at 76 it is 5,000; this discrepancy goes
unnoticed in performance. Holinshed numbers the
French at 60,000 but makes the proportion six to one
(p. 552).

6 *God bye you*: God be with you (F, *God buy' you*). Forms
of the phrase include 'God be wi' you', 'God buy ye'
and 'Goodbye'.
charge: Military forces under his command.

7–10 *If we no more ... adieu*: Seems to foreshadow *Julius
Caesar*, V.1.114–18: 'whether we shall meet again I know
not. | Therefore our everlasting farewell take ... | If
we do meet again, why, we shall smile; | If not, why
then this parting was well made.'

10 *my kind kinsman*: Addressed to Westmorland, whose
younger son was married to Salisbury's daughter.

14 *framed*: Composed.

14 *truth of valour*: Constancy of courage. Taylor compares
Chapman's Homer, *Iliad*, ll. 364–5: 'He that affects
renown in war must like a rock be fixed, | Wound or
be wounded: valour's truth puts no respect betwixt.'

16–18 *O that we ... today*: In Holinshed (p. 553), this speech
is given merely to 'one of the host' and Westmorland
is not at Agincourt. Shakespeare, however, makes him
one of the main supporters of the Bolingbroke line and
a leader in the battle.

18 *work*: I.e., fighting (as often in Shakespeare).

20 *enow*: Enough.

21 *To do our country loss*: For England to feel the loss.

22 *The fewer ... honour*: 'The more danger, the more
honour' was proverbial. In *Edward III* the King refuses
to send a single man to reinforce the Black Prince, who
is in mortal peril, so as not to diminish his glory
(III.5.40).

24 *Jove*: Jupiter, the supreme god in Roman mythology.

26 *yearns*: Grieves.

28–9 *But if it be ... alive*: Cf. Hotspur's claim in *Henry IV,
Part I* that he would be willing 'To pluck bright honour
from the pale-faced moon' if it meant that he could
'wear | Without corrival all her dignities' (I.3.200–
205).

30 *faith*: Truly.
coz: Cousin.

35 *stomach*: (1) Appetite *or* (2) courage.

37 *for convoy*: I.e., to pay for the journey home.

39 *fears his fellowship ... us*: Fears his duty as a member
of our armed band to die with us. Cf. IV.3.60, *we band
of brothers*, and IV.8.100, *Here was a royal fellowship of
death!*

40 *Feast of Crispian*: 25 October, the religious feast day of
Saints Crispinus and Crispianus (cf. 57), brothers who
fled from Rome under Diocletian's oppression but were
martyred in AD 287. Shakespeare's use of the spelling
Crispianus rather than the usual 'Crispinian' makes
Thomas Deloney's *The Gentle Craft* (Part I, 1597; Part
II, 1598) a likely source. In Deloney's fiction, Crispianus

and Crispine are third-century Kentish princes who
evade Roman persecution by posing as apprentice shoe-
makers and eventually succeed in re-establishing a
British bloodline to rule over Britain. As a reward for
his bravery in the wars in Gaul, where he fought as a
conscript, Crispianus secures the Emperor's assent to
Crispine's secret marriage to the Emperor's daughter
(Part I, chs. 5–9).

45 *vigil*: Evening before the feast day.

48 *And say, 'These wounds I had on Crispin's day.'*: This
line occurs in Q but appears to have been omitted acci-
dentally from F. As Craik notes: 'F's colon at the end
of l. 47 may indicate that something was to follow, and
the omission would be an easy error because l. 46 had
also begun with the words *And say*.'

49–50 *yet all ... remember*: I.e., yet when all else shall be
forgotten he'll remember.

50 *advantages*: Embellishments (a humorous observation).

54 *Warwick and Talbot*: Neither Warwick nor John
Talbot, first Earl of Shrewsbury, were at Agincourt,
but both feature prominently in the French wars in
Henry VI, Part I and their names would resonate with
the audience, which may account for their inclusion
in this list.

56 *the good man*: I.e., every good man. Taylor suggests a
play on 'goodman' = 'householder, yeoman'.

60 *happy*: Fortunate.

62 *vile*: Of little account, low-ranking; similarly Q's *base*
= low in the social scale.

63 *gentle his condition*: Ennoble him, dignify his social rank
(figuratively; actual social elevation is not envisaged).

68 *bestow*: Place, i.e. prepare for battle.

69 *bravely in their battles set*: Handsomely, splendidly drawn
up in their battle formations.

70 *expedience*: Haste, speed.

77 *likes*: Pleases.

80 *compound*: Agree terms.

82 *gulf*: Whirlpool. Cf. II.4.10, *As waters to the sucking of
a gulf.*

83 *englutted*: Swallowed up.

84 *mind*: Remind.

91 *achieve*: Gain, capture; but Henry immediately makes clear that he does not intend to be captured alive, so all the French will gain are his bones.

93–4 *The man . . . hunting him*: Proverbial idea, deriving from Aesop's fable of the hunter who sold a bear's skin before he had killed the bear; in the fable he himself escaped death, but only narrowly.

96 *native*: English, i.e. they will survive the battle.

97 *in brass*: Inscribed on brass memorials.

102 *clime*: Region.

104 *abounding*: Abundant.

105 *crasing*: Shattering. Many editors amend to 'grazing', but both Q and F agree on *crasing*, and no change is needed.

107 *in relapse of mortality*: (1) In returning to the condition of non-existence *or* (2) by a deadly rebound. The English will continue to kill after they are dead because their decomposing bodies will cause a fatal outbreak of disease.

109 *for the working-day*: I.e., clothed for work.

110 *gayness*: Brightness of colour, pomp.

111 *painful*: Toilsome.

112 *feather*: Ornamental plume.

114 *slovenry*: Slovenliness, untidiness, dirtiness.

115 *in the trim*: In good order, i.e. ready for action.

117–19 *pluck . . . service*: I.e., demobilize them by removing their liveries. An Elizabethan servant wore his master's liveried coat, which was taken from him when he was dismissed from service.

118 *gay*: Fine, brightly coloured.

122 *gentle*: Noble, courteous.

123 *joints*: Limbs.

123–5 *They shall have . . . little*: Holinshed reports that, when the French herald asked what ransom he would give, Henry replied 'that his dead carcass should rather be a prize to the Frenchmen than that his living body should pay any ransom' (p. 554).

131   *vaward*: Vanguard. Henry 'appointed a vaward, of the which he made captain Edward Duke of York, who of an haughty courage had desired that office' (Holinshed, p. 553).

133   *dispose the day*: Determine the day, i.e. award the victory.

IV.4

  o   *Excursions*: Theatrical term for stage skirmishes and/or sorties across the stage by several actors.

2–3   *Je pense ... qualité*: 'I think that you are a gentleman of good quality.' F's French in this scene has been regularized but not completely corrected. Verbs and pronouns in the second person vacillate between singular and plural forms.

  4   *Calitie! 'Calen o custure me'*: F reads *Qualtitie calmie custure me*. Pistol mimics the French soldier's last word uncomprehendingly. By sound-association it prompts Pistol to mispronounce a popular Irish refrain, *'Cailin og a' stor'* ('Maiden, my treasure'), of an Elizabethan song, given in Clement Robinson's *Handfull of Pleasant Delites* (1584) as 'A sonnet of a lover in praise of his lady'.

  5   *Discuss*: Declare.

  6   *O Seigneur Dieu*: 'O Lord God!'

  8   *Perpend*: Weigh, ponder. Shakespeare uses the word five times, always with speakers who are mock-solemn – Touchstone in *As You Like It*, the Clown in *Twelfth Night* – or pompous-pretentious – Pistol here, Falstaff in *The Merry Wives of Windsor* and Polonius in *Hamlet*.

  9   *fox*: Sword. The maker's mark of a wolf on some sword-blades was mistaken for that of a fox.

 11   *Egregious*: Extraordinary. Cf. II.1.43.

12–13   *O, prenez ... moy*: 'O, take mercy! Have pity on me!'

 13   *moy*: Now spelt *'moi'*, in sixteenth-century French pronunciation it rhymed with other words ending in '-oy', for example, with 'destroy' in *Richard II*, V.3.118–19). Cf. *le Roy*, IV.1.49.

 14   *Moy*: Pistol takes this to be a coin; the word occurs in French and English for a measure of quantity (about a bushel).

15 *rim*: The 'rim of the belly', i.e., the peritoneum, the stomach-lining. Pistol is threatening to rip Le Fer's guts out by the throat.

17–18 *Est-il impossible . . . bras*: 'Is it impossible to escape the strength of your arm?' '*bras*' ('arm') was pronounced 'brass' in the French of the time.

19 *Brass*: I.e., a non-precious metal; Pistol misinterprets the French word for 'arm'.

20 *luxurious*: Lascivious, lecherous.

mountain goat: Goats are associated with lechery. The line suggests the Frenchman has a pointed beard.

22 *O, pardonne-moy*: 'O, pardon [spare] me', i.e., save me.

26 *Écoutez: comment êtes-vous appelé*: 'Listen: what are you called?'

27 *le Fer*: French for 'iron' – a name at odds with his cowardice.

29 *fer*: Used here as a nonce-word suggesting 'beat'.

firk: (1) Beat *or* (2) get money from *or* (3) puns on 'fuck'. Craik notes that it is 'used with overtones of "fuck" in Thomas Dekker's *Shoemaker's Holiday* (1.232; 7.44; 13.28)'.

ferret: Worry, tear at (as a ferret does its prey), with wordplay on 'fuck'.

33–6 *Que dit -il . . . gorge*: 'What does he say, sir?' 'He orders me to tell you that you [should] make yourself ready, for this soldier here is disposed this very hour to cut your throat.'

37 *Owy, cuppele gorge, permafoy*: 'Yes, cut the throat, by my faith.'

40–42 *O, je vous supplie . . . écus*: 'O, I beg you, for the love of God, to spare me! I am a gentleman of a good house. Save my life, and I will give you two hundred crowns.'

49 *Petit monsieur, que dit-il*: 'Little sir, what says he?'

50–53 *Encore . . . franchisement*: 'Again that it is contrary to his oath to spare any prisoner; nonetheless, for the crowns that you have promised, he is content to give you liberty, enfranchisement.'

54–7 *Sur mes genoux . . . d'Angleterre*: 'On my knees I give you a thousand thanks, and esteem myself happy that

I have fallen into the hands of a knight, I think, the most brave, valiant, and most [literally 'very'] distinguished lord of England.'

63 *suck blood*: (1) Kill *or* (2) the characteristic horse-leech simile which, at II.3.53, was merely predatory. Craik compares Lyly's *Endymion*, 3.2.26–31: 'I marvel Corsites, that you being a captain, who should sound nothing but terror and suck nothing but blood, can find in your heart to talk such smooth words, for that it agreeth not with your calling to use words so soft as that of love.'

I will some mercy show: Pistol is breaking military law. Thomas Digges's *Stratioticos* (1579) declares: 'Every soldier shall present such prisoners as are taken to their captain immediately at their return to the camp, and none shall either kill them or license them to depart' (pp. 278–9).

65 *Suivez-vous le grand capitaine*: 'Follow the great captain.'

66–7 *so empty a heart*: I.e., a person so lacking in courage.

67–8 *'The empty vessel makes the greatest sound'*: Proverbial.

69–70 *roaring devil . . . dagger*: This refers to what was apparently a popular morality play incident. The Clown in *Twelfth Night* sings of 'the old Vice . . . | Who with dagger of lath . . . | Cries, "Ah, ha!" to the Devil' and who offers to 'Pare [his] nails' (IV.2.120–26).

73–5 *The French . . . boys*: The Boy anticipates the French could plunder the lightly guarded luggage but does not anticipate the massacre to follow in which he will be killed (IV.7.1–4), though the language of predation hints at it.

IV.5

1–2 *O diable . . . perdu*: 'O the devil!' 'O Lord! The day is lost, all is lost!'

3 *Mort Dieu! Ma vie*: See note to III.5.11.

confounded: (1) Ruined *or* (2) put to shame.

5 *O méchante fortune*: 'O wicked fortune!'

7 *perdurable*: Everlasting (stressed on the first syllable).

11 *in honour! Once*: F reads *in once*, a word evidently having been omitted. Q's version of 23 is *Lets dye with honour*,

our shame doth last too long, and this probably supplies
the omission. Other suggestions are 'in harness', 'in
arms' and 'instant'.

14 *pander*: Pimp.

15 *gentler*: (1) Better born, nobler *or* (2) kinder.

16 *contaminated*: Defiled, sullied (by being raped).

17 *spoiled*: (1) Destroyed, *or* (2) injured (reputation).
   friend: Befriend.

18 *on heaps*: In heaps.

20 *in our throngs*: I.e., with the weight of our massed bodies.

22 *throng*: Crowd, i.e., where the fighting is thickest.

23 *Let life ... long*: 'Better to die with honour than live
   with shame' was proverbial. Bourbon does not die in
   battle, however; he later enters as Henry's prisoner in
   IV.7.

IV.6

0 *train*: Followers.

7 *array*: Outfit.

8 *Larding*: Enriching, i.e., with his blood.

9 *Yoke-fellow*: See II.3.51 and note.
   honour-owing: (1) Honour-owning, i.e., honourable *or*
   (2) wounds to which honour is owed.

11 *haggled*: Hacked.

12 *insteeped*: Immersed.

14 *yawn*: Gape.

18 *well-foughten field*: Well-fought battle.

21 *raught*: Reached.

23 *Commend*: Remember.

26 *espoused to death*: Pledged (figuratively married) to
   death. York upholds the proverb Bourbon cites at
   IV.5.23 but fails to fulfil, a contrast the dramatic
   sequence underscores when Bourbon reappears as
   Henry's prisoner in IV.7.

28 *pretty*: Admirable.

29 *waters*: I.e., tears.

31 *my mother*: 'Womanly' qualities inherited from the
   mother, i.e., tenderness. Cf. *Twelfth Night*, II.1.35–8:
   'My bosom is full of kindness, and I am yet so near the
   manners of my mother that upon the least occasion

more mine eyes will tell tales of me.' The identification of tearful compassion as an 'unmanly' loss of
control suggests the specific sense of 'the mother', as
hysteria was called. Cf. *King Lear*, II.4.54: 'Oh how
this Mother swells up toward my heart! *Histerica passio*,
down thy climbing sorrow.'

33 *perforce*: Of necessity.

33–4 *compound | With mistful eyes*: Come to terms with
tearful eyes by allowing them to be misty or by
conceding he must wipe his eyes to prevent tears falling.

35–8 *But hark ... through*: Shakespeare follows Holinshed
in having Henry issue the order to kill the prisoners in
the mistaken belief that the alarum prompted by the
French raid on the luggage in fact signalled that
the enemy was rallying and an assault on his army was
imminent:

> But when the outcry of the lackeys and boys, which run away
> for fear of the Frenchmen thus spoiling the camp, came to
> the king's ears, he doubting lest his enemies should gather
> together again, and begin a new field; and mistrusting further
> that the prisoners would be an aid to his enemies, or the very
> enemies to their takers in deed if they were suffered to live,
> contrary to his accustomed gentleness, commanded by sound
> of trumpet, that every man (upon pain of death) should incon-
> tinently slay his prisoner (p. 554).

In Q, after Henry's order, Pistol (present but silent
until now) ends the scene with his catchphrase, *Couple
gorge*. (See The Play in Performance, p. xciv.)

IV.7

1 *Kill the poys ... luggage*: Fluellen's passion causes him
to suggest that the luggage has also been murdered.
'Fluellen's error may have been prompted by the
analogy with *baggage*, which could mean (as *luggage*
nowhere does, outside this passage) "the men guarding
the baggage-train of an army" (*OED sb.* 2b, first
example 1603)' (Taylor).

2 *knavery*: Dishonest and crafty dealing.

8–10 *wherefore the King . . . throat*: Gower mistakenly believes that Henry gave the order to kill the French prisoners in retaliation for the slaughter of the boys guarding the luggage. (See note to 54.)

  9 *worthily*: Deservedly, justly.

 10 *gallant*: Admirable, praiseworthy, excellent.

 11 *Monmouth*: Southern Welsh town located near the English border by one of the tributaries of the Wye river.

12–13 *Alexander the Pig*: Alexander the Big, by which Fluellen means Alexander the Great (reigned 336–323 BC), son of Philip II of Macedon.

 17 *are all one reckonings*: All amount to the same thing.

 19 *Macedon*: Macedonia, a region that overlaps with what is now northern Greece.

 26 *Wye*: The River Wye, on the English–Welsh border.

 31 *is come after it indifferent well*: Has resembled it fairly well.

31, 42 *figures*: Similitudes, patterns, comparisons.

 33 *cholers*: Fits of anger.

42–4 *As Alexander . . . his cups*: Inflamed with wine after a banquet, Alexander quarrelled with and killed his friend and general Cleitus in 328 BC in a dispute over whether Alexander had exceeded his father, Philip II.

 46 *great-belly doublet*: Doublet (close-fitting jacket for the upper body) whose lower part, known as the 'belly', was stuffed with padding. The reference is to Falstaff's immense belly; the actor who played the part may have worn such a doublet to achieve the physical effect.

 47 *gipes*: Gibes/jibes.
    knaveries: Roguish pranks.

47–8 *I have forgot his name*: 'Probably a joking allusion to the name having had to be changed (from Oldcastle to Falstaff)' (Taylor).

 54 *this instant*: Henry has just learnt of the French raid on the tents in which the boys were killed. (See note to 8–10.)
    trumpet: Trumpeter.

 57 *void*: Clear, leave.

59 *skirr*: Scurry.

60 *Enforcèd*: Forcibly shot.

Assyrian slings: The allusion is to Judith 9:7 (Geneva Bible, 1587): 'The Assyrians ... trust in shield, spear, and bow, and sling.' Cf. *Henry IV, Part II*, V.3.102.

67 *fined*: I.e., pledged.

69 *charitable licence*: Permission granted out of Christian charity.

71 *book*: Record.

75 *vulgar*: Commoners.

77 *Fret*: Chafe, struggle.

78 *Yerk out*: Kick out, lash out.

83 *peer*: Appear.

89 *Crispin Crispianus*: See note to IV.3.40.

90 *grandfather*: I.e., Edward III, who was Henry's great-grandfather.

97 *garden where leeks did grow*: It is not clear whether Fluellen refers to the battle of AD 540 (cf. note to IV.1.55) or to Crécy; the episode he cites has not been traced.

98 *Monmouth caps*: Round, brimless caps worn by sailors and soldiers and originally made in Monmouth.

99–101 *and I do believe ... day*: Elizabeth commemorated St David's Day in honour of the Tudors' Welsh ancestry. Dover Wilson cites Francis Osborne, *Works* (8th edn, 1682): 'Nor did he [the Earl of Essex] fail to wear a leek on St David's Day, but besides would upon all occasions vindicate the Welsh inhabitants and own them for his countrymen, as Queen Elizabeth usually was wont, upon the first of March' (p. 610).

105 *Welsh plood*: Henry's tenuous claim to Welsh ancestry derives from the husband of his great-grandmother Eleanor Plantagenet of Lancaster, who was distantly related to a daughter of a Welsh king, Llywelyn the Great.

114 *just notice*: Accurate information.

123 *swaggered*: Quarrelled.

124 *take*: Strike.

130 *craven*: Confessed or acknowledged coward.

133 *sort*: Rank.

133 *from the answer of his degree*: Exempt (because of his high rank) from the obligation to answer a challenge from one of William's low social rank.

134–5 *as good a gentleman as the devil is*: Traditional idea, the devil being of the highest rank among angels; cf. *King Lear*, III.4.136: 'The prince of darkness is a gentleman.'

138 *Jack-sauce*: Saucy or impudent fellow.

140 *sirrah*: Sir (a term of address used by a person of authority to an inferior).

146 *literatured*: Well-read, learned.

149 *favour*: I.e., the glove, given by the king as a mark of favour.

150 *Alençon*: A French duke.

152 *helm*: Helmet.

156 *fain*: Gladly.

158 *aggriefed at*: Aggrieved by, annoyed by.

168 *haply*: Perhaps.

175 *touched with choler*: I.e., short-tempered. 'The implied metaphor is that of applying fire to the gunpowder in a cannon' (Craik).

176 *return an injury*: Repay an insult (with a blow).

IV.8

4 *peradventure*: Perhaps.

9 *'Sblood*: God's blood.

11 *You villain*: Addressed to Williams for striking an officer.

12 *be forsworn*: Swear falsely, i.e., break his word.

14 *into plows*: Possibly 'in two blows'.

16 *lie in thy throat*: Outright lie. Allegations of lying were categorized according to their deliberateness (see, for example, William Segar's *The Book of Honour and Arms* (1590)). Fluellen's allegation is the most insulting: a lie in the throat was one uttered deliberately and inexcusably; a lie in the teeth was a degree less grave and objectionable. Touchstone mocks these categorizations in *As You Like It*, V.4.65–101.

36 *avouchment*: Assurance.

49 *abuse*: Insult.

52 *lowliness*: Seeming low rank.

63 *mettle*: Spirit, courage.

65 *prabbles*: Brabbles (i.e., petty quarrels).

70–71 *good silling*: Good shilling, i.e., not counterfeit.

74 *good sort*: High rank.

75–99 *Charles ... Lestrake*: This transcribes Holinshed (p. 555) nearly word for word.

81 *bearing banners*: 'Entitled to bring their vassals to the field under their own banner, i.e., all ranks of nobles down to a knight banneret' (Craik).

89 *blood*: Nobility.

94 *Great Master*: Chief officer of the royal household.

97 *lusty*: Strong, vigorous.

103 *Kikely*: Spelt thus in Holinshed; *Ketly* in F.

104 *name*: Note, high social rank.

105 *five-and-twenty*: Holinshed gives this figure 'as some do report', though he records immediately after that 'other writers of greater credit affirm, that there were slain about five or six hundred persons' (p. 555). Modern historians estimate about 7,000 French dead and 400–500 English, a discrepancy striking enough.

108 *plain shock*: Direct clash of armed forces.
   even play: Equal contest.

122 *Non Nobis ... Te Deum*: Opening words of Psalm 115 (part of 113 in the Vulgate): 'Give praise not unto us, O God', and of the canticle *Te Deum laudamus*, 'We praise Thee, O God'.

123 *with charity enclosed in clay*: I.e., given Christian burial.

V.*Chorus*

1 *Vouchsafe*: Grant.

3 *admit*: Accept.

3–4 *th'excuse | Of time*: Between Agincourt (1415) and the Treaty of Troyes five years elapsed; cf. 38–41 and note.

9 *Athwart*: Across.

10 *Pales in*: Fences in (*pales* = stakes).
   flood: Sea.

11 *deep-mouthed*: Deep-voiced, sonorous.

12 *whiffler*: Attendant who clears the way for a procession or at a spectacle.

16 *Blackheath*: Large open common just outside London to the south of Greenwich on the road from Dover.

18 *bruisèd*: Dented, battered.

bended: Bent.

19 *He forbids it*: Holinshed reports that:

> The king like a grave and sober personage, and as one remembering from whom all victories are sent, seemed little to regard such vain pomp and shows as were in triumphant sort devised for his welcoming home from so prosperous a journey, in so much that he would not suffer his helmet to be carried with him, whereby might have appeared to the people the blows and dints that were to be seen in the same (p. 556).

21 *full trophy, signal, and ostent*: Every sign, token and display of honour.

23 *quick*: (1) Lively *or* (2) rapid.

forge and working-house: Furnace for heating and shaping metal or the workshop where this is done.

25–8 *The Mayor ... Caesar in*: 'The mayor of London, and the aldermen, apparelled in orient grained scarlet, and four hundred commoners clad in beautiful murrey [cloth of mulberry colour], well mounted, and trimly horsed, with rich collars, and great chains, met the king on Blackheath, rejoicing at his return' (Holinshed, p. 556).

25 *brethren*: Fellow aldermen.

in best sort: (1) In their civic robes *or* (2) in a group comprising the highest civic officials.

26 *antique*: Ancient.

27 *swarming*: See Virgil, *Georgics*, 4.67–87. Annabel Patterson notes that bees swarm when they desert the hive to follow a new leader (*Shakespeare and the Popular Voice*, p. 86). On the metaphor and its application to Essex, see Patterson, pp. 81–8.

29 *lower*: Lesser, less exalted.

loving: (1) Praiseworthy *or* (2) loyal. F reads *but by loving* and has been variously emended to 'high-loving' (Taylor), 'as loving' (Craik), 'behoving' (Proudfoot) or 'loving' (Rowe and this edition).

likelihood: (1) Probability *or* (2) similitude.

30 *General*: Probably a reference to Robert Devereux, the second Earl of Essex, who had departed for Ireland on 27 March 1599 as commander of the royal army to suppress the revolt in Ireland (see Introduction, p. xxxii–xxxiii.)
our gracious Empress: Queen Elizabeth I.

32 *broachèd*: (1) Spitted *or* (2) figuratively, chiselled *or* (3) set on, introduced. (See Introduction, p. xxxiii.)

34 *Much more, and much more cause*: Many more and with much more cause.

38–41 *The Emperor's coming . . . to France*: The Holy Roman Emperor Sigismund came to England to negotiate on behalf of France on 1 May 1416; further English invasions of France took place in 1416–19; and the Treaty of Troyes was signed in 1420. The play recognizes no appreciable interval between the events of IV.8 and those of V.1 (Dr Johnson indeed thought that V.1 should be the last scene of Act IV).

39 *order*: Arrange.
omit: Pass over.

44 *brook*: Tolerate.

V.1

4 *ass*: As, with wordplay on 'ass' and 'arse'.

5 *scauld*: Scabby, vile, contemptible.
lousy: Infested with lice.

7 *fellow*: Person of no esteem or worth (contemptuously).

10 *breed no contention*: Start an argument.

14 *swelling like a turkey-cock*: Puffed up with vanity and aggressiveness (proverbial).

15–16 *swellings . . . turkey-cocks*: With possible phallic wordplay.

16 *scurvy*: Worthless, contemptible.

18 *bedlam*: Mad, i.e., a resident of the Hospital of St Mary of Bethlehem, an asylum for mentally deranged persons located near Bishopsgate in London.
Troyan: Often, like Corinthian, Ephesian, Greek, etc., used for a 'good companion', but here a knave.

19 *Parca's fatal web*: I.e., kill you. In classical mythology the web of life is spun, measured and cut by the three Parcae or Fates.

20 *qualmish*: Faint, nauseous.

27 *Cadwallader*: Famous seventh-century Welsh warrior.

33 *sauce*: I.e., to sharpen Pistol's appetite, the *sauce* being the blood running from Pistol's wounded scalp.

34 *mountain-squire*: Landlord of the barren Welsh hills.

35 *squire of low degree*: An allusion to the title of a medieval romance.

37 *astonished*: Stunned, stupefied.

39 *pate*: Head, more particularly the scalp.

40 *green*: Fresh.
   coxcomb: Fool's head.

49 *cudgel*: Club.

52 *broken*: Wounded (not 'fractured').

55 *groat*: Small coin worth four old pence.

60 *in earnest of*: As a down-payment for.

62 *woodmonger*: Timber merchant.

67–9 *an ancient tradition . . . valour*: See note to IV.1.55.

70–71 *gleeking and galling*: Mocking and jeering.

75 *condition*: Disposition, i.e., a lesson in respect.

76 *play the housewife with*: I.e., jilt.
   housewife: Hussy, prostitute (pronounced 'hussif').

77 *Doll*: Both Q and F read *Doll*, but, since Doll Tearsheet was Falstaff's woman and Nell Quickly Pistol's, many editors change to 'Nell'. Some argue that Falstaff originally appeared in *Henry V* (as promised in the epilogue to *Henry IV, Part II*) and that his part was later transferred to Pistol, 'Doll' remaining unchanged through an oversight though it should have been altered to 'Nell'. This theory is unlikely, and *Doll* is probably a mere slip, arising from the similarity of the two women's positions and names. Apart from many difficulties in envisaging Falstaff in France, this speech and the action preceding it are very appropriate to Pistol, very inappropriate to Falstaff.
   spital: Hospital.

78 *malady of France*: Syphilis, popularly known in England as the 'French disease'.

79 *rendezvous*: See note to II.1.15.

80 *wax*: Grow.

81 *bawd*: Pimp.

82 *cutpurse*: See note to III.6.61.

84 *patches*: Bandages.

85 *Gallia*: I.e., French, alluding to Caesar's *Gallic Wars*,
in which the Roman general recounts his triumph over
the Gauls.

V.2

2 *brother*: Fellow monarch. *sister* (addressed to Queen
Isabel) and *cousin* (addressed to Katherine and
Burgundy) are similarly marks of courtesy.

5 *royalty*: Royal family; more generally, collection of
royal persons.

12 *issue*: Outcome.

   brother England: *brother Ireland* in F; *brother England* in
   F2.

16 *bent*: (1) Line of sight *or* (2) punning on line of fire.

17 *balls*: (1) Eyeballs *or* (2) cannonballs.

   basilisks: (1) Fabulous reptile whose breath and gaze
   were fatal *or* (2) large cannon named after the fabled
   reptile.

23 *on*: From.

27 *bar*: Tribunal, court, i.e., meeting place for negotiating
a treaty of peace.

31 *congreeted*: Greeted each other.

33 *rub*: See note to II.2.188.

35 *arts*: Learning.

37 *put up*: Lift up.

39 *husbandry*: Crops.

   on: In.

40 *it*: Its (the old genitive form).

42 *even-pleached*: Evenly intertwined.

44 *fallow leas*: Uncropped arable grassland.

45 *darnel, hemlock, and rank fumitory*: Weeds particularly
liable to grow on cultivated land; in *King Lear* they are
included among 'the idle weeds that grow | In our
sustaining corn' (IV.4.3–6).

   rank: Excessively luxuriant, overabundant.

46 *coulter*: Blade on a plough.

47 *deracinate*: Uproot.

47 *savagery*: Wild vegetation.

48 *even mead*: Flat meadow.

   erst: Formerly.

49 *freckled cowslip, burnet, and green clover*: I.e., useful
   plants.

50 *uncorrected*: Unchecked by cutting, uncultivated.

51 *teems*: Flourishes.

52 *kecksies*: (Plants with) dry hollow innutrient stems.

55 *Defective*: I.e., fallen. 'At the Fall the natural world
   became degenerate and corrupt; because of this defect
   of nature, it reverts to *wildness* unless constantly cultivated and corrected' (Taylor).

58 *sciences*: Skills.

61 *diffused*: Disordered.

63 *reduce*: Restore.

   into our former favour: To its former appearance (of
   orderliness and beauty).

65 *let*: Hindrance, impediment.

68 *would*: Would have, desire.

69 *want*: Lack.

72 *tenors*: Meanings.

73 *enscheduled*: Listed.

77 *cursitory*: Cursory.

79 *presently*: Immediately.

80 *better heed*: Greater care and attention.

82 *Pass*: Pronounce.

   accept: Accepted, agreed.

   peremptory: Decisive, final.

90 *consign*: Subscribe, agree (by signing or marking with
   a seal).

94 *nicely*: With insistence on detail, strictly.

   stood on: Insisted on.

96 *capital*: Principal. The marriage was in fact the first
   article of the Treaty of Troyes; cf. 97, 326.

108 *Pardonnez-moi*: 'Excuse me'.

111–12 *Que dit-il . . . ainsi dit-il*: 'What does he say? That I
   am like the angels?' 'Yes, truly, saving your grace, he
   says so.'

115–16 *O bon Dieu . . . tromperies*: 'O good God! The tongues

of men are full of deceits.' (Henry translates her statement accurately.)

121 *the better Englishwoman*: More like an Englishwoman
(in distrusting flattery).

124 *plain*: Plain-spoken. Johnson expressed surprise that
'Shakespeare now gives the king nearly such a char-
acter as he made him formerly ridicule in Percy' (see
Henry IV, Part I, II.4.100–109).

129 *clap hands*: Shake hands.

131 *Sauf votre honneur*: 'Saving your honour'.

134 *measure*: (Skill in) poetic metre.

135 *strength in measure*: Ability at dancing.

136 *measure in strength*: Amount of physical strength.

136–41 *If I could win ... off*: Among other praises of Henry,
Holinshed writes: 'In wrestling, leaping and running,
no man [was] well able to compare with him' (p. 583).
As Prince Hal, when fully armed for war Henry 'vaulted
with such ease into his seat' that he seemed the angelic
rider of a fiery Pegasus, to 'witch the world with noble
horsemanship' (*Henry IV, Part I*, IV.1.107–10.)

139 *leap into*: (1) Attain *or* (2) have sex with.
buffet: Box, fight.

140 *bound my horse*: Make my horse jump.

140–41 *lay on*: (1) Strike blows *or* (2) have sex.

141 *sit*: (1) On his horse *or* (2) on his wife, i.e., have
prolonged sex.
jackanapes: Tame ape or monkey (trained to sit on a
horse).

142 *greenly*: Like an inexperienced lovesick youth.

146 *not worth sunburning*: One that the sun could not make
worse. A sunburnt face was thought unbecoming; cf.
Troilus and Cressida: 'The Grecian dames are sunburnt
and not worth | The splinter of a lance' (I.3.282–3).

148 *be thy cook*: Dress the dish (his face) to your taste.

149–51 *If thou canst love ... too*: Cf. Rosalind's mockery of
romantic extravagance in *As You Like It*, IV.1.83–94.

152 *uncoined*: (1) Not counterfeit, genuine *or* (2) uncircu-
lated (sexually).

155–6 *rhyme themselves into ladies' favours*: Cf. Benedick's admission in *Much Ado About Nothing*, V.2.36, that he 'was not born under a rhyming planet'; Berowne's claim in *Love's Labour's Lost*, IV.3.177, that, being 'honest', he would never 'write a thing in rhyme'; and Hotspur's mockery of Glendower's 'mincing poetry' in *Henry IV, Part I*, III.1.128.

156 *ladies' favours*: Friendly regard, with wordplay on sexual favours.

157 *prater*: One who speaks much to little purpose, a chatterbox.

158 *but a ballad*: Ballads were often mere doggerel, and scorned as such.

fall: Wither.

160 *full*: Perfect, clear.

160–61 *wax hollow*: (1) Become sunken *or* (2) grow insincere.

180–82 *Je – quand sur le possession ... mienne*: 'I – when on [I have] the possession of France, and when you have the possession of me, ... then yours is France, and you are mine.' Q suggests a lively stage adaptation of this; see Collations, p. 127.

181 *Saint Denis*: Patron saint of France.

182 *be my speed*: Help me.

186–7 *Sauf votre honneur ... parle*: 'Saving your honour, the French that you speak, it is better than the English that I speak.'

189 *truly-falsely*: Sincerely but incorrectly.

196 *closet*: Private room.

200 *cruelly*: Fiercely.

202 *scambling*: Struggling indecorously.

206 *Constantinople*: The city did not fall to the Turks until 1453, thirty-one years after Henry died, but its recovery was thereafter a project which haunted Christian leaders. The *boy* whom Henry foresees winning it was in fact Henry VI, under whom England lost France and suffered the Wars of the Roses.

206–7 *take the Turk by the beard*: Humiliate the Turks (by driving them from Constantinople).

208 *flower-de-luce*: Fleur-de-lis (lily), emblem on the French royal coat of arms.

210 *know*: With wordplay on 'have sex'.

212 *part*: Portion, possibly with wordplay on 'genitals'.

213 *moiety*: Half, portion.

214–15 *la plus belle ... déesse*: 'the most beautiful Katherine of the world, my very dear and divine goddess'.

216 *fausse*: 'False', i.e., (1) incorrect *or* (2) deceitful, insincere.

217 *sage demoiselle*: 'wise [prudent] young lady'.

220 *blood*: (1) Passion *or* (2) sexual desire.

222 *untempering*: Unsoftening.

     beshrew: Cursed be (a humorous imprecation).

223 *civil wars*: I.e., deposing Richard II.

224 *got*: Conceived.

228 *ill layer-up*: Poor preserver because it causes wrinkles, like a 'wet cloak ill laid up' (*Henry IV, Part II*, V.1.78).

230 *wear me*: (1) Alter me through use *or* (2) endure me *or* (3) wear me out sexually.

237 *Plantagenet*: The royal dynasty to which Henry V belonged.

239 *fellow with*: Equal to.

240–41 *broken music*: Music arranged in parts for a number of voices and/or instruments.

244 *de Roi mon père*: 'the king my father'.

245 *shall*: Must.

250–53 *Laissez ... seigneur*: 'Let go, my lord, let go, let go! My faith, I do not at all wish you to abase your greatness by kissing the hand of one [who is] – our Lord – [your] unworthy servant. Excuse me, I beg of you, my most mighty lord.'

255–6 *Les dames ... France*: 'For ladies and young ladies to be kissed before their marriages, it is not the custom in France.'

261 *Your majestee ... moi*: Your majesty 'understands' better 'than I'.

264 *Oui, vraiment*: 'Yes, truly.'

265 *nice*: (1) Unimportant, trivial *or* (2) fastidious *or* (3) coy.

267 *list*: Limit, boundary (literally, the barrier enclosing a jousting yard or duelling area).

268 *places*: (High) rank.

281 *apt*: (1) Quick to learn *or* (2) sexually keen.

284 *conjure up*: Raise up (spirits).

284–5 *conjure up . . . in her*: I.e., make her love me.

288 *conjure in*: I.e., have sex with.

289 *make a circle*: (1) Draw a magic circle around yourself like a conjuror *or* (2) open (i.e., penetrate) her vagina. Cf. Mercutio in *Romeo and Juliet*, II.1.23–9: "Twould anger him | To raise a spirit in his mistress' circle | Of some strange nature, letting it there stand | Till she had laid it and conjured it down . . . | I conjure only but to raise up him'.

conjure up: Raise up (spirits, but here a penis in a state of erection).

290 *naked and blind*: (1) Like Cupid (Roman god of love, commonly represented as a naked and blindfolded boy) *or* (2) as a penis (with its 'blind eye').

291 *maid*: Virgin.

291–2 *rosed over . . . modesty*: (1) Blushing in modesty *or* (2) flushed in sexual arousal.

292–3 *she deny . . . in her*: (1) She denies that she feels love (for Henry) within her *or* (2) she refuses to consent to having sex with you (strictly, she refuses to allow your penis inside her).

293 *naked seeing self*: (1) Emotionally exposed (and physically naked) state *or* (2) vulva (drawing on sexual puns that compare the exterior female genitals to an eye) (Eric Partridge, *Shakespeare's Bawdy* (1968)).

294 *hard condition*: (1) Severe demand *or* (2) the penis in a state of erection.

consign: Agree, consent. Cf. note to 90.

295 *wink and yield*: Close both their eyes and give in.

295–6 *love is blind and enforces*: (1) Cupid exerts his power over the will *or* (2) the penis forces its way in.

300 *consent winking*: Express her consent by closing her eyes and yielding.

301 *wink on her*: Wink at her, i.e., signal to her.

302 *know my meaning*: Understand what I am signalling she should consent to, i.e., sex.

302–3 *well summered*: Well nurtured (as cattle are on summer pastures).

303 *warm kept*: (1) Richly, comfortably kept *or* (2) kept sexually aroused.

303–4 *Bartholomew-tide*: St Bartholomew's Day, 24 August (when flies supposedly feel the late summer's warmth and grow sluggish).

305 *handling*: With sexual connotations.

307 *moral ties me over to*: Lesson constrains me to wait for.

309 *latter end*: (1) Late summer *or* (2) lower body *or* (3) behind (as a sluggish fly is caught unawares from behind).

    blind: (1) Lacking in judgement *or* (2) unaware.

310 *before it loves*: (1) Until it sees the person that inspires love *or* (2) in the presence of the beloved *or* (3) before it's consummated sexually.

315 *perspectively*: As in a 'perspective' (a picture or figure that appears distorted or confused when viewed from one particular angle).

317 *maiden walls*: (1) Unbreached walls *or* (2) inviolate chastity.

    war: (1) Military force *or* (2) sexual force, rape.

    entered: (1) Invaded *or* (2) penetrated sexually.

320 *so*: So long as.

321 *wait on her*: Follow her (as part of her dowry).

322 *will*: (1) Political and military objectives *or* (2) sexual desire.

328 *subscribèd*: Signed in agreement.

330 *matter of grant*: Deed conferring lands or titles.

331 *addition*: Title.

332–4 *Notre très cher fils ... Franciae*: 'Our most beloved son Henry, King of England, Heir of France', and thus in Latin, 'Our most renowned son Henry, King of England and Heir of France'. The discrepancy in meaning between the French and Latin words ('most beloved', 'most renowned') arises because '*praeclarissimus*' is a misprint in Shakespeare's sources for '*praecharissimus*' (i.e., '*praecarissimus*', 'most beloved').

341 *Issue*: Descendants.

342 *pale*: White (because of the chalk cliffs).

344 *dear*: (1) Beloved, precious *or* (2) costly.

354 *spousal*: Marriage, union.
355 *ill office*: Disservice.
    fell: Deadly.
357 *paction*: Pact, agreement.
358 *incorporate*: United in one body (as marriage is said to make man and woman one flesh).
363–4 *My Lord of Burgundy . . . peers'*: In an unusual staging that defies theatre convention and possible audience expectations, Burgundy and the Dauphin do not swear their oaths on stage. Cf. *Famous Victories* sc.xx and Holinshed, p. 572, and see Introduction, pp. xl.
366 *Sennet*: Set of notes on the trumpet or cornet signalling a ceremonial entrance or exit.

Epilogue

1 *rough*: Coarse, uneven.
  all-unable: Wholly inadequate.
2 *bending*: (1) I.e., over his work *or* (2) bowing.
3 *room*: Space (possibly referring to the *wooden O* of the theatre).
4 *by starts*: I.e., by telling the story in fits and starts, intermittently.
5 *Small time*: Henry V died aged thirty-five in 1422, having reigned for nine and a half years.
6 *This star of England*: Cf. Holinshed: 'for conclusion, a majesty was he that both lived & died a pattern in princehood, a lode-star in honour, and mirror of magnificence' (p. 584).
7 *world's best garden*: I.e., France. Cf. V.2.36.
9 *infant bands*: Strips of linen used to wrap babies, i.e., swaddling clothes. Henry VI was less than a year old when his father died.
12–13 *That they lost . . . hath shown*: The loss of France and the beginning of the civil wars over the succession that had been portrayed in Shakespeare's three plays on the reign of Henry VI.
13 *their*: I.e., Shakespeare's three plays concerning Henry VI's reign.
14 *this acceptance take*: This play find favour.